**Second Edition**

# Small-Group Reading Instruction

## Differentiated Teaching Models for Intermediate Readers, Grades 3–8

intervention

evolving

maturing

advanced

## Beverly B. Tyner
## Sharon E. Green

**INTERNATIONAL**
**Reading Association**
800 BARKSDALE ROAD, PO BOX 8139
NEWARK, DE 19714-8139, USA
www.reading.org

D0473518

The International Reading Association attempts, through its publications, to provide a forum for a wide spectrum of opinions on reading. This policy permits divergent viewpoints without implying the endorsement of the Association.

**Executive Editor, Publications**    Shannon Fortner
**Managing Editor**    Christina M. Terranova
**Editorial Associate**    Wendy Logan
**Design and Composition Manager**    Anette Schuetz
**Design and Composition Associate**    Lisa Kochel

**Cover**    Design, Lise Holliker Dykes; Photographs (top) Beverly Tyner, (bottom) © Creatas Images

The publisher would appreciate notification where errors occur so that they may be corrected in subsequent printings and/or editions.

**Library of Congress Cataloging-in-Publication Data**

Tyner, Beverly B.
  Small-group reading instruction : differentiated teaching models for intermediate readers, grades 3-8 / Beverly B. Tyner and Sharon E. Green. -- 2nd ed.
     p. cm.
  Includes bibliographical references and index.
  ISBN 978-0-87207-843-7
  1. Reading (Elementary) 2. Group reading. 3. Reading--Remedial teaching. I. Green, Sharon E., 1970- II. Title.
  LB1573.T97 2011
  372.41'62--dc23

                                        2011028262

**Suggested APA Reference**

Tyner, B.B., & Green, S.E. (2012). *Small-group reading instruction: Differentiated teaching models for intermediate readers, grades 3–8* (2nd ed.). Newark, DE: International Reading Association.

To our precious children: Leslie, Susan, Jennifer, Harrison, Jack, Benjamin, and Thomas. They are truly our greatest gifts and our most important students.

# CONTENTS

**B**everly **B. Tyner**, EdD, is an educator with more than 30 years of experience. Her career includes positions as a teacher, principal, and school district curriculum director. She was also a graduate professor and the director of student teaching at Kennesaw State University in Atlanta, Georgia, USA.

In 2004, Beverly published her first book, *Small-Group Reading Instruction: A Differentiated Teaching Model for Beginning and Struggling Readers*, with the International Reading Association. In 2005, she published a sequel to her first book: *Small-Group Reading Instruction: A Differentiated Teaching Model for Intermediate Readers, Grades 3–8*. Beverly has also produced training DVDs that accompany her books. In addition, she has published research in the *Journal of Educational Psychology* that supports her reading intervention model.

Currently, Beverly is a private literacy consultant. Her work includes presenting at national and international conferences, consulting with schools and school districts, and writing curricular materials. Most recently, she has been assisting school districts with the implementation of Response to Intervention using her reading intervention model. Beverly is well known for her practical yet research-based models in reading instruction. She feels that her most important work continues to be with students and teachers within the classroom setting.

Beverly resides in Chattanooga, Tennessee, USA, with her husband, Paul, and is the mother of four grown children.

**S**haron **E. Green**, PhD, is currently an independent education consultant residing in Hong Kong. Before relocating to Asia, she was awarded tenure in the School of Education at Fairleigh Dickinson University in Madison, New Jersey, USA. Previously, she served on the faculties of Emporia State University and the University of Kansas and has been an adjunct professor at several other institutions in the United States. Prior to her career in higher education, she was an elementary and special education teacher. Sharon received her BA from Duquesne University in 1992, her MSEd from Simmons College in 1998, and her PhD from the University of Virginia in 2002.

In addition to the first edition of this book, she also coauthored *Cue-Up and Unpack: Effectively Teaching Science, Mathematics and Social Studies*, published by Kendall Hunt in 2010. Sharon regularly publishes in both peer-reviewed journals and online publications. Additionally, she routinely presents at conferences, including those of the International Reading Association, the Literacy Research Association, the Association of Literacy Educators and Researchers, the National Association for Professional Development Schools, and the National Association for the Education of Young Children.

In her current role as an independent consultant, Sharon is continuing her previous staff development work with teachers, focusing on the practical aspects of differentiated reading instruction in the international school setting. She also continues to assess and work with individual students. Her areas of research include small-group reading instruction, developmental spelling, and metacognition as it relates to comprehension and the parents' role in a child's reading development.

Sharon is married and has a vested interest in the future of education as the mother of three young boys.

---

**Author Information for Correspondence and Workshops**

The authors welcome questions and comments about this book. Beverly can be contacted at beverly@literacylinks.net, and Sharon can be contacted at sharongreen@me.com.

# PREFACE

This second edition reflects our knowledge and insight gained over the past six years through our experiences working with students and teachers in many different classrooms across the country. Our goals in revising this book were first, to refine the small-group model to reflect the challenging Common Core Standards that have been adopted by a majority of the states; second, to acknowledge the concerns from teachers for meaningful follow-up extension activities; and third, to provide an intervention model for students performing well below grade level. These additions will affect intermediate classrooms in powerful ways both within and outside of small-group instruction.

We believe that all children have the right to quality reading instruction. To become successful in today's society, all students must become proficient readers, writers, and critical thinkers. With the pressure of high-stakes assessments and heightened demands through the Common Core Standards, the quest for effective reading instruction continues to be at the forefront of education. The intermediate years are the last opportunity for students to receive focused reading instruction, which is critical to both academic and future career success.

Teaching reading in the intermediate grades brings the added pressure of content area mandates, which present a daunting task for many upper elementary and middle school teachers. Traditional whole-class instruction for these students often fails for the same reasons that it does in the primary grades: In any classroom, there are multiple levels of readers. If we are serious in our desire to make all students competent readers, then we must provide differentiated reading instruction geared to the specific needs of students as they matriculate through the upper grades.

For most intermediate readers, the transition from learning to read to reading to learn has been clearly established. However, left unsupported, these readers may fail to develop the critical skills necessary to pave the way to more advanced reading levels. Intermediate readers vary in their levels of literacy learning and, as such, reading instruction must be differentiated to meet these needs. Differentiation as it relates to this text is reading instruction based on the developmental needs of the reader. Differentiating instruction may not always be convenient or easy, but it is a necessity if we are to provide quality reading instruction for all students. Unfortunately, one-size-fits-all instruction is not effective because there is no one standard student profile. Instead, we must be able to assess a student's literacy knowledge and be prepared to provide focused reading instruction based on the student's identified needs.

This second edition presents small-group differentiated teaching models with effective teaching strategies for growth in fluency, word study, comprehension, and vocabulary. The key to this book is the focus on differentiated instructional practices both within and outside of small groups.

Intermediate teachers often do not have the time to select materials and develop appropriate instruction to meet the specific needs of all of their students. This book is intended for those teachers. We provide both the research base and the practical implementation models to assist in meeting the literacy needs for all intermediate students. Further, we provide meaningful extension activities designed to meet the needs of students in all stages of reading development.

This book will be useful for regular and special education teachers, administrators, staff developers, teacher educators, reading educators, and other professionals looking for help in the intermediate classroom. The models are practical and powerful and will allow teachers to provide effective reading instruction for the diverse student needs in their classrooms. These intermediate students must continue to be supported in literacy development as they grow toward reading independence.

# Acknowledgments

First, we would like to thank the many teachers and students who unknowingly provided the motivation for this book. We are especially grateful to our husbands, Paul and Brian, for their steadfast support as we toiled, which has sometimes meant doing more than their part with household and parental duties.

Without the support of the International Reading Association, this endeavor never would have been possible. We thank Shannon Fortner, Danny Miller, Susanne Viscarra, and Christina Terranova for their patience, valuable input, and talents in editing and publishing this book.

# CHAPTER 1

# Intermediate Reading Instruction and Small-Group Differentiated Reading Models

Despite nearly two decades of policy and investment focused on improving reading achievement for all students, the most recent National Assessment of Educational Progress report (National Center for Education Statistics, 2010) showed dismal results. The achievement scores of fourth- and eighth-grade students in reading have barely budged since 1992. This troubling information has ignited an unprecedented concern about how we are educating our students. Parents, educators, business leaders, and politicians are adamant that our students deserve a better education.

Reading ability is the barometer that measures the success or failure of students. There is a valid reason for this, especially when it comes to students in grades 3–8. Intermediate students who are deficient in reading are most likely deficient in other curricular areas as well.

Most intermediate teachers are fully aware of the importance of students' reading abilities but are also faced with the task of making sure that students gain content knowledge. Student access to content-related information is largely dependent on a student's ability to be able to read and understand the text.

What does it mean to teach reading in the intermediate grades? Currently, the culture of many classrooms around the country is primarily one of standards-driven, whole-class instruction. An increased accountability for student achievement is often determined by high-stakes assessments in the intermediate grades. In some instances, teacher pay is tied to student success. This situation only increases the pressure for teachers to ensure that their students achieve.

Faced with the need to teach a large quantity of information to a wide range of learners, many teachers in intermediate classrooms primarily engage in whole-group instruction. With a three- to four-year reading range in most intermediate classrooms, teachers are struggling to meet the needs of all their students. When teachers review assessment data, many are disappointed with the results. They can do a thorough job of teaching the standards, but if the students cannot independently read and understand the grade-level assessments, teachers will continue to find disappointing results.

In our observations, time and lack of knowledge of the developmental reading process are the biggest obstacles that many teachers face. In order to meet the needs of their diverse students, intermediate teachers need to be better prepared for this challenge. With the increased pressure to succeed, teachers and administrators are scrambling to find the quick fix that will have all students reading at grade level. This mind-set has led to a purchasing frenzy of scripted, neatly boxed, "research-based" reading programs. Additionally, teachers are forced to address reading deficits in segmented instruction that does not allow students to engage in *real*, authentic reading. Without a true understanding of the reading process or developmental models that address all of the reading needs in a classroom, teachers and students will continue to fall short of expectations. The bottom line is that teachers, rather than shiny, new boxed reading programs, teach students to become better readers.

Teachers are also faced with a shrinking instructional day and are scrambling to find enough time to teach. There needs to be a balance of whole-group and small-group instruction that takes into account the various reading levels of students. Struggling readers, for example, will need more time and support in small-group instruction. That said, *all* students need supported instruction to make gains along the reading continuum. The questions for teachers then become, What should I be doing to differentiate instruction based on the developmental reading needs of my students? What do I do for my struggling readers as well as my gifted readers to add value to their literacy development?

This book provides both the theoretical knowledge base and practical application models necessary to implement effective small-group differentiated reading instruction for a wide range of readers in the intermediate grades.

# Small-Group Differentiated Reading Models

## Development of the Models

Beverly's original work with small-group differentiated reading instruction began with her development of models to accommodate the needs of beginning and struggling readers in grades K–2. Her initial work was an outgrowth of her association with Darrell Morris (2005), who developed the Howard Street Tutoring Program in Chicago. The success of his model has been documented with both urban and rural populations (Morris, Tyner, & Perney, 2000; Santa & Høien, 1999). Although Morris's one-on-one tutoring program was highly successful with individual students, it became apparent that this kind of effective instruction was needed in most regular classroom settings. Further, one-on-one tutoring programs were becoming less feasible because of economic constraints. This was the impetus for Beverly's first book, *Small-Group Reading Instruction: A Differentiated Teaching Model for Beginning and Struggling Readers* (Tyner, 2004).

An important component of this model is the use of a balanced approach to developmental reading instruction. Rather than relying on one reading component or another, the instruction is inclusive of all the critical reading components that have been verified through research (National Institute of Child Health and Human Development [NICHD], 2000). This balanced approach is fundamental in producing well-rounded readers. We need to teach all of the components that contribute to an individual reader at any given time.

With the success of the model in the primary grades, it became apparent that the model needed to be extended. After a chance meeting, we began discussing this exact topic. Sharon, a former regular education and special education teacher, had been working with her graduate students using a similar balanced approach with older struggling readers. Our combined work with preservice and inservice teachers made us keenly aware of the continued needs of teachers and their students as the students matriculated into the intermediate grades. We realized that the needs of the teachers and the students at the intermediate level were not very different from those in the primary grades.

As a follow-up to Beverly's first book, this book includes the later stages of reading development as well as models for implementing small-group differentiated reading instruction in the intermediate classroom.

## Differentiating the Stages of Reading Development

Most researchers agree that reading acquisition occurs in stages (Chall, 1983). Just as children pass through developmental milestones in physical development, students move through reading stages toward the goal of becoming an advanced reader. Understanding the differences between these reading stages is critical because it allows for the differentiation of instruction based on readers' needs within each particular stage.

Typically, in an intermediate classroom, readers are often grouped together with little discrimination regarding their abilities. Most classrooms contain some students who struggle with reading, others who read well above grade level, and still others who fall somewhere in between. Small-group differentiated reading instruction allows teachers to accommodate the diverse needs of readers at any given stage.

For example, in the beginning reading stages, a stronger emphasis is placed on decoding than on comprehension. As readers progress, this focus shifts to a stronger emphasis on comprehension because of readers' increased word recognition abilities within more complex texts. In effect, readers are able to spend more of their mental energy on what the words mean rather than on what the words are. Table 1 details the five stages in beginning reading development. Table 2 shows the subsequent stages of intermediate reading development.

# The Stages of Intermediate Reading

Chall (1979) was one of the first reading researchers to discuss the developmental stages through which a reader passes. Her research was based on the work of developmental psychologists as they described the typical psychological development of a child. Since Chall's first publication, many other researchers have followed in her footsteps and developed similar stages of reading development (e.g., Fountas & Pinnell, 1996; Gunning, 2002). Delineation and names of reading stages vary from researcher to researcher. The stages presented in this text reflect our philosophy.

**TABLE 1**
**Stages of Beginning Reading Development**

| Stage | Appropriate Grade Level | Beginning Student Characteristics | Major Focuses |
|---|---|---|---|
| 1 Emergent Reader | Late pre-K/ mid-K | • Recognizes and produces less than half the alphabet<br>• Has little concept of word<br>• Has little phonemic awareness<br>• Recognizes few, if any, sight words | • Using memory and pictures<br>• Recognizing and reproducing letters of the alphabet<br>• Tracking print<br>• Distinguishing beginning consonant sounds<br>• Recognizing 15 sight words<br>• Using concepts of print |
| 2 Beginning Reader | Mid-/late K | • Recognizes and produces more than half the alphabet<br>• Tracks print with return sweep<br>• Is able to hear some sounds<br>• Recognizes 15 or more sight words | • Completing alphabet recognition and production<br>• Using beginning and ending consonant sounds, blends, and digraphs<br>• Recognizing 50 sight words<br>• Reading simple text<br>• Using sentence context and pictures or word recognition cues to decode<br>• Reading books without a pattern |
| 3 Fledgling Reader | Early/mid-first grade | • Recognizes beginning and ending consonant sounds, blends, and digraphs<br>• Recognizes 50+ sight words<br>• Reads simple text | • Recognizing and using word families and short vowels in reading and writing<br>• Recognizing 100+ sight words<br>• Reading more complex text<br>• Developing fluency<br>• Developing comprehension strategies<br>• Self-correcting errors using phonics and comprehension knowledge |
| 4 Transitional Reader | Mid-/late first grade | • Applies word family and short vowel knowledge in reading and writing<br>• Recognizes 100+ sight words<br>• Reads developed text | • Using common vowel patterns in reading and writing<br>• Developing decoding and comprehension strategies<br>• Developing fluency<br>• Writing to demonstrate comprehension |
| 5 Independent Reader | Early/late second grade | • Reads and writes to comprehend<br>• Uses strategies to figure out new words<br>• Reads fluently<br>• Uses vowel pattern knowledge to support reading and writing | • Using complex vowel patterns<br>• Developing fluency in a variety of texts<br>• Responding to text to demonstrate comprehension<br>• Applying diverse strategies to comprehend text<br>• Using common word features in reading and writing |

*Note.* Modified from *Small-Group Reading Instruction: A Differentiated Teaching Model for Intermediate Readers, Grades 3–8* (p. 5), by B. Tyner and S.E. Green, 2005, Newark, DE: International Reading Association. Copyright 2005 by the International Reading Association.

**Stages of Intermediate Reading Development**

| Stage/Grade Level | Beginning Student Characteristics | Major Focuses |
|---|---|---|
| Intervention Reader Mid-first to late second grade | **Reading**<br>• Has limited sight vocabulary<br>• Lacks fluency<br>• Focuses on decoding<br>• Finger points and subvocalizes<br>**Word Study**<br>• Knows most short vowels, blends, and digraphs | **Fluency**<br>• Developing speed, accuracy, and expression<br>**Word Study**<br>• Learning common and less common vowel patterns/common word features<br>**Comprehension**<br>• Transitioning from decoder to comprehender of text |
| Evolving Reader Late second to late fourth grade | **Reading**<br>• Has an extensive sight vocabulary<br>• Begins to read more fluently and expressively<br>• "Chunks" unknown words<br>• Depends less upon finger pointing and subvocalizing (these strategies phase out during the stage)<br>**Word Study**<br>• Knows most common word features<br>• Knows most common and less common vowel patterns<br>• Begins to make connections between spelling and meaning<br>• Begins to learn about the meaning connections of simple prefixes and suffixes | **Fluency**<br>• Developing smooth, quick, accurate, automatic word recognition while using expression to interpret the author's meaning<br>**Word Study**<br>• Learning about syllable patterns<br>• Learning complex vowel patterns in multisyllabic words, contractions, complex digraphs and blends, homophones, and compound words, as well as prefixes, suffixes, and simple Greek and Latin roots<br>**Comprehension**<br>• Learning and experimenting with before-, during-, and after-reading strategies |
| Maturing Reader Late fourth to late sixth grade | **Reading**<br>• Reads fluently<br>• Reads longer text in a variety of genres<br>• Uses a variety of strategies to comprehend text<br>**Word Study**<br>• Spells most one-syllable words<br>• Continues to study the meaning connection of spelling and vocabulary<br>• Understands meaning changes when prefixes and suffixes are added to words | **Fluency**<br>• Independent practice for fluency<br>**Word Study**<br>• Learning about syllable stress in multisyllabic words<br>• Mastering the principle of preserving short- or long-vowel patterns as a syllable is added; learning more difficult affixes as the spelling–meaning connection is explored<br>• Learning polysyllabic words with Latin and Greek roots<br>**Comprehension**<br>• Developing and expanding before-, during-, and after-reading strategies |
| Advanced Reader Late sixth to late eighth grade | **Reading**<br>• Fluent, often avid readers<br>• Develops competency with knowing when and how to use effective comprehension strategies based on text structure<br>**Word Study**<br>• Understands basic and more complex syllable patterns | **Fluency**<br>• Independently practicing for fluency<br>**Word Study**<br>• Mastering additional complex syllable patterns<br>• Learning polysyllabic words with Latin and Greek roots<br>**Comprehension**<br>• Developing independent use of strategies and developing critical insight |

*Note.* Modified from *Small-Group Reading Instruction: A Differentiated Teaching Model for Intermediate Readers, Grades 3–8* (p. 6), by B. Tyner and S.E. Green, 2005, Newark, DE: International Reading Association. Copyright 2005 by the International Reading Association.

An intermediate reader is best described as one who has made, or is in the process of making, the transition from learning to read to reading to learn. Intermediate reading can be further broken down into the following stages: Evolving Reader, Maturing Reader, and Advanced Reader. Combined, these stages typically cover grades 3–8. It also is important to note that these stages build on one another in a continuum; therefore, the beginning and end points of the stages are not always clearly defined. Rather, some overlap occurs. For example, the maturing reader may be able to comprehend text on a higher level; however, he or she may still need some practice with ambiguous vowel patterns in polysyllabic words, which is a word study feature generally studied in the Evolving Reader stage. Therefore, we examine these stages in terms of typical grade-level development and expectations. In our experience with intermediate students who show deficits, particularly in the area of word study, we find that most did not receive appropriate developmental instruction in this area in the earlier grades. It is critical as students reach the intermediate grades that teachers are aware of these deficits and adjust their instruction accordingly.

We realize that in the intermediate grades some readers function below the third-grade level and some function above the eighth-grade level. The Intervention Reader stage outlined in this book addresses the needs of readers who are functioning six months or more below the third-grade reading level. The needs of students reading above the eighth-grade level are met in the Advanced Reader lesson plan model. In the following sections, we introduce these reading stages and the instructional lesson plan model components that meet the needs of these diverse readers. Table 2 provides an overview of the early characteristics of each stage, as well as the instructional focuses with appropriate literacy components.

## Intervention Reader Stage

The needs of intermediate readers who are functioning six months or more below the third-grade reading level are addressed in the Intervention Reader stage. This lesson plan model is appropriate for all struggling readers, including those with special needs and those who are English learners (ELs). These students need strong support in fluency, word study instruction (particularly basic phonics), comprehension in instructional-level text, and reading vocabulary. This small-group model of instruction is used within the reading block, but the model can also be used for additional intervention. Please note that this model meets the needs and criteria outlined in the Response to Intervention guidelines (Hale, 2008).

## Evolving Reader Stage

According to *Webster's Tenth New Collegiate Dictionary* (Merriam-Webster, 2000), *evolutionary* is defined as "a process of change in a certain direction" (p. 397). This epitomizes the state of the evolving reader who has moved from being a basic decoder of text to a comprehender of text. Fluency development is critical for evolving readers who lack the speed, accuracy, and expression needed to comprehend the text. These evolving readers need support in word study as defined by their individual needs and grade-level standards with regard to multisyllabic words, syllabication, and simple Greek and Latin prefixes and suffixes. Reading and understanding complex grade-level text is of utmost importance. Expanding reading vocabulary as students engage in text is also incorporated in the instructional models to support comprehension of various text types. Although the evolving reader is typically found in grades 3 and 4, readers at this stage may include lower level fifth or sixth graders reading below grade level or second graders reading above grade level. The first section in Table 2 presents an overview of the characteristics and major instructional focuses for the evolving reader.

## Maturing Reader Stage

The maturing reader is best characterized as one who has successfully completed the foundational stages of reading development and is continuing to grow in his or her abilities to independently understand and evaluate text. The maturing reader requires less directed teacher support than an evolving reader does, and is developing the critical behavioral characteristics necessary to become an advanced reader. The second section of Table 2 outlines characteristics and instructional focuses that are representative of the maturing reader. Although maturing readers will continue to practice oral reading fluency, it is not a lesson plan component. Word study instruction centers on complex syllabication as well as the study of Greek and Latin roots. The majority of the lesson is focused on reading and comprehending complex text and the vocabulary associated with the text. Maturing readers read a substantial amount of text within and outside of the small-group setting. Students are expected to compose written comprehension pieces in response to the varied text types.

## Advanced Reader Stage

The final stage for intermediate readers is the Advanced Reader stage. Advanced readers have well-developed reading skills and are able to comprehend and critique a variety of texts and genres. The teacher's role increasingly involves modeling and facilitating the critical thinking skills that are necessary to evaluate complex text. The instructional plan for small groups is adapted to allow most of the reading to be completed outside of small-group instruction. These readers continue to grow in word study with a focus on sophisticated Greek and Latin roots. It is unnecessary to meet with these advanced readers on a daily basis, but it is important to set aside time during the week to meet consistently. Advanced readers are exposed to complex narrative and informational text. These readers need to respond to text critically, both orally and in writing. The final section of Table 2 shows the characteristics and instructional focuses of the advanced reader.

# Lesson Plan Components

The components of the Small-Group Differentiated Reading Models include fluency practice for struggling intermediate readers as well as for evolving readers. Explicit word study instruction as well as in-depth comprehension and vocabulary are also components of the lesson plans. Research supports that fluency, word study, and comprehension are integrated processes (Bear, 1991; Bear, Invernizzi, Templeton, & Johnston, 2007; Moats, 2000). Thus, effective reading instruction must include a balanced focus. With proper instruction, these three processes develop in unison (Bear et al., 2007).

## Fluency

Fluency is the ability to read smoothly, accurately, quickly, and with expression. Even though a student might be able to accurately decode the words in a given text, if the student cannot read those words automatically and with expression, then he or she cannot fully understand the author's message. Fluency instruction helps build automatic word recognition so that the text can be read effortlessly, and the reader can focus on meaning rather than word recognition. Research suggests that faster, accurate readers tend to have better comprehension and, therefore, are more proficient readers (Rasinski, 2000). Fluency instruction requires practice with independent-level texts, which are texts that a student can read and understand without teacher support.

We have worked with some school districts that use fluency rates as the primary benchmark for assessing reading achievement. Fluency passages, often above the student's independent reading level, are assigned, practiced, and assessed during the week for tracking purposes. Those students who score below the designated benchmark are assigned to reading intervention with little regard for other critical assessment data. Fluency development is best accomplished through the repeated readings of independent-level texts (Samuels, 1979), which leads to improvement in decoding, reading rate, expression, and comprehension. Rereading previously read instructional text gives students in the Intervention Reader stage supported fluency practice. Evolving readers need to continue to hone their fluency skills both within and outside of small-group instruction, using various short pieces of text. Maturing and advanced readers are given opportunities outside of small-group instruction to practice their fluency skills.

## Word Study

Word study is the systematic, developmental study of words (Bear et al., 2007; Ganske, 2000; Henderson, 1990). Based on the stages of developmental spelling, word study addresses the needs of phonics, spelling, and vocabulary development for all students. The word study scope and sequence outlined in this text reflects a developmental model coupled with grade-level expectations. Typically, word study for an intermediate reader includes studying features including but not limited to vowel patterns in polysyllabic words, syllabication, Greek and Latin affixes (i.e., prefixes, suffixes), and morphemic units (i.e., root words).

A developmental word study approach allows students to internalize word features rather than memorize spelling rules. Thus, students can take the information beyond the isolated classroom lesson and transfer it meaningfully while they read text and write their own text. Using the word study approach, students categorize words, which enables them to compare and contrast similar features in words. Further, students are able to generalize these word patterns when they are faced with reading or spelling an unknown word. This approach is particularly helpful for intermediate students when they are studying specialized, content-specific vocabulary. Developmental word study for each of these reading stages serves the important purpose of increasing readers' vocabulary knowledge, which, in turn, supports and increases comprehension.

## Comprehension

Simply stated, comprehension is the ability to understand text. Good readers have a purpose for reading and are active participants in the thinking processes that make understanding text possible. In other words, skillful readers are able to think critically as they navigate a text.

The goal of reading is to understand and learn from text, not merely identify words. Contrary to popular belief, most students do not automatically know how to comprehend information; they have to be taught through systematic, guided instruction in meaningful text (Fielding & Pearson, 1994; Keene, 2002). This allows students to more fully understand the text and make higher level thinking connections. Effective comprehension strategies include generating questions, evaluating text structure, activating background knowledge or schemata, making predictions, visualizing, summarizing, and inferring.

For many educators, the terms *strategy* and *comprehension* seem to be synonymous. In fact, the two are very different. Comprehension is the ability to understand text, and a strategy is a tool used to help a reader understand the text. We use comprehension strategies to achieve a specific reading purpose. For example, if a teacher wants to deepen comprehension, he or she might pose questions at various levels of understanding. A summarizing strategy might be to retell important main ideas and details. Comprehension strategies can be divided into those tools that are used before, during, and after reading. All are important to ensure that a reader understands a given text.

Prior to reading, the teacher provides the support necessary for students to navigate the text. These strategies include previewing vocabulary, building background knowledge, and previewing text features. During the reading of the text, questioning by the teacher as well as the students will increase understanding. Ultimately, students need to be able to question as they read independently to increase their understanding. This questioning needs to reflect thinking beyond a literal aspect. After reading the text, students should be able to summarize and evaluate the information. In this edition, we have developed instructional activities that require students to complete written comprehension responses as extensions of their small-group instruction.

In our opinion, the isolation of comprehension strategies has led to a loss of true comprehension. For example, focusing instruction for an entire week on cause-and-effect relationships with little regard for any of the other strategies that are needed to understand the text is absurd. In other words, we want teachers to recognize the importance of all of the facets of comprehension and not just focus on one for an extended period of time. Our small-group models are adapted so that teachers can use strategies interchangeably to best support students' understanding of a given text.

# Gaps in Other Small-Group Reading Models

*Guided reading* is a common term used to describe small-group reading instruction, especially in grades K–2. Guided reading is gaining popularity in the intermediate grades; unfortunately, many models do not offer the explicit, systematic instruction in word study and comprehension that we know is essential for growth in all readers. In the intermediate grades, we often find that guided reading is replaced with literature circles. This change is problematic because although literature circles can be useful in motivating students and generating discussion, they do little to support or provide explicit teacher instruction. Daniels (1994) describes literature circles as student directed rather than teacher directed. In our opinion, literature circles alone do not typically provide the basic teacher instruction necessary to guide and develop proficient readers. Students are given the freedom to choose and independently read a book for the purpose of small-group discussion. Although this may motivate some students to read more challenging texts, students are often left with texts that are either too easy or too difficult. We believe that students make optimal gains only when paired with instructional-level text and support by the teacher. Students are motivated to read when they can actually read their texts. In reality, we recognize that small-group reading instruction might not take place every day. On the days when teacher-directed small groups do not meet, student-directed literature circles could serve as an alternative activity, but only if the students are reading books that are at their independent reading level.

Similar to literature circles, a readers' workshop approach by itself does not offer students enough teacher-directed instruction at a student's instructional level. As described by Atwell (1998), the workshop lesson consists of minilessons that focus on some aspect of literature or a reading strategy, and independent reading time, which requires students to keep a journal and respond to the literature in terms of what they think or how they feel about what they are reading. Also during this time, the teacher engages in student conferences on an individual or group basis or can engage in guided reading with groups of students who need additional support. Additionally, students have sharing time, during which they share with another person their journal entries, and the other person gives feedback. If students are only reading at their independent level, they are not being challenged to reach their true potential. If they are reading in their instructional level without proper guidance or support, they are most likely missing important information that they need in order to fully understand a given text.

Recently, basal reading programs have included small-group options. These are accompanied by leveled text identified as below, on, and above grade level. The quality and levels of these texts seem questionable at times. Often, the focus of the leveled text lesson is simply a repetition of what was taught in the whole-group "story of the week" lesson. This is not differentiated instruction, nor does it meet the development needs of individual readers.

# Literacy Venues for Intermediate Readers

Small-group differentiated reading is a critical part of a comprehensive literacy program which, when implemented effectively, gives every student the opportunity to become a more successful reader. Although this book focuses on small-group differentiated reading instruction and its importance, the additional venues for delivering literacy instruction cannot be overlooked. It is unrealistic to think that small-group instruction can be used exclusively for instructional delivery in any classroom. Whole-class instruction allows opportunities for the teacher to model and share literacy experiences with the students. Additionally, meaningful independent practice gives students the time to master their literacy skills. Together, these venues provide a powerful model for effective delivery and practice of literacy skills. Table 3 shows the literacy venue options in an intermediate classroom.

**TABLE 3**
**Instructional Literacy Venues in the Intermediate Classroom**

| Venue | Teacher Read-Alouds Teacher Models Writing | Shared Reading Shared Writing | Small-Group Differentiated Reading | Independent Reading and Writing |
|---|---|---|---|---|
| Text selections | • Narrative, informational text, poetry<br>• At or above grade level | • Short choral readings, poetry, short narrative and informational text<br>• Grade-level text | • Short narrative pieces, informational text, poetry<br>• Instructional-level text | • Student choice<br>• Text from small group<br>• Independent reading level |
| Focuses | • Listening/ speaking comprehension<br>• Listening/ speaking vocabulary<br>• Modeling written comprehension | • Comprehension in grade-level text<br>• Addressing grade-level standards<br>• Developing grade-level vocabulary<br>• Composing written comprehension pieces | • Fluency<br>• Reading/writing vocabulary<br>• Orchestrating reading strategies for comprehension<br>• Developmental word study | • Fluency practice<br>• Reading to comprehend<br>• Writing to demonstrate comprehension<br>• Reading/writing vocabulary |
| Provides | • Access to text written above grade level<br>• Motivation<br>• Connections from reading to writing | • Access to grade-level text with teacher support<br>• Teacher support for grade-level standards | • Access to instructional-level text<br>• Growth opportunities for all students<br>• Increased reading by students | • Practicing reading and writing strategies<br>• Motivation<br>• Writing to demonstrate comprehension<br>• Connections from reading to writing |
| Appropriate for | • Whole group<br>• Heterogeneously grouped students | • Whole group<br>• Heterogeneously grouped students | • Small groups (six or fewer students)<br>• Homogeneously grouped readers | • Individuals<br>• Partners<br>• Small groups |

*Note.* Modified from *Small-Group Reading Instruction: A Differentiated Teaching Model for Intermediate Readers, Grades 3–8* (p. 11), by B. Tyner and S.E. Green, 2005, Newark, DE: International Reading Association. Copyright 2005 by the International Reading Association.

## Teacher Read-Alouds

An effective venue to address the wide range of reading levels in a classroom is through a teacher read-aloud. Having the teacher read text to the class allows text access to all students while building listening comprehension and vocabulary knowledge. Please note, however, that reading aloud and discussing text with students will not, in and of itself, produce better readers. During this time, we can teach students about and model reading strategies as well as increase background knowledge needed for the text. The ultimate goal is to have students use these strategies intuitively when they read on their own.

Teacher read-alouds provide the following benefits:

- Offer whole groups of students an opportunity to experience text that is often above their instructional reading level
- Allow teachers to model proficient, fluent reading while also demonstrating effective think-aloud strategies
- Provide students with a model for comprehending a variety of texts and genres as well as for developing listening vocabulary and listening comprehension

Teacher read-alouds are effective in the following situations in intermediate classrooms:

- Working with heterogeneously grouped readers
- Sharing content-specific information related to grade-level standards in a whole group
- Motivating students through engaging genres in a whole-group setting
- Building background knowledge in content areas

## Modeled Writing

Modeled writing provides an opportunity for students to observe the teacher as he or she responds to texts with various writing types (e.g., narrative, informational, persuasive). Although traditionally thought of in terms of teaching writing, modeled writing is an important venue for extending reading comprehension. Teachers demonstrate their own understanding of the text through a combination of thinking aloud and writing. For example, if your focus in writing is to create a well-organized report, and your focus in comprehension is to determine main ideas and supporting details, you could begin with a well-chosen read-aloud. Then, the modeled writing focus could be the process of determining main ideas and details. The teacher can then model how to assimilate those into a well-written report.

Modeled writing provides the following benefits:

- Allows students to observe the teacher using think-aloud strategies and constructing the text piece
- Demonstrates the connection between reading and writing comprehension
- Creates a written piece that can be used for shared reading

- Gives a visual representation for important content
- Provides writing models for students to refer to as they are writing independently

Modeled writing is effective in the following situations in intermediate classrooms:

- Working with a heterogeneous group of readers and writers
- Responding to a read-aloud
- Demonstrating comprehension of a text
- Modeling different forms of writing, such as narrative, informational, and persuasive

## Shared Reading

Simply defined, the shared reading venue is one in which both the teacher and the students share in the reading and discussion of the text. That said, the students must have access to the text that is being read and discussed. The teacher is primarily responsible for reading the text, although students should be held accountable for whispering along or reading chorally with the teacher. It is not appropriate to ask individual students to read the text aloud in the shared reading setting. Short text pieces, such as poems or brief informational texts, are more appropriate than longer selections for this reading venue.

Shared reading provides the following benefits:

- Allows students to share a common piece of grade-level text
- Allows all students access to grade-level text that they may not be able to read independently
- Offers students exposure to content-area information in accordance with prescribed standards
- Provides effective instructional support for a wide range of readers
- Enables the teacher to engage students in a purpose-driven writing activity
- Supports vocabulary and comprehension development

Shared reading is effective in the following settings:

- Working with heterogeneously grouped students
- Sharing content-specific or grade-specific text

## Shared Writing

Similar to modeled writing, shared writing also gives students the opportunity to participate in the writing process as it is orchestrated by the teacher. Although the teacher is responsible for the writing of the text, the students contribute as the text is composed. Inclusive of the benefits of modeled writing, shared writing also provides these additional benefits:

- Allows students to participate in the thinking and composing process with teacher support
- Establishes clear examples for students to apply to their own understanding of a text
- Provides scaffolded support for students as they move toward independent written responses

## Small-Group Differentiated Reading

This small-group instructional venue is instrumental in increasing the reading abilities for intermediate students. During this time, the teacher carefully provides systematic instruction in the teaching of fluency, word study, and comprehension. Appropriate instructional-level text is used during instruction. Small-group differentiated reading provides the following benefits:

- Maximizes optimal reading instructional time
- Affords the opportunity for all students to move forward in their reading abilities
- Allows the teacher to pinpoint students' difficulties and adjust instruction appropriately
- Supports reading comprehension and word study skills that are necessary for more advanced reading
- Provides the text necessary for successful independent reading and writing extensions

Small-group reading instruction should be used in an intermediate classroom during the literacy block time. Additionally, intermediate readers who are performing significantly below grade level need to be given additional small-group instruction outside of the regular reading block. This can be provided by supplemental personnel, such as a special education, EL, Title I, or reading specialist.

## Independent Reading

Intermediate readers need ample time to practice reading at their own reading levels. Without independent practice, students will lack the confidence to become more advanced readers. This independent practice should take place while the teacher is providing small-group instruction to other groups of students.

This is an activity that promotes students' reading at their independent levels. In other words, this is an opportunity for students to do the *real work* (i.e., decoding, comprehending) of reading on their own. Independent reading provides the following benefits:

- Supports fluency and comprehension development
- Provides students with many opportunities to practice reading on their own

- Motivates students because they are allowed to choose their own independent-level reading material
- Motivates students with materials that they can independently read and understand

Independent reading should be used in an intermediate classroom while the teacher is conducting small-group reading instruction.

## Independent Writing

This venue offers students time to practice focused writing skills as they deepen their written comprehension. These writing opportunities might extend from a book previously read by the teacher, a shared reading selection, a text that is read in their small group, or even an independently selected text. In addition, independent writing is an activity that promotes writing fluency and student choice in topic and format.

Independent writing provides the following benefits:

- Offers students many opportunities to practice targeted writing skills
- Motivates students when they are allowed to write on their choice of topic, format, or both
- Offers quality writing assignments that allow students to demonstrate their text comprehension
- Helps students develop confidence in their writing skills
- Allows the teacher to evaluate individual student writing and set realistic goals for improvement
- Supports individual students and is respectful of their developmental writing levels

Independent writing should be used in an intermediate classroom while the teacher is conducting small-group reading instruction. Individual writing conferences provide support to students as they are developing their own writing skills. Just as readers go through developmental stages, writers also progress in this manner.

## Other Considerations

### Leveled Text

Although more commonly associated with beginning readers, using leveled books with intermediate readers is important to students' reading development. Leveled books are those that vary in readability based on the structure of the text, content, vocabulary, theme, and grammatical structure. Using a leveled book approach allows teachers to differentiate reading instruction as students continue through upper elementary school and middle school. There are many leveling systems in place by a multitude of publishers and researchers. Throughout this book, we refer to four commonly used leveling systems: (1) Developmental Reading Assessment (DRA; Beaver & Carter, 2005),

(2) Fountas and Pinnell (1996), (3) Lexile levels, and (4) Reading Recovery levels as they pertain to the Intervention Reader stage. Each school should decide on a leveling system that is appropriate for the books available to them. Once this decision is made, all books should be leveled using this system.

## *Motivation*

Motivation is essential if students are to become successful readers and writers. This can be a difficult area to address in the intermediate grades. Intermediate readers' difficulties are often attributed to a lack of motivation. If motivation were the issue, then incentives such as grades, privileges, and rewards would likely be effective remedies. However, incentives are rarely enough to adequately address the issue. Lack of motivation is often a secondary consequence of underlying problems rather than the primary cause of poor reading. Students become frustrated when they are constantly forced to attempt to read material that is above their reading level. This, in turn, leads to teacher frustration in having to teach content-area standards when their students cannot read their textbooks. Many content-area teachers have neither the understanding of reading development nor the knowledge of differing venues to meet both student needs and curricular requirements.

In our experience, students become motivated when they are given text or activities that they can successfully read and master. Additionally, teacher and student frustration is reduced when reading instruction is perceived as a doable task. Reading becomes a challenging yet achievable goal when students are presented with appropriate instructional-level materials.

It is difficult to imagine motivating students without a literacy-rich environment that includes a variety of leveled text types (e.g., novels, magazines, newspapers, content-specific books, poetry, digital media) for students to explore, read, and enjoy. It is impossible to motivate both teachers and students when they do not have the materials needed to succeed. Securing these materials must become a priority for the school and district-level administration. It is only with their support that teachers will feel empowered to teach, and students will feel empowered to learn.

# Common Core Standards: Classroom Implications

In the 21st century, the reality of the need for our students to possess diverse skill sets has become a must in the United States. Although mandates such as the No Child Left Behind Act of 2001 have supported the development of state standards and assessments, the United States still lags behind other countries in student academic achievement (Hechinger, 2010). The changing nature of work, technology, and the global economy finds our nation scurrying to make the changes needed to remain as a competitive nation. Other countries have outpaced the U.S. education system in meeting these future job skill realities.

The adoption of the Common Core Standards is considered a critical piece needed to help close the gap between U.S. students and students from other top-performing countries. The U.S. Department of Education expects the gap to begin to close by 2014 (Daggett & Gendron, 2010).

Over the last two decades, states, school districts, and even individual schools have spent millions of dollars and untold time developing standards, only to have them continually rewritten. Many teachers have become so confused with the turnover of standards that they have trouble even finding the most current standards document.

Today, most states have chosen to adopt the Common Core Standards (National Governors Association Center for Best Practices & Council of Chief State School Officers [NGACBP & CCSSO], 2010c). How will these standards affect the nature of everyday classroom instruction? The implications for educators of the Common Core Standards are both exciting and daunting. Educators need to shift how they teach and how they assess students. With this in mind, we were attentive to the standards as we revised the lesson plans for this edition. This will assist teachers as they become knowledgeable about and plan for the standards.

The Common Core Standards expect upper elementary and middle school students to read grade-level texts and respond to them independently. How will we address the needs of those students still unable to meet this expectation? *Small-Group Reading Instruction* can help increase reading achievement for all students. Placing a grade-level text in the hands of a student who is reading significantly below grade level is not the answer. The small-group models provided in this book support teachers and students as they strive to meet these new standards.

The Common Core Standards are certainly a challenge but also an opportunity to improve student achievement and help direct teacher instruction. These standards reflect what all students are expected to know and be able to do, rather than dictate how teachers should teach. Beginning with the goal in mind can help teachers design instruction that produces the desired results.

We want to be clear about our inclusion of the Common Core Standards information: We are not agreeing or disagreeing with the current standards movement, as we realize as educators that we will always have guidelines to follow and benchmarks to strive for. It is our goal to assist and support teachers with this endeavor.

# A Look Ahead

Chapter 2 takes an in-depth look at each of the lesson components: fluency, word study, and comprehension. Vocabulary instruction is embedded in both word study and comprehension, as appropriate. Each component is defined, and research is cited as a rationale for the inclusion of each component. Activities and routines that support each lesson component are thoroughly discussed, with an explanation for differentiation of these activities between stages.

Chapters 3–6 provide an in-depth look at each of the intermediate reader stages: Intervention Reader, Evolving Reader, Maturing Reader, and Advanced Reader. A lesson plan model for each stage is presented, along with in-depth teacher–student dialogue centered on each lesson component. A variety of text genres are used in sample lessons for both narrative and informational texts. Additionally, appropriate text levels are suggested for each reading stage.

Chapter 7 discusses the extensions for and management of small-group differentiated instruction in the intermediate classroom. Extension activities that include quality reading and writing assignments directly related to the students' small-group instruction are provided. Further, classroom routines, organizational models, and sample schedules are included for successful small-group implementation.

Finally, Chapter 8 discusses pre-, post-, and ongoing assessments that support the Small-Group Differentiated Reading Models. These informal assessments include a review of informal reading inventories that can be used to assess word recognition and comprehension. Qualitative and quantitative fluency assessments can provide guidance in determining student progress. Spelling assessments are also included and can be used to guide word study instruction. These assessments provide valuable information for curricular planning, flexible grouping, and individual assessment. Using the information gained through these assessments allows teachers to make informed decisions as they assign students to small groups based on individual literacy needs. These assessments are used routinely throughout the school year to track student progress in fluency, word study, and comprehension.

# CD Materials

A series of PDFs is on the accompanying CD for you to print and use in your classroom. For your convenience, there are also thumbnail samples of these materials throughout the chapters and in the CD Contents section at the back of the book. The CD includes materials in the following three content areas:

1. *Assessment materials:* Includes informal assessment materials for fluency, word study, and comprehension as well as scoring guides for word study assessments

2. *Word study materials:* Includes a word study glossary and, for each of the four reader stages, a word study scope and sequence, word sort directions, and word study cards

3. *Support materials:* Includes resources for use within small-group and extension activities

# Components of and Activities for the Small-Group Differentiated Reading Models

In developing the lesson plan models for small-group differentiated reading instruction, careful attention was given to balancing the important research-based components, which include fluency, word study, and comprehension. Another component that is vital to student reading ability is vocabulary. You will notice that we embedded vocabulary development into word study (as it relates to the structure and meaning of words) and comprehension (as it relates to the understanding of words in text). These components have been identified as essential in the process of learning to read (Bear et al., 2007; Samuels, 2002; Sweet & Snow, 2002); therefore, the power of our lesson plan models lies in the inclusion of each of these critical components, as they are relevant in the different stages of reading development, into a manageable, cohesive plan.

This chapter provides the research base that validates the use of each component in the Small-Group Differentiated Reading Models. Further, we provide differentiated instruction and activities based on the developmental stages of the reader, which allows teachers to plan for and execute meaningful instruction for all of their students.

In Chapter 7, we provide instructional extension activities for each component. Different from that of literacy centers or learning stations, where all students work on the same thing, these extensions are meant to supplement individual learning. The instructional activities presented in this chapter are more appropriate for use within small-group instruction.

## Fluency

Reading fluency is an important milestone in reading achievement. The foundation of fluency is in the ability to identify words quickly and accurately in context. Therefore, students' attention can be directed toward constructing meaning from the text rather than decoding text. The National Reading Panel report (NICHD, 2000) describes fluency as the ability to read "with speed, accuracy, and proper expression" (p. 11). These three areas are further defined as follows:

1. *Speed:* Relates to the student's rate of reading and is usually determined in words per minute (WPM) or correct words per minute (CWPM)

2. *Accuracy:* Determined in reading by the student's ability to recognize words correctly, without omissions, insertions, or substitutions

3. *Expression:* Relates to the student's ability to read using correct phrasing, intonation, tone, and pitch so that the reading reflects the author's intended meaning. The word *prosody* is also used to describe these elements (Dowhower, 1991). Expression is subjective; therefore, it is more difficult to assess.

## Research Base

Historically, fluency has been considered the most "neglected reading goal" (Allington, 1983, p. 556). The connection between decoding, fluency, and comprehension has often been overlooked. However, thanks in part to the National Reading Panel report (NICHD, 2000) and the subsequent publication, *Put Reading First: The Research Building Blocks for Teaching Children to Read: Kindergarten Through Grade 3* (Armbruster, Lehr, & Osborn, 2001), fluency is currently one of the most widely discussed topics in reading, and the research in this area is flourishing, particularly with regard to a focus on aspects of fluency and fluency assessment (Hasbrouck & Tindal, 2006; Pikulski & Chard, 2005). Research in fluency in the early 1970s (LaBerge & Samuels, 1974) focused on the relationship between automatic word recognition and reading achievement. This concept is known as automaticity. Research now solidifies the link that fluency offers between automatic word recognition and comprehension (Bashir & Hook, 2009; Hook & Haynes, 2009; Katzir et al., 2006; NICHD, 2000). Although automaticity is essential for proficient reading, there are students who have this skill yet lack the prosody that allows them to interpret the author's meaning of a given text. Obviously, without automaticity and prosody, a student cannot fully comprehend the text.

Pinnell and colleagues (1995) found that only 13% of all fourth graders could read with enough expression to interpret the author's meaning. The same study also found that the fourth-grade reading rates were linked with overall reading proficiency. Faster reading has long been associated with increased comprehension (Carver, 1990; Samuels, 1976). Clearly, we cannot ignore the implications of fluency as they relate to intermediate readers. That said, when assessing fluency, we must look at all aspects rather than just one. For example, simply assessing word accuracy does not take into account speed or prosody. Likewise, if we are assessing only speed (WPM), we do not get the whole picture of a student's ability. All aspects—accuracy, speed, and expression—are vital for a reader to not only be fluent but also comprehend at a higher level.

A limited number of activities can be used to address both word recognition and prosody issues as they relate to fluency. Arguably, the most effective and widely researched instructional activity is repeated readings. Studies indicate that repeated readings of a given text allow students the opportunity to practice reading fluency (Rasinski & Padak, 1998; Samuels, 1979; Samuels, Schermer, & Reinking, 1992). The National Reading Panel report (NICHD, 2000) concluded that "repeated and monitored oral reading improves reading fluency and overall reading achievement" (as cited in Armbruster et al., 2001, p. 21). Additionally, when students are given guidance and feedback during a repeated reading activity, fluency and comprehension development are both optimized (Meyer & Felton, 1999; NICHD, 2000). For this strategy to be effective, a student must reread independent- or instructional-level text. Although a teacher read-aloud provides a model of a fluent reader, this activity will not necessarily increase a student's oral reading fluency.

Common sense tells us that if we want students to become more fluent readers, they need to have time each day to practice this skill. In our own observations, many fluency issues remain unresolved because students are not given ample time to read the appropriate levels of texts in a supported environment. We know from research and our own clinical observations that time spent in fluency practice results in dramatic increases in word recognition, speed, accuracy, and prosody (Samuels, 1979; Topping, 1987). It is similar to learning how to play a musical instrument. To play a piece by Mozart, one has to sit down at the piano and start with "Old MacDonald Had a Farm." Reading skills must be practiced as well. More often than not, students in the intermediate grades are required to read silently and, therefore, do not practice their oral reading fluency.

Although silent reading is faster and can increase comprehension, many intermediate students are still evolving readers. These readers struggle with automatic word recognition or have passed the decoding phase but continue to read in a word-by-word fashion, disregarding punctuation and using little expression. For many evolving readers, fluency is an area in which they are lacking; therefore, the Small-Group Differentiated Reading Models include this component. For maturing and advanced readers, this component should still be practiced; however, it is done independently, outside of the small-group instructional time. Keep in mind that there may be times when a teacher would want to listen to a maturing or advanced reader to assess oral reading fluency. For example, this is appropriate when students are reading a piece of literature that requires the correct prosody to fully understand the text. As a side note, it is important to realize that although fluency progress can be made with older struggling readers, it can often be a long, time-consuming process. Thus, studies have shown that it is more effective to use preventative fluency interventions rather than remedial measures (Torgesen et al., 2001).

Recently, the number of teachers using informational text for fluency practice and development has increased. The decision which text to use, narrative versus informational, should take individual student needs into consideration. There are also district and school mandates to consider. In both our small-group and extension activities, we use both narrative and informational texts, including songs, poetry, and theater scripts, to engage and motivate these intermediate readers.

## Small-Group Activities for Fluency

Within a small-group setting, the following rereading activities are used with intervention and evolving readers. Independent- or instructional-level text must be used for each of these activities. Note that there are times when evolving readers can also practice fluency on their own; it does not necessarily always have to be done in the small group on a daily basis (see the extension activities in Chapter 7). This decision should be based on an assessment (see the 4 × 4 Oral Reading Fluency Rating Scale in the Assessment Materials section on the CD ) that measures all aspects of fluency. However, intervention readers should practice fluency daily in small-group sessions.

**Choral Reading:** Using short selections, such as pieces of selected text or poems, the group reads and rereads the whole text or part of the text in unison. The teacher begins this activity by modeling the fluent reading of the text prior to the group's unison read. Choral reading cannot take the place of individual reading practice, but it can be used to provide support for students when necessary. This activity is most appropriate for intervention and evolving readers.

**Partner Reading:** Each student is paired with another student in the small group. The students take turns reading previously read text. One student reads while the other student gives assistance and feedback. Then, the process is reversed. The teacher monitors by listening in on the reading pairs, assisting when necessary. This activity provides more practice for students as they reread text.

**Whisper Reading:** Students are asked to reread a text that has been read by the group. They read at their own pace in a whispering voice that allows the teacher to monitor and offer support when necessary.

**Lead Reading:** In this activity, a teacher or student reads aloud, and the other students in the group whisper read along with the leader.

Finally, we want to stress the importance of using independent- or instructional-level text with any oral reading fluency activity. Additionally, we stress using a balance of materials; it is not always appropriate to use informational text when working on fluency, nor is it appropriate to use only poetry. A teacher must use a variety of materials, keeping in mind the result: faster, more efficient readers. For the purposes of time and motivation, we recommend the use of poetry and/or song lyrics during small-group fluency instruction.

# Word Study

*Word study* is a term that is often overused and misunderstood. As stated in Chapter 1, we refer to word study as the systematic, developmental study of words (Bear et al., 2007; Ganske, 2000; Henderson, 1990). In considering the word study component for intermediate readers, we have included systematic phonics and vocabulary instruction. Although a word study or phonics component can be found in most published reading basal series, in our opinion, many of these lack a logical scope and sequence for instruction and fail to meet the developmental needs of all students. This scope and sequence is exactly what is most important when engaging students in the study of words at their developmental level. Invernizzi and Hayes (2004) attribute the lack of systematic classroom instruction in word study to a combination of deficient teacher knowledge in this area and confusing information provided by both publishers and policymakers. Our students need higher level decoding skills to read higher level texts. We believe that by providing teachers with a logical scope and sequence for word study, they will be able to implement this component in their small-group instruction, which will ultimately allow for differentiated instruction that will better meet the needs of all of their students.

Developing word study with intermediate readers is crucial to their continued success with reading and writing development. This is particularly important for those third- or fourth-grade students who are just beginning to have reading and writing difficulties. Their difficulties might be due to a heavy focus on phonics and phonemic awareness and a lack of focus on comprehension skills in the early grades. However, the difficulties may be caused by the fact that they are relying on rote memorization for word identification. Thus, these students are unable to decode more difficult text. In reality, the challenges that some students face are probably a combination of both factors. Memorization will take a student only so far; they need explicit, sequential instruction along with specific decoding skills.

Beginning in third grade, a greater emphasis is placed on informational text because content area instruction becomes integral to meeting state standards. Consider, for instance, the new Common Core Standards initiative. Our goal in addressing the standards in this edition is not to agree or disagree with the merits of the standards; rather, our goal is to inform teachers and address the issues.

When reviewing the Common Core Standards, we have clearly raised the bar for the word knowledge that we expect kids to know. For example, in third grade, students are expected to be able to do the following:

> Know and apply grade-level phonics and word analysis skills in decoding words.
>
> a. Identify and know the meaning of the most common prefixes and derivational suffixes.
>
> b. Decode words with common Latin suffixes.
>
> c. Decode multisyllable words.
>
> d. Read grade-appropriate irregularly spelled words. (NGACBP & CCSSO, 2010a, p. 17)
>

Our higher level readers will be able to meet the challenge of decoding words with common prefixes and suffixes; however, our average or below-level readers will most certainly need more explicit word analysis and vocabulary instruction. We know that intermediate teachers are more likely to embed spelling instruction within their writing instruction (Cramer, 2001); however, many fail to explicitly illustrate spelling patterns and/or spelling–meaning relationships (Johnston, 2000). Further, we know that some intermediate teachers simply cannot find time for systematic word study instruction (Templeton, 2002). As a result of these factors, we have many intermediate students who are missing the opportunity to improve their spelling and reading as well as their writing ability.

## Research Base

Word study for beginning readers focuses on phonemic awareness and phonics (Armbruster et al., 2001). *Phonemic awareness*, typically taught in kindergarten and first grade, is defined as the student's "ability to hear, identify, and manipulate the individual sounds—phonemes—in spoken words" (Armbruster et al., 2001, p. 3). Phonemic awareness development does not introduce letters as it relates to sounds, which is known as phonics. There is an important difference: Phonemic awareness is an auditory skill, whereas phonics is the ability to make the connection between the sounds (phonemes) and the written letters (graphemes). Phonemic awareness is considered the precursor to phonics ability and is a powerful predictor of later reading success (Snow, Burns, & Griffin, 1998). Many students come to the intermediate classroom lacking these basic phonics skills. Therefore, phonics must be retaught in order for these students to progress in their reading development. The need for systematic phonics instruction delivered in small-group settings is well documented (Morris et al., 2000; NICHD, 2000; Santa & Høien, 1999); therefore, we have included it in the Small-Group Differentiated Reading Models.

Much of what is currently known as word study grew out of developmental spelling research and theory (Invernizzi & Hayes, 2004). Research on developmental spelling is vast and has been done for decades (e.g., Bear, 1989; Bloodgood, 1991; Gill, 1992; Henderson & Templeton, 1986; Invernizzi, Abouzeid, & Gill, 1994; Nelson, 1989; Templeton & Morris, 1999). However, it has been only in the past 15 years that we have seen developmental spelling data driving classroom word study and the link to reading instruction.

We believe this is due to a growing body of research that supports the connection between a student's ability in spelling and reading. Invernizzi and Hayes (2004) have found that spelling scores for almost 70,000 first graders correlated with both word recognition in isolation and oral reading accuracy. Word recognition in isolation is arguably the best predictor of a student's reading level. If a student can read given words in isolation, it is likely that the student can read the words in context as well. Being able to accurately decode words allows the reader to focus on meaning rather than structure. The processes of spelling and reading are clearly related; in fact, they can be considered two sides of the same coin.

As readers mature, vocabulary development is widely considered to be the cornerstone of reading achievement (Blachowicz & Fisher, 2000; Hennings, 2000). As students transition from learning to read to reading to learn, vocabulary instruction becomes essential. This is increasingly important for maturing and advanced readers because they encounter much more content-specific vocabulary. Research shows that students who lack word knowledge or cannot access their word knowledge have difficulty understanding what they read (Chall, 1987; Daneman & Reingold, 1993). Thus, we have purposely embedded vocabulary development in our models through both explicit word study and comprehension instruction.

## Scope and Sequence

To fully understand the reading, writing, and spelling processes, teachers need a solid foundation in the structure of the English language (Moats, 2000). Henderson and

Templeton (1986) refer to this structure as being divided into layers: alphabet, pattern, and meaning. When teachers become familiar with the aspects of each of these layers, they can use this information to assess students' developmental levels and then guide the classroom instruction to best meet the needs of the students.

### *Alphabet Layer*

The alphabet layer is taught in the beginning reader stages and consists of the basic letter–sound relationships in the left-to-right manner. For example, the word *big* is broken down into three sounds: /b/, /i/, and /g/. Each sound is directly represented by a letter. However, the word *ship* still has three sounds even though there are four letters. *Sh* is a digraph that makes one sound. This layer has no silent or unsounded letters. Each sound is represented by one letter or sometimes by a pair of letters. (For more information on a word study scope and sequence for the beginning reader, see *Small-Group Reading Instruction: A Differentiated Teaching Model for Beginning and Struggling Readers* [Tyner, 2009].)

### *Pattern Layer*

The pattern layer typically is taught in the beginning reader stages and continues into the Evolving Reader stage. The pattern layer includes studying words that have silent and unsounded letters, and words with more than one syllable (i.e., syllabication). Initially, this layer includes a focus on vowel patterns in single-syllable words. In the word *time*, for example, we hear three sounds: /t/, /i/, and /m/; however, there are four letters, and the *e* does not act with another letter. The focus in this layer progresses to examining more complex vowel patterns, such as the "air" in *chair*, and words having more than one syllable.

### *Meaning Layer*

The meaning layer generally covers the end of the Evolving Reader stage and continues throughout the Advanced Reader stage. This layer primarily focuses on the morphology of words, that is, a group of letters directly associated with a particular meaning. For example, *spec(t)* means look; thus, we know that *inspector, spectator,* and *spectacle* are related in meaning and have something to do with looking. This layer explores the Latin and Greek base words and root words. A base word can stand alone as a word (e.g., *train*). A root word cannot stand alone as a word, and its origin is in Latin or Greek (e.g., *spec(t)*).

## Common Core/Curricular Standards

As previously stated, to meet grade-level standards, word study for intermediate students is a critical component of a language arts curriculum. The following are examples of the word knowledge expectations for fifth and seventh graders according to the Common Core Standards:

**Grade 5**

Know and apply grade-level phonics and word analysis skills in decoding words.

a. Use combined knowledge of all letter-sound correspondences, syllabication patterns, and morphology (e.g., roots and affixes) to read accurately unfamiliar multisyllabic words in context and out of context. (NGACBP & CCSSO, 2010a, p. 17)

**Grade 7**

Determine or clarify the meaning of unknown and multiple-meaning words and phrases based on *grade 7 reading and content*, choosing flexibly from a range of strategies.

a. Use context (e.g., the overall meaning of a sentence or paragraph; a word's position or function in a sentence) as a clue to the meaning of a word or phrase.

b. Use common, grade-appropriate Greek or Latin affixes and roots as clues to the meaning of a word (e.g., *belligerent, bellicose, rebel*).

c. Consult general and specialized reference materials (e.g., dictionaries, glossaries, thesauruses), both print and digital, to find the pronunciation of a word or determine or clarify its precise meaning or its part of speech.

d. Verify the preliminary determination of the meaning of a word or phrase (e.g., by checking the inferred meaning in context or in a dictionary). (NGACBP & CCSSO, 2010a, p. 53)

Without a doubt, we cannot overlook the importance of a word study component in the small-group reading model as it relates to intermediate readers. As evidenced in the previous table, after grade 5, there is a progression from simply decoding words to decoding words in order to figure out their meaning; this is what we refer to as vocabulary development. The scope and sequence that we have created for word study (see the Word Study Materials section on the CD 💿 ) is based on both the aforementioned layers and curricular standards that dictate what students will encounter in state testing. In today's classrooms, both of these factors *must* be considered in structuring an effective word study sequence. Each word study feature (e.g., a specific word pattern or root) is studied for at least one week. We suggest one week as an appropriate amount of time to ensure that students understand the feature.

One question that we encounter often from teachers is, "What if there is a difference between my students' reading and word study abilities?" Unlike younger students, older readers may have a discrepancy between their reading and spelling ability. Teachers often tell us that they have difficulty addressing the different word study needs within their small reading groups. Although we firmly believe that it is beneficial to individual students to solidify incomplete word knowledge before moving on to learning new features, this is not always easily accomplished in the small-group setting. Thus, teachers need to make the instructional decisions (e.g., modifying the group and/or features studied) that will be of greatest benefit to their students at any given time. For example, some students may benefit from just the exposure to features that they might see later on a standardized test. For other students, it may be an appropriate time to study a given feature in depth. In either scenario, word study instruction remains in the small-group setting. Students need teacher support when finding, discussing, and analyzing specific word patterns.

As with the other small-group components, assessment is key. A teacher must first assess students (see the Assessment Materials section on the CD 📀 ) to properly place them in the word study scope and sequence.

## Small-Group Activities for Word Study

In the small-group setting, the following activities are used during the word study component of the lesson. However, for purposes of differentiated instruction, we have noted which activities are appropriate for each stage of reader. Some of the activities in this section have corresponding reproducibles in the Support Materials section on the CD 📀 ; this information is noted after each activity. As with fluency and comprehension, you can find extension activities in Chapter 7 that support word study features.

As previously noted, features are typically studied for one week. During this time, students work with the same group of words. Every week, each student is given a copy of the words (word study cards are available in the Word Study Materials section on the CD 📀 ). Students should cut out the word study cards prior to small-group instruction, saving valuable instructional time when students come to their small group. These word study cards can be used for small-group and independent word study activities. (The teacher can provide students with envelopes or plastic bags to store their cards.)

**Intervention Reader Word Study Cards**
Level 1, Week 1: Consonant-A Vowel Patterns

| cat | flat | flag |
| hat | clap | slap |
| trap | crab | bat |
| make | shake | gave |
| take | page | tape |

**Word Study Notebooks:** Many activities here and throughout the book can be completed in word study notebooks. In basic terms, a word study notebook is a bound notebook that houses all word study information (e.g., spelling sorts, writing sorts, sentences). These notebooks are an important resource for intermediate students because they use them to keep track of the word features that they have studied. In addition, the word study notebook can serve as a resource for students as they work independently. For example, if students are editing written work and have misspelled words with features that they already studied, the teacher can direct students to the appropriate section in their word study notebooks, so students can correct the words. These notebooks are also the link between in-group and extension activities.

### Word Sorts

Sorting is fundamental to word study. Through this activity, students compare and contrast word features (e.g., pattern, meaning). Students categorize words based on the features being studied. Students can sort words into an "oddball" category for

**FIGURE 1**
**Completing a Word Sort in Small Group**

*Note.* Photo courtesy of Heather Hughes.

those words that do not follow a specific generalization. After students have sorted their words, the teacher should lead a discussion about categories the students used and what they discovered about the words through the activity. In addition, the teacher should lead a discussion about the meaning of the words. See Figure 1 for a completed word sort.

The discussion during the small-group time is the most important aspect of word study instruction. Word study success should not be measured by how quickly students can sort their word cards. Rather, success should be measured by students' increased knowledge and interest about words. Do the students find words that match their pattern (without being told) in other pieces of text? Can the students pick out a pattern, or are they logical in their thoughts about how words are put together? Are the students using their knowledge to figure out words while reading? During small-group discussion is the time to ask questions such as

- What do we notice about the words?
- What patterns do we see?
- Have you seen this pattern before?
- What are some of the words that we do not recognize?

- Are we sure that we know the meaning of all of the words?
- How do we know? Can we explain the meaning in our own words?

This group discussion is critical for word study success.

### Types of Sorts

**Closed Sort:** In a closed sort, the teacher gives the students explicit instructions regarding the word study features and provides header cards showing these features. For example, in the Evolving Reader stage, when studying suffixes, a teacher can choose to use header words (e.g., *dropped, waved, checked*) or header patterns (e.g., *E-Drop, Doubling, Nothing*). Students then sort the word study cards based on these features. Please note that we have left the header words to the discretion of the teacher, thus they are not provided in the Word Study section on the CD 💿.

**Open Sort:** An open sort gives students the opportunity to sort the word study cards without explicit teacher directions regarding the word features. This process allows students to use critical thinking skills to discover patterns in words.

**Spelling Sort:** A spelling (or writing) sort is used after the students have worked with the specific features for at least one day. This type of sort is critical for solidifying students' ability to recognize and reproduce the patterns being studied. In this activity, the teacher calls out words for students to simultaneously sort and spell. This activity can be completed with intervention, evolving, and maturing readers when more than one feature is being studied. There is a three- or four-box spelling sort sheet to use depending on the number of features studied (see the Spelling Sort sheet in the Support Materials section on the CD 💿 ). This particular sort is essential for students to make the knowledge transfer from sorting to their writing. A spelling sort would not be appropriate when students are studying one feature (e.g., root words), as we want students to be able to recognize and replicate patterns.

### Other Word Study Activities

**Student-Generated Sentences:** In this activity, students create their own sentence (they can also practice different types of sentences and questions) to demonstrate both accurate spelling and the meaning of a given word. This activity helps students make the transition from sorting word patterns to spelling word patterns in context, as well as demonstrate their understanding of the given word. This activity is appropriate for all readers and can also be completed as an extension activity outside of small-group sessions.

**Meaning Discussions:** Teachers have told us that they struggle with having to show a product—something completed in writing at the end of a lesson. With word study, the process, rather than the product, is essential; students must go through the thought process to fully understand the words they are studying. The only way to accomplish this is through a rich discussion. This can be time-consuming if there are many words whose meanings students do not know, but this dialogue is important at all of the reading stages. We believe that it is important for teachers to have a full understanding of the words their students are studying; thus, it is worth the time for teachers to purposely plan their discussion within a small-group lesson.

Note: Although sorting is at the crux of word study instruction, this activity cannot be the only one that students do with the words. Students need to be involved with writing activities (e.g., spelling sorts, writing sentences) and oral discussions in order for the features to transfer to their everyday writing.

### Additional Word Study Activities for Intervention Readers

In addition to the sorting activities previously listed, the following activities would be beneficial for intervention readers.

**Sound Boxes:** This activity has two purposes: First, students segment sounds in a given word (oral language activity). Then, students use the boxes to write the corresponding letters of that word (see the Sound Boxes sheet in the Support Materials section on the CD  ).

**Word Scramble:** Students are given letter cards, and the teacher provides a word for students to spell. They make the word by choosing the correct letters from their cards and writing the correct word in their word study notebooks.

**Dictated Sentences:** Prewritten sentences are dictated to students each day. Each sentence contains a word (or words) that includes the feature(s) studied that week.

# Comprehension

Improving comprehension is one of the most important goals of intermediate-grade teachers. A student's ability to comprehend text affects every aspect of his or her educational endeavors. While beginning readers are cracking the alphabetic code and developing automaticity, intermediate readers continue to develop important word study knowledge because the focus at this stage shifts to comprehending the text's message. Although comprehension seems to develop as a natural process for some students, occurring after they master basic decoding skills, this is not true for all students. As previously noted, comprehension must be taught through systematic instruction across the content areas.

Comprehension should be a focus of all beginning reading instruction and should begin in preschool. Just as phonemic awareness is a precursor to phonics, listening comprehension is a precursor to reading comprehension. For example, strategies associated with story structure, sequence, or summarizing that a kindergarten teacher directs after a read-aloud of the Three Little Pigs are essentially the same strategies that an intermediate student will engage in as he or she reads text independently. Comprehension for intermediate readers is focused on students' reading as well as their ability to use and refine their comprehension skills—in essence, knowing what strategy to use and when to use it.

Comprehension is a critical thinking skill, not simply a series of questions that students answer while they read or a worksheet that they fill out after they read. Comprehension is a continual thought process. Students need explicit modeling of comprehension strategies and time to practice applying those strategies rather than the assign and assess model that is often used in the intermediate grades. We firmly believe that comprehension instruction should follow the gradual release of responsibility model (Duke & Pearson, 2002; Pearson & Gallagher, 1983). This model includes a teacher, or more experienced guide, giving an explicit explanation of how to perform the skill while modeling exactly what should be done. Then, the student works with the teacher to practice the skill together. Gradually, the teacher provides less and less guidance until the students are able to perform the skill on their own. This notion of a newcomer learning from a more adept individual stems from Vygotskian theory (Vygotsky, 1978). Learning occurs during language-rich interactions between the skilled and less skilled, whether the learners are adults or children. The zone of proximal development, also an element of Vygotskian theory, suggests that a teacher should provide scaffolded learning opportunities for students while slowly withdrawing more and more support as it becomes less needed.

Our students need opportunities for modeling and guided practice in the same way that medical students need constant practice as they are learning their skills. Would we want a newly trained doctor performing a surgery on us after simply listening to someone talk about it? Or, would you rather the surgeon read about it, discuss it with an attending physician, and then practice it under guided supervision before attempting it alone? Comprehension instruction should follow a similar model.

Many teachers model asking questions while they are reading. They tell students the importance of asking different types of questions along the way in order to understand what is being read. What is often missing, however, is *how* they came up with those questions. As skilled readers, what made the teachers decide which questions to ask first, and how did they know which questions to ask next? This is the piece of modeling that students are missing. What we are talking about is using modeling to help students develop their critical thinking skills.

Although an abundance of research exists on developing reading comprehension, our focus is on comprehension as it relates to instruction within the Small-Group Differentiated Reading Models. Although not explicitly stated in the lesson plans, modeling of metacognitive strategies is a vital piece of good instruction. As teachers conduct small-group instruction, we want them to be cognizant of their students' metacognitive skills and development. This may include rereading passages, discussing others' perceptions of the text, recognizing how to use word structure and syntax knowledge, or simply reminding students to make a conscious effort to think about the text they are reading and connect it to their own knowledge base.

This instruction includes the following strategies:

- Previewing the text, including predicting, accessing prior knowledge (making connections), and building background knowledge if needed
- Identifying the text structure and previewing specialized vocabulary
- Generating questions by the teacher and the students (e.g., literal, inferential, and application questions)
- Summarizing, including identifying the main idea, supporting details, and the sequence of events; the ability to compare and contrast and examine cause-and-effect relationships; and identifying major story elements

As readers progress through the developmental stages of reading, comprehension becomes more important; therefore, we adjusted the lesson plans to support more advanced comprehension skills. That is, we have scaffolded the strategies to best meet the needs of readers at any given stage because the comprehension skills build on one another from simple to complex. In addition, teacher support should decrease as students become more competent in their abilities to fully understand the text.

One of the most critical aspects of comprehension development is the dialogue that occurs between the teacher and the students as well as the dialogue that occurs between students. These conversations are worth their weight in gold when it comes to student understanding. What naturally occurs in a conversation (not teacher lecturing) is the exchange of ideas, knowledge, and perceptions. What are the particular aspects that each student brings to a text, and how does that enable or impede his or her understanding? This exchange can happen only through lively dialogue; thus, we have made this feature explicit in the lesson plans for this edition.

## Issues of Text Complexity

Text complexity (previously known as text difficulty) is not limited to readability. According to the Common Core Standards for English Language Arts in grades K–12, text complexity is multifaceted. The research cited in Appendix A of the Common Core Standards argues, "Despite steady or growing reading demands from various sources, K–12 reading texts have actually trended downward in difficulty in the last half century" (NGACBP & CCSSO, 2010b, p. 3). Basically, as the demand on students to read difficult and complex text in college has increased, the text demands in grades K–12 have decreased. As such, the Common Core Standards measure text complexity with quantitative (e.g., words per sentence, syllable information, sentence length) and qualitative (e.g., purpose, structure, language used, clarity) factors and issues related to the reader (e.g., motivation, experience, perception). As a result of the inclusion in the Common Core Standards, text complexity will undoubtedly become increasingly important. As we discuss comprehension, we touch on text complexity as one of the topics of consideration when choosing texts for students to read.

## Research Base

The amount of research that supports systematic comprehension instruction is vast. Comprehension is a complex cognitive undertaking with many facets working in collaboration. Based on the findings of the National Reading Panel report (NICHD, 2000), Armbruster and colleagues (2001) identified strategies, including story structure, questioning, and summarizing, as "appear[ing] to have a firm scientific basis for improving text comprehension" (p. 42). Furthermore, strategies related to background knowledge, previewing, and predicting text also have shown to be effective for improving comprehension (Guthrie, 2005). In fact, research also verifies that these strategies can and should be systematically taught (Dowhower, 1999; Menke & Pressley, 1994; Pearson, 1993; Pressley & Afflerbach, 1995). Furthermore, there is an evidence base that supports students using these strategies in independent reading situations when the strategies have been explicitly taught (Griffin, Malone, & Kame'enui, 1995; Pressley, Symons, Snyder, & Cariglia-Bull, 1989).

### *Assessing, Activating, and Building Background Knowledge*

In the small-group model, we cannot ignore the value in finding out what students know about a given topic before they begin reading a piece of text. This step is critical in order for them to understand the text beyond a literal level. To be clear, there is a difference between assessing and activating background knowledge. *Activating* infers that the information is there, and a teacher just needs to help students find the correct file in their heads that contains the information. When assessing, a teacher needs to find out if the information has ever been filed. Once a teacher has established students' current knowledge base, he or she may then need to build some of the knowledge that they lack.

This can be done in a variety of ways, including through multimedia resources such as virtual field trips, YouTube, and online WebQuests. Although the use of online videos is sometimes considered to be a time waster, there are many video clips and series that are excellent and appropriate for classroom use. Although the above is not feasible during most small-group sessions, a teacher could choose to use the resources provided in whole-class instruction or as extension activities.

### *Predicting, Previewing, and Identifying Text Structure*

Previewing the text includes making predictions based on the title and illustrations (for narrative text), making connections related to background knowledge, discussing possible unknown vocabulary, and identifying the text features that assist in comprehension (for informational text). All of these techniques are used to support comprehension prior to the reading of the text. Research supports the notion of actively engaging students before reading a text (Guthrie, 2005; Stevens, 1982; Tierney & Pearson, 1985). Previewing is similar to reading the jacket of a book before reading the entire book. The quick blurb whets a reader's appetite for the book and provides a glimpse of what is to come.

Identifying text structure enables students to identify critical elements, which allows students to differentiate between narrative and informational text. This, in turn, aids in their understanding of the purpose and content of the text. In narrative text, this structure typically includes characters, setting, plot, events, and conflict and resolution. Informational texts have many different structures; the five most common are descriptive, sequence, cause and effect, comparison and contrast, and problem and solution. Special features such as graphs and diagrams are also included in informational text structures. The following are descriptions of each of these structures:

1. Descriptive Text Structure (the most common structure for textbooks)

   - Provides information about a topic, concept, event, object, person, idea, and so forth
   - Describes facts, characteristics, traits, and features, usually qualifying the listing by criteria, such as size or importance
   - Connects ideas through description by listing the important characteristics or attributes of the topic

2. Sequence Text Structure

   - Puts facts, events, or concepts in order
   - Traces the development of the topic or gives the steps in the process
   - Makes references to time that are explicit or implicit, but a sequence is evident in the pattern

3. Cause-and-Effect Text Structure

   - Shows how facts, events, or concepts (effects) happen or come into being because of other facts, events, or concepts (causes)

4. Comparison-and-Contrast Text Structure

   - Points out similarities or differences among facts, people, events, concepts, and so forth

5. Problem-and-Solution Text Structure

   - Shows the development of a problem and one or more solutions to the problem

Currently, identifying text structure often is found on state-mandated assessments for intermediate readers (Armbruster, Anderson, & Ostertag, 1989; Cudd & Roberts, 1987; Fowler, 1982). Because the purpose of narrative and informational text differs, students need to be able to adapt their knowledge of comprehension strategies to meet the demands of the text. When students are able to identify how a text is organized, they are better equipped to extract an author's intended meaning. It is important for students to understand that within a given piece of text, they might find more than one structure; in such cases, students need to consider the overall purpose of the piece. For example, in the following text excerpt, the author describes longitude and latitude. The overall purpose of the piece compares and contrasts the two aspects rather than merely describing them.

> Notice that the globe has a network of vertical and horizontal lines. The horizontal lines are called *parallels* because they run parallel to each other, and the vertical lines are called

*meridians* because any one shows all the places that have the same local time. Each location along a parallel has the same *latitude,* or distance from the equator. Each location along a meridian has the same *longitude,* or angle between it, the north pole, and the prime meridian.

Latitude and longitude are two very different things: on the surface of the earth, latitude is a distance while longitude is an angle. You cannot tilt the earth on its side and expect the latitude lines to match the old longitude lines. The meridians converge to two points: the north and south poles, but the parallels don't converge anywhere; they stay the same distance apart everywhere. (Strebe, 2009, paras. 2–3)

## *Questioning*

Two types of questioning occur in a classroom: (1) questioning that the teacher generates and (2) questioning that the students generate. Both are important and are steeped in supportive research (Cohen, 1983; Wixson, 1983). Teacher questioning in oral or written form is probably the oldest and most commonly used comprehension strategy. Questioning helps clarify the teacher's knowledge of the students' understanding: Do students really understand? Did they catch the important parts? Can they make inferences from the text?

By asking questions during small-group time, the teacher is better able to assess student thought processes and understanding because there is more time for individual student responses. This discourse scenario acknowledges comprehension as a collaborative process, which is more process oriented rather than product oriented (Palincsar, 2003; Palincsar & Brown, 1984). The ultimate goal of questioning is to develop advanced readers who intuitively question their own reading; thus, demonstrating self-questioning is a strategy that must be modeled and taught (Pearson & Fielding, 1991; Wong, 1985). Many students view questioning as a form of interrogation, a way for a teacher to find out what they know and do not know. On the contrary, when used appropriately, questioning is meant to extend students' understanding of the text's message.

Another aspect of questioning that has received much attention as it relates to reading comprehension is the type of questions that both a student and a teacher ask (Wixson, 1983). These types of questions align with Bloom's taxonomy, which classifies six levels of thinking (Bloom, 1956). Many teachers tend to ask questions in the lower tier of the taxonomy rather than the higher tiers. In most cases, this is not done intentionally, but it becomes a habit. In a classroom where time is a precious commodity, it is much faster to ask a question that can be answered in three words versus a question that requires students to fully explain their thinking. Simply asking these types of recall questions leaves many aspects of comprehension unaddressed. Rather, questions should be varied to ensure that all levels of thinking are addressed.

Effective questioning requires careful planning and appropriate feedback to student responses. It is just as important to ask appropriate questions as it is to give appropriate feedback to student responses. The following are key points to remember to increase comprehension:

- Provide immediate feedback to all question responses whether correct, incorrect, or partially correct

- Offer information with regard to why an answer was correct or have other students explain why the information was correct
- Probe to solicit a correct response before asking another student to answer the question

### *Types of Questions*

Questions are categorized as literal, inferential, and application.

- *Literal questions:* These require basic recall of facts from the text; that is, the answer is directly stated in the text. Although these questions require little reflection by the reader, basic recall is an important aspect of the foundation for comprehension. These questions are the bottom two tiers of Bloom's taxonomy: knowledge and comprehension.
- *Inferential questions:* These require students to synthesize information found in more than one place in the text or surmise information to form an answer. Although the answers to these types of questions may be provided in the reading, the students must look in several places to find them. However, students also may have to rely on their own background knowledge to read between the lines. These questions are in the middle of Bloom's taxonomy: application and analysis.
- *Application questions:* These require students to draw on their own prior knowledge and experiences to interact with the text. This type of question requires students to formulate and justify an opinion. In other words, students must go beyond the printed words and evaluate the text to respond appropriately. These questions are at the top of Bloom's taxonomy: synthesis and evaluation.

### *Summarizing*

We believe that summarizing is the most necessary comprehension component because it requires students to provide a general analysis and synthesis of key text components, whether using a narrative or informational text selection (Pearson & Dole, 1987; Pressley, 1990). Summarizing in narrative text involves synthesizing major story elements. Summarizing as it relates to informational text engages the reader in activities that allow him or her to extrapolate the main ideas and supporting details, explore relationships, sequence important information, and evaluate causal relationships. With each type of text, students must select certain features and omit others, in effect differentiating essential from nonessential details (Rinehart, Stahl, & Erickson, 1986). This skill must be modeled and taught explicitly as students struggle with extracting critical information. We see this demonstrated when we ask students to highlight important information; they tend to highlight everything, the bold words, or nothing. This shows the difficulty students have with extrapolating the information that an author deems important.

## Small-Group Activities for Comprehension

We firmly believe that comprehension involves much more than handing out blackline masters. We cannot stress enough the importance of meaningful teacher-led discussions and questioning that needs to happen during small-group instruction. In most cases, small-group time is the only time during the school day when students have the opportunity to engage in meaningful, instructional conversations related to reading at their own instructional level.

We encourage teachers to be mindful of the time involved in using these in-group activities and balance these with discussions about students' reading and understanding. For example, a teacher may want some way for students to keep track of events that have occurred while reading a chapter book. Rather than giving each student a graphic organizer to fill out during small-group time, the teacher may act as the scribe, while the students each contribute orally to complete the visual aid. There is no substitute for the insight that both students and teachers bring to the reading table. The following can be collaborative in-group activities or extension activities (see Chapter 7), depending on the lesson objectives. (Some of the activities have a corresponding reproducible in the Support Materials section on the CD 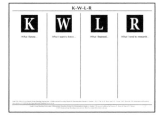.)

### *Before Reading*

**K-W-L-R:** This activity (adapted from Ogle, 1986) is useful for assessing background knowledge. When beginning to discuss a new concept, the teacher leads the discussion of what the students *know* about the topic. The teacher then asks the students what they *want* to learn about it. After the topic has been studied, the teacher then asks the students what they *learned* about it. Identifying what students learned is often overlooked; however, it is critical to the intended learning process. The *research* item allows students to identify points that they still do not know or have enough information about. These points can then be used as the basis for future research (see the K-W-L-R sheet in the Support Materials section on the CD ).

**Inquiry Chart (or I-Chart):** Originally developed by James Hoffman in 1992, this activity requires students to identify ideas that they know or think they might know about a particular topic. Then, students are required to find evidence that supports their hypotheses from at least three different sources. Teachers can tweak this activity to meet their own instructional goals (see the Inquiry Chart sheet in the Support Materials section on the CD ).

**Fact or Fib?:** Similar to an anticipatory set, the teacher provides students with a set of statements before they start reading the text. The students need to decide if the statements are true or false (fact or fib). After reading, the students review their initial assumptions and correct any that were incorrect (see the Fact or Fib? sheet in the Support Materials section on the CD  ).

### Predicting and Previewing

**Directed Reading–Thinking Activity:** This activity (adapted from Vacca et al., 2011) includes having students make predictions about what they think will be the first thing that happens in a story before reading it. The teacher writes down a prediction from one student. After reading a few pages, the teacher stops and asks the students to revisit the prediction. The teacher then asks the remaining students what their predictions were and what actually happened. The teacher writes down a prediction from another student. The teacher continues this process of predicting and revisiting until the entire book is read (see the Directed Reading–Thinking Activity Sheet in the Support Materials section on the CD  ).

**Text Feature Preview:** Because of the nature of previewing, this activity is done orally. After distributing the books, the teacher leads the students in examining the informational text by pointing out features such as chapters, pictures, photographs, maps, charts, headings, and subheadings. In addition, to help students navigate informational text, the teacher should be sure to point out the table of contents and appendixes.

### Vocabulary

**Vocabulary Discussion:** Teachers should preselect vocabulary that is essential to a given text. When discussing these words within small groups, it can be helpful to have a visual image of the vocabulary words when appropriate. Google Images is a great resource for this purpose. Teachers should be sure to revisit the identified vocabulary throughout the teaching of the text.

**Very Important Predictions (VIP):** For this activity, the teacher preselects important words from the story that relate to the characters, setting, problem, action, or solution. Each student contributes to the VIP Map (see the Very Important Predictions [VIP] Map in the Support Materials section on the CD 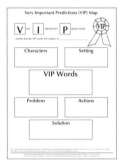 ) by predicting which words will correspond to which story elements before reading the story. Then, students check their predictions either during or after reading the story. Teachers can ask students to justify their responses. (See Figure 2.)

### During Reading

**Making Connections:** With this oral activity, students are encouraged to make personal connections to the text based on their experiences. These connections can be to students' own lives, to other texts, or to the outside world. Teachers should explicitly model the quality of the connections they are seeking. For example, consider the following scenario: Students are reading a piece of text in which the main character is torn between two decision points and does not know the right thing to do.

## FIGURE 2
### Completed Very Important Predictions (VIP) Map

*Note.* Photo courtesy of Jennifer Tyner.

Thomas:     I have a connection: I had a decision to make, and it was hard.

Teacher:     Good connection, Thomas. You are making a link to your own life.

In this example, Thomas needs some additional feedback, such as

• How do you think the character feels about making a hard decision?

• Did this remind you of your feelings? Why?

• Why do you think that the decision was hard for him, and how did his thought process resemble yours?

Just the fact that a student makes a connection is not enough. Teachers need to think about *how* students are connecting with the text. They need to be connecting with the important aspects rather than minuscule details, as demonstrated in the previous dialogue.

## Questioning

**Questioning Guides:** These guides can be a catalyst for in-depth questioning by the teacher. Questions are provided for all levels (i.e., literal, inferential, application) and geared specifically to increase comprehension in both narrative and informational text (see the Questioning Guides for Narrative and Informational Text in the Support Materials section on the CD  ). Some teachers find it helpful to have the questioning guides close by as they are teaching.

**The 5 Ws:** This is another type of questioning activity that promotes identifying the main idea from a text and can be done before, during, or after reading a text. Each student draws a card on which is written one of five question words (*who, what, where, when,* or *why*). Students are asked to use their word as a stem for a question that they generate as they read the next section of the text. Then, students pose their questions to the group to generate discussion about the reading.

## Summarizing

**Stop and Go!:** This activity can be used either during or after reading. If used during the reading, the teacher stops at strategic points to ask students (who should be called on randomly) to summarize what has happened in the text thus far. As the student summarizes the text, the teacher stops the student abruptly and asks another student to take over the summarizing. This process continues until all of the events or details have been discussed.

## After Reading

**Story Map:** This graphic organizer (adapted from Beck, McKeown, McCaslin, & Burkes, 1979) is a visual aid that represents the elements of narrative text (see the Story Map in the Support Materials section on the CD ).

**Cause and Effect:** This graphic organizer helps students collaborate and discuss examples of cause and effect in narrative and informational text (see the Cause and Effect sheet in the Support Materials section on the CD ). We often find cause and effect difficult to teach and difficult for students to learn. Emphasize that students should try to describe why they think the outcome (effect) was caused by a particular event.

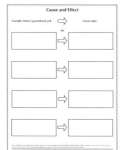

**Problem–Solution:** This organizer (see the Problem–Solution sheet in the Support Materials section on the CD ) allows

students to list the particular problems in a text and the solution that solved the problem. Be sure to discuss how this text type is different from cause and effect. In a problem, the reader can find an answer to the issue rather than a causal relationship.

**Compare and Contrast With Meaning:** This graphic organizer (see the Compare and Contrast With Meaning sheet in the Support Materials section on the CD ) is used by students to compare and contrast characteristics of given topics. Adapted from an activity on the ReadingQuest website (readingquest.org), this activity requires students to think about how given aspects are related or different.

**Timeline:** This graphic organizer (see the Timeline sheet in the Support Materials section on the CD ) helps students recall important events and place the events in the order in which they occurred in the story.

## *Summarizing*

**Sum It Up:** This strategy (adapted from an activity on the ReadingQuest website, readingquest.org) can be started in small-group sessions and extended outside of group. Sum It Up helps students write concise summaries that focus on the main idea of a text. Students imagine that they are placing a classified ad or sending a telegram, and every word costs them a certain amount of money. (This activity is also great for teaching math!) The teacher determines how much each word will cost and how much students can spend. For example, a teacher might determine that students have

$5 to spend and that each word costs 10 cents. Then, students have to write a summary using 50 words or less. This may seem like a large number of words, but teachers can adjust the number and cost based on the text that students are summarizing (see the Sum It Up sheet in the Support Materials section on the CD ).

**ABC Brainstorm/Summary:** This activity (adapted from an activity on the ReadingQuest website, readingquest.org) can be used to either activate or assess prior knowledge, or summarize/ assess what has been learned. The strategy also helps students brainstorm and summarize the key ideas associated with a given concept by thinking of words or phrases associated with that concept; each concept begins with a letter of the alphabet (see Figure 3 and the ABC Brainstorm/ Summary sheet in the Support Materials section on the CD ).

**What's the Big Idea?:** This activity can be used during or after reading as students summarize key points from the text.

*Note.* Photo courtesy of Jennifer Tyner.

Students use this strategy to identify the main ideas and supporting ideas in informational text (see the What's the Big Idea? sheet in the Support Materials section on the CD  ).

**Bio-Poem:** This activity can be used after reading a narrative text or a biography. Students contribute pertinent attributes about a character in the form of poetry. The poem follows an established, free verse pattern (see Figure 4 and the Bio-Poem sheet in the Support Materials section on the CD ).

**The Essentials:** After reading a piece of text or a text in its entirety, students are asked to individually identify the essential details (see The Essentials sheet in the Support Materials section on the CD ). Then, in small-group sessions, the teacher leads a discussion of common essential details and interesting facts. The group moves on to discuss differing details. During the discussion,

**FIGURE 4**
**Completed Bio-Poem**

Line 1:     First Name: _Jess_

Line 2:     Four traits that describe # 1: _Imaginative,_
_caring, patient, talented._

Line 3:     Related to: _May Belle_

Line 4:     Cares about: _Leslie_

Line 5:     Who feels: _Sad that Leslie is dead._

Line 6:     Who needs: _Courage_

Line 7:     Who gives: _understanding_

Line 8:     Who fears: _Being without Leslie_

Line 9:     Who would like to see: _the bridge to_
_Terabithia rebuilt._

Line 10:    Resident of: _Terabithia_

Line 11:    Last name: _Aarons_

Note. From *Small-Group Reading Instruction: A Differentiated Teaching Model for Intermediate Readers, Grades 3–8* (p. 33), by B. Tyner and S.E. Green, 2005, Newark, DE: International Reading Association. Copyright 2005 by the International Reading Association.

students need to be able to justify why they think their details are essential rather than just interesting facts, and vice versa. After the discussion, students create another list to provide closure to the text.

Comprehension instruction should not be limited to reproducibles or blackline masters. Rather, teachers need to engage students in a balance of authentic, meaningful activities that include discussion, visual aids, and writing opportunities. Small-group instructional time is an ideal venue for allowing students to understand how they, as individuals, make meaning from text. Many of the previous activities can be modeled in small-group sessions as a shared experience and then used as an extension activity with future texts.

We would like to emphasize that when teaching any given strategy (not an activity), it is important to integrate the strategies as they are appropriate to the understanding of a given text. Teachers often identify comprehension as a major issue for their students. Comprehension issues can be a combination of many factors, including vocabulary, level of text, decoding, and background knowledge. Often, it is difficult to tease out where the comprehension process is breaking down. Therefore, all aspects of comprehension need to be addressed on a continual basis.

# Conclusion

The vast theoretical base of reading can contain conflicting information and at times be difficult to navigate. However, even more challenging is the ability to apply the research to practical classroom instruction. Until we apply current research to the classroom level, the research remains an untapped resource. In extracting what we feel are the most important research-based components and strategies, we hope to make this transition for teachers more effective and efficient. In our experience, teachers are overwhelmed with training and information about "research-based" strategies without a model for practical classroom application. Thus, in this chapter, we kept to our goal of helping teachers *work smarter not harder* by providing the important research base along with ideas for immediate classroom use that will benefit both teachers and students.

# CHAPTER 3

# The Intervention Reader Stage

An intermediate student reading six months or more below grade level can be described as a struggling reader and in need of intervention. This intervention begins in the regular reading block with small-group differentiated reading instruction and continues with additional support outside of the allotted reading block time. Not only do these struggling readers face obstacles in the demands of the language arts curriculum, but they also struggle in content areas that are historically supported by text written above grade level. As the standards for intermediate readers become more complex and time demands increase, many teachers are at a loss to find the time necessary to address the specific needs of these struggling readers. With this in mind, it becomes important to work strategically within the classroom and include appropriate reading materials that address grade-level standards.

It is important to note that all intervention readers who are struggling do not look the same and will not need the same support strategies. A good example of this was when Beverly was assigned as a swimming instructor to a group of nonswimmers. Among them, there were various levels of readiness. The "rocks" would not get in the pool and were hanging onto the surrounding fence. The "tadpoles" were in the pool but would not put their faces in the water. Yet the "frogs" were jumping into the deep end of the pool, totally unaware of their inability to swim. It is similar for struggling readers. For this reason, most boxed intervention kits do not work for all struggling readers. Many basal reading programs tout intervention programs that pay little more than lip service to the differences among these readers. This chapter discusses three differentiated models for struggling intermediate readers based on their needs.

## How to Determine the Intervention Level

Table 4 displays the three levels of intervention. Typically, students do not struggle with one aspect of reading; they have deficits in multiple areas. Their deficits are often cyclical. For example, if a student struggles with decoding, this leads to fluency deficits and difficulty understanding the text. Or, students could be fluent decoders but do not have the vocabulary or background knowledge to fully understand the text. In our experience, we found that generally, intermediate students lack the ability to comprehend because the text is too difficult; that is, students do not decode it accurately, so their comprehension breaks down. Additionally, students struggle with the meaning of words or lack the background necessary to understand the text's message. For these reasons, the intervention models presented in this chapter are inclusive of each reading component.

**T A B L E  4**

**Intervention Stages for Intermediate Readers**

| Intervention Level | Grade-Level Equivalent | Instructional Reading Level | | | | Instructional Word Study Level | Assessments |
|---|---|---|---|---|---|---|---|
| | | Reading Recovery | Lexile Bands | DRA[a] | Fountas and Pinnell[b] | | |
| 1 | Mid– to late first grade | 8–16 | 200–400 | 8→16 | E–I | Common vowel patterns | • Running Record (93–97% accuracy with comprehension)<br>• Common vowel patterns<br>• Spelling assessment level 1 |
| 2 | Early to mid-second grade | 16–20 | 300–500 | 18→30 | J–L | Less common vowel patterns | • Running Record (93–97% accuracy with comprehension)<br>• Less common vowel patterns<br>• Spelling assessment level 2 |
| 3 | Mid– to late second grade | 20–22 | 500–700 | 24→34 | M–O | Common word features | • Running Record (93–97% accuracy with comprehension)<br>• Common word features (spelling and meaning)<br>• Spelling assessment level 3 |

[a]*Developmental Reading Assessment: Kindergarten Through Grade 3* (2nd ed.), by J. Beaver and M.A. Carter, 2005, Upper Saddle River, NJ: Pearson. [b]*Guided Reading: Good First Teaching for All Children*, by I.C. Fountas and G.S. Pinnell, 1996, Portsmouth, NH: Heinemann.

It is critical that teachers have access to all the information necessary to provide the most appropriate instruction, especially as it relates to struggling students.

The needs of many struggling intermediate readers can be addressed in the Evolving or Maturing Reader stages. For example, a fifth-grade reader who is significantly below grade level may be best served in the Evolving Reader stage. The Intervention lesson plan models accommodate intermediate students performing below the Evolving Reader stage. There are three different levels of intervention that accommodate readers performing at the mid–first-grade level through the end of the second-grade level.

Teachers need to assess each struggling reader in areas such as fluency, word study, and overall reading levels. Teachers should be sure to review all formal and informal assessment data that have been previously completed. Many times, generic data (e.g., standardized test scores) show that a student is functioning below grade level, but the data lack the specific diagnostic information needed to guide the teacher in a concrete progression plan. To construct such a plan, basic assessment information is needed. First, the instructional reading level must be established; that is, the text level that a student can read and understand with around 93–97% accuracy. Independent-level text, however, is text that the student can read and understand at 98–100% accuracy. Most schools that we have worked with already have a way to determine and track students' individual reading levels. Use all available data and assess if any critical information is missing. In order to provide the most effective instruction, the student must be reading instructional-level texts in a small-group setting.

A scope and sequence for the three levels of word study in intervention is presented in Table 5. Assessing word study levels (e.g., basic phonics patterns and word features) for these struggling readers is also essential in selecting the most appropriate level of intervention. (See the Assessment Materials section on the accompanying CD 💿.) Begin by assessing the students' ability to spell the most common vowel patterns that are foundational to phonics instruction. Using the level 1 spelling assessment for common vowel patterns, call each word out as you would in a traditional spelling test. When grading the assessment, the entire word must be spelled correctly. If a student scores below 80% on this assessment, guide the student through the seven-week scope and sequence outlined in Intervention level 1. If the student passes the level 1 assessment, administer the level 2 spelling assessment for the less common vowel patterns. If the student scores below 80% on this assessment, begin with the seven-week scope and sequence outlined in Intervention level 2. When the student passes the level 2 assessment, proceed to the level 3 assessment, which assesses both the spelling and meaning of common word features such as compound words, simple prefixes, and suffixes. If the students scores below 80% on this assessment, begin with the seven-week scope and sequence outlined in Intervention level 3.

Based on instructional reading levels and information from word study assessments, place each student in the most appropriate intervention level. It is very important to remain mindful of each of the reading components necessary for struggling readers. There are no shortcuts in the process of getting these students to become grade-level readers.

**TABLE 5**
**Word Study Scope and Sequence for Intervention Reader**

| Word Study | Week 1 | Week 2 | Week 3 | Week 4 | Week 5 | Week 6 | Week 7 | Spelling Assessments/Recommendations |
|---|---|---|---|---|---|---|---|---|
| **Level 1 Common vowel patterns** | Short a (cat)<br>aCe (make)<br>ar (car)<br>ay (day) | Short i (sit)<br>iCC (kind)<br>iCe (bike)<br>ir (girl) | Short o (top)<br>oa (coat)<br>oCe (rope)<br>or (born) | oo (look)<br>oo (pool)<br>ou (found)<br>ow (cow) | Short u (mud)<br>uCe (cute)<br>ur (fur) | Short e (red)<br>ee (keep)<br>er (her)<br>ew (few) | Review All r-Controlled<br>ar (car)<br>ir (girl)<br>or (born)<br>ur (burn) | >80%: Move on to level 2<br>60–80%: Review and reteach<br><60%: Redo |
| **Level 2 Less common vowel patterns** | ai (paid)<br>are (care)<br>au (fault)<br>aw (saw) | ie (field)<br>igh (high)<br>y (cry) | oar (roar)<br>oCC (cold)<br>oi (join)<br>oy (joy) | ou (cloud)<br>ou (would)<br>ow (how)<br>ow (mow) | ue (blue)<br>ui (build)<br>ui (fruit) | ea (bread)<br>ea (team)<br>ei (eight)<br>ey (they) | air (fair)<br>ear (near)<br>oar (roar)<br>ore (sore) | >80%: Move on to level 3<br>60–80%: Review and reteach<br><60%: Redo |
| **Level 3 Common word features** | Contractions<br>have<br>is<br>not<br>will | Homophones<br>ate/eight<br>by/bye/buy<br>hear/here<br>plane/plain<br>rode/road<br>sail/sale<br>tail/tale<br>there/their/they're | Homophones<br>cents/sense/since<br>deer/dear<br>hall/haul<br>made/maid<br>new/knew<br>not/knot<br>wear/where<br>write/right | Compound<br>any<br>every<br>night<br>over | Plurals<br>-es<br>-s<br>-y to -i | Simple Prefixes<br>dis-<br>pre-<br>re-<br>un- | Simple Suffixes<br>-er<br>-est | >80%: Move on to evolving reader stage<br>60–80%: Review and reteach<br><60%: Redo |

As assessment data is reviewed, there may be areas that are not well defined. For example, a student may read at an instructional reading level that is appropriate for level 3 intervention, but still lack basic phonics skills taught in level 1. If a student needs more help in one area or another, it can be provided by the EL or special education teacher. The most important aspect of supplemental instruction is the coordination among all of those who are working with these struggling readers.

# Levels of Intervention

## Level 1

Level 1 intervention is appropriate for students reading at the mid– to late first-grade level. These students need to reread books often. Word study focuses on the review of common vowel patterns that are necessary for foundational reading and writing. Although these level 1 students are still in the decoding phase of reading, the lesson plan also focuses on comprehension strategies that are appropriate to these students' developmental reading level. This weekly plan cycles through and reviews common vowel patterns that assist in filling the gaps of basic phonics knowledge and then progresses to the less common vowel patterns in level 2.

At the end of the seven-week cycle, administer the level 1 spelling assessment. Students scoring at 80% or higher should move on to level 2. Be sure to look critically at the mistakes that each student is making and reteach around the mistakes that are consistent within the group. For example, Juan scored 70% on the assessment, but upon analysis, the teacher realized he made only two common errors. He confuses the *sh* and *ch* digraphs as well as short and long vowels. The teacher can reteach around these errors and reassess before advancing him to the next level. If students continue to score below 80%, they should repeat the cycle.

Comprehension is addressed before, during, and after strategies. Additionally, out-of-group written comprehension extension activities support these readers as they demonstrate their comprehension through writing.

## Level 2

Students at this intervention level perform much like beginning to mid–second-grade readers. Again, fluency practice with rereading is important. As book selections get longer, the book may be used as a new read one day and a reread the next day. These students progress to less common vowel patterns that are critical to increased reading and writing levels. Before, during, and after comprehension strategies support these readers as they work toward the goal of successful grade-level reading and understanding. Grade-level standards in reading and comprehending are addressed as appropriate to the texts.

After the sequence is completed, give the level 2 assessment. Based on students' scores, you may move on, reteach certain features, or repeat the entire sequence.

## Level 3

This is the final level of intervention prior to beginning the Evolving Reader stage. These readers typically perform at the mid– to late second-grade level, where they begin to focus less on decoding and more on the comprehension of text. Word study focuses on a review of common word features that are associated with grade-level standards. In this level, there should be a stronger emphasis on the comprehension of both narrative and informational texts.

The assessment for common word features is modified to determine not only spelling but also the meaning of the words. The teacher first administers the spelling portion of the test. Then, students are asked to write a sentence with each word. The assessments are scored by looking at the correct spelling as well as the ability to accurately use the words in context.

## Assessments and Pacing

Generally speaking, plan for seven weeks of focused instruction for each intervention level. Pacing is critical, as a teacher needs to be sure that the material is neither too hard nor too easy. You will need to monitor progress with weekly spelling assessments, comprehension assessments, and informal running records (see Chapter 8).

# Instructional Components of the Intervention Reader Lesson Plan

For convenience, this lesson plan was designed for all three levels of intervention. Fluency, word study, and comprehension with accompanying vocabulary are all included in the plan along with suggested activities. The plan should assist teachers in effective planning and implementation of the lessons. Keep in mind that each text piece will require a lesson plan. The plan also serves as documentation for the intervention process.

A lesson plan model adapted for all three levels of intervention can be found in Figure 5. Although the components in the plan are consistent, the book level, word study levels, and comprehension strategies will vary based on the needs of the students. Each lesson component is discussed in this chapter, along with the strategies used during the lesson.

## Fluency

Each lesson begins by rereading the book that was read the day before. These students require rereading to improve fluency. All students must be engaged in the rereading of the text. Choral leading, lead reading, and whisper reading are good strategies to keep students engaged in the process.

**Intervention Reader Lesson Plan**

| FLUENCY (REREADING) | FLUENCY EXTENSION(S) |
|---|---|
| ☐ Reread text, selected pages, or poetry<br><br>Text: _____ | |

| WORD STUDY | WORD STUDY EXTENSION(S) |
|---|---|
| Level 1 ☐   Level 2 ☐   Week: _____<br>Vowel Pattern Focus: _____<br>☐ Open Sort: (day 1 only)<br>☐ Sound Boxes (day 2)<br>☐ Spelling Sort (days 3–5)<br>☐ Teacher-dictated sentence:<br><br>_____<br><br>Level 3 ☐   Feature Focus: _____<br>☐ Open Sort: (day 1 only)   ☐ Spelling Sort<br>☐ Word Meaning discussion<br>☐ Student-Generated Sentences to show<br>  meaning | |

| COMPREHENSION (NARRATIVE TEXT) | COMPREHENSION (INFORMATIONAL TEXT) |
|---|---|
| New text: _____<br><br>Before Reading<br>☐ Activate and build background knowledge<br>☐ Preview vocabulary: _____<br><br>_____<br>☐ Set a purpose | New text: _____<br><br>Before Reading<br>☐ Activate and build background knowledge<br>☐ Preview text features and structure<br><br>_____<br>☐ Preview vocabulary: _____<br><br>_____ |
| During Reading<br>☐ Teacher/student questions: _____<br><br>_____<br>☐ Discussion/teaching points: _____<br><br>_____<br>_____<br><br>Notes: | During Reading<br>☐ Teacher/student questions: _____<br><br>_____<br>☐ Discussion/teaching points: _____<br><br>_____<br>_____<br><br>Notes: |
| After Reading<br>Summarize<br>☐ Plot/story elements<br>☐ Character (traits, motivations, point of view)<br>☐ Setting (mood, importance)<br>☐ Events (sequencing)<br>☐ Conflict and resolution<br>☐ Theme<br>Notes: | After Reading<br>Summarize<br>☐ Main ideas and essential details<br>☐ Compare and contrast<br>☐ Sequence<br>☐ Cause and effect, or problem and solution<br>Notes: |

**WRITTEN COMPREHENSION EXTENSION(S):** _____

_____

Notes:

## Word Study

The word study routines included in the lesson plan model provide a variety of strategies. Students need to be able to talk about patterns in words, thus demonstrating their knowledge orally. Each lesson begins with a one- or two-minute introduction that includes explicit instruction. Then, the students are involved in a written activity to practice sorting and writing the words. Again, we have found that not only must students sort and be able to read the words, but also they must be able to effortlessly write the words.

**Open Sort:** Begin working with new patterns on the first day with an open sort, which allows students to sort the cards into categories without prior explicit discussion of the focus patterns. This allows students the opportunity to compare and contrast words and discover how the patterns work. The teacher engages students in a discussion about the patterns and provides more direct instruction when needed. It also includes an opportunity to explore word meanings.

**Spelling Sort:** After providing a quick review of the focus vowel pattern, students write the isolated pattern in the boxes provided (see the Spelling Sort sheet in the Support Materials section on the CD  ). Then, the teacher calls out one of the words and asks the students to repeat it, and they visually sort and write the word under the appropriate pattern. You can expect to complete two words for each pattern in the lesson. After each student writes the word correctly, the teacher takes the word card and sorts it for the group under the correct pattern as a visual check.

**Sound Boxes:** Writing words in sound boxes where each box represents only one sound is especially helpful for intermediate students who still lack phonemic awareness and are confused when asked, "How many sounds do you hear in the word?" or "What vowel pattern represents that sound?" For example, the word *shirt* written in sound boxes would look like this:

All students should have their own sound boxes to use in this activity (see the Sound Boxes sheet in the Support Materials section on the CD  ). (Hint: If you put the Sound Boxes sheet in a sheet protector, you can use it multiple times.) It is important that the teacher sort each card after the students complete the boxes. This gives students an additional visual of the patterns so that they can recognize them automatically.

**Dictated Sentences:** In Intervention levels 1 and 2, the teacher dictates a sentence daily so that students have the opportunity to apply their pattern knowledge in writing. Prewritten sentences are provided for teacher convenience, but any sentence that contains the words with the focus vowel patterns can be used (see the Intervention Reader Dictated Sentences in the Word Study Materials section on the CD ). The sentence could also be used for a quick grammar check. For example, after the sentence has been written correctly, the teacher could ask students to circle the nouns, find the subject and predicate, and so forth. This additional activity will only take an extra minute or so and can give the teacher valuable data while giving the student valuable grammar instruction.

**Student Sentences:** In the final Intervention phase, level 3, the students are asked to compose a sentence with a particular word or words. For example, if contractions were the focus of the lesson, students might be asked to write a sentence using a contraction correctly. The teacher might ask each student to use a different word and then share the sentence with the group. The following are other examples:

- **Homophones:** Give each student a homophone pair to construct correct sentences using the homophones.

- **Plurals:** Give each student a singular word and ask them to use it as a plural in a sentence.

These activities could also be used as an extension for the students to complete on their own.

# Informational Lesson Model: Level 1 Intervention

## Description of the Group

The following group is composed of students from four different classrooms. After assessing the students, the third-grade teachers realized that these students could best be served in a group with common word study and reading abilities. The four teachers agreed to trade several students so that these struggling readers could receive more focused instruction. Edward, Juana, Shavon, Nevah, and Anna are the group members. Edward and Juana are EL students, Shavon has been assessed and receives special education services, and Nevah and Anna are new to the school and have a long history of moving multiple times during the school year. The following assessment information was gathered by the teachers:

| Student | Instructional Reading Level | Spelling Assessment Level |
|---|---|---|
| Anna | 12 | 40% |
| Edward | 10 | 40% |
| Juana | 8 | 30% |
| Nevah | 10 | 55% |
| Shavon | 14 | 35% |

Based on this assessment information, the teacher knew that these students were performing at the mid–first-grade level. Although they mastered basic sight words, they still lacked basic decoding skills, as evidenced by the spelling assessments. Considering that these third graders are a full two years behind in reading, it will take small-group instruction in the regular classroom setting along with additional small-group intervention instruction to begin closing their achievement gap.

The teacher reviews all spelling assessments and thinks that it will be valuable for all of the students in the group to review basic vowel patterns. It is also important for the teacher to communicate with the EL teacher, the special education teacher, and the interventionist so that additional small-group instruction is cohesive. These level 1 students will focus on common *O* patterns in today's lesson.

In selecting an appropriate text, the teacher considers the fact that many books at this level will be geared to younger children. If the students are to stay motivated, they need a book that they view as interesting or one that they can make a connection with on a personal level. The new text for the day is *The Dolphins* by Rose Inserra. Informational texts are good choices for intervention readers. Prior to reading the new text, the teacher piques students' interest by asking several "Fact or Fib" questions. When they finish reading, students check their answers to determine the winner with the most correct answers. Following the short quiz, the teacher introduces important text vocabulary. Additionally, the teacher points out several text features that are part of this informational text. Figure 6 shows the completed lesson plan for this group.

## Lesson Goals/Objectives

### Fluency

The fluency goal for this group is to increase speed, accuracy, and expression in reading to ultimately improve comprehension.

### Word Study

The lesson objective for word study is for students to recognize common *O* vowel patterns and to quickly and automatically read and write words that contain these patterns.

### Comprehension

Comprehension objectives include being able to identify main ideas and details in informational text and create a poster that incorporates this information.

## Fluency

Fluency practice for this group takes place both within and outside of the students' small group. Today's lesson begins by rereading the text that was read the day before. The teacher assigns partners to practice reading the text after group time, which gives students the opportunity to read the text three times.

**FIGURE 6**
**Completed Intervention Reader Lesson Plan for Level 1**

| FLUENCY (REREADING) | FLUENCY EXTENSION(S) |
|---|---|
| ☑ Reread text, selected pages, or poetry<br><br>Text: _The Nest on the Beach by Annette Smith_ | |

| WORD STUDY | WORD STUDY EXTENSION(S) |
|---|---|
| Level 1 ☐  Level 2 ☐  Week: ___3___<br>Vowel Pattern Focus: _Short o, o_e, _or_<br>☑ Open Sort: (day 1 only)<br>☐ Sound Boxes (day 2)<br>☐ Spelling Sort (days 3–5)<br>☐ Teacher-dictated sentence:<br>_Were you born on the west shore?_<br><br>Level 3 ☐  Feature Focus: _____<br>☐ Open Sort: (day 1 only)   ☐ Spelling Sort<br>☐ Word Meaning discussion<br>☐ Student-Generated Sentences to show<br>  meaning | • Sort cards and write sorts in word study notebooks.<br>• Choose one word from each pattern and write a sentence. |

| COMPREHENSION (NARRATIVE TEXT) | COMPREHENSION (INFORMATIONAL TEXT) |
|---|---|
| New text: _____ | New text: _The Dolphins by Rose Inserra_ |
| Before Reading<br>☐ Activate and build background knowledge<br>☐ Preview vocabulary: _____<br>_____<br>☐ Set a purpose | Before Reading<br>☑ Activate and build background knowledge<br>☑ Preview text features and structure<br><br>☑ Preview vocabulary: _breathe, smooth, fin, hole,_<br>  _whole_ |
| During Reading<br>☐ Teacher/student questions: _____<br>_____<br>☐ Discussion/teaching points: _____<br>_____<br>_____<br><br>Notes: | During Reading<br>☑ Teacher/student questions: _____<br>_____<br>☑ Discussion/teaching points: _How do dolphins_<br>  _breathe?_<br>_____<br><br>Notes: |
| After Reading<br>Summarize<br>☐ Plot/story elements<br>☐ Character (traits, motivations, point of view)<br>☐ Setting (mood, importance)<br>☐ Events (sequencing)<br>☐ Conflict and resolution<br>☐ Theme<br>Notes: | After Reading<br>Summarize<br>☑ Main ideas and essential details<br>☐ Compare and contrast<br>☐ Sequence<br>☐ Cause and effect, or problem and solution<br>Notes: |

| WRITTEN COMPREHENSION EXTENSION(S): _Design a poster: "The Top Five Things_ |
|---|
| _About Dolphins"_<br>Notes: |

| Teacher: | Yesterday, we read the book *The Nest on the Beach* by Annette Smith [2001]. Today, I want to hear you reread the book. I am going to set the timer for six minutes. I want everyone to begin whisper reading. When I tap your book, I want you to read a little louder so that I can listen. I want you to try to read in the same way that you talk. Go ahead and get started. Remember to pay attention to punctuation. |
|---|---|

The teacher does some informal assessment with fluency during the lesson. She makes notes as she listens in to each student.

### *Fluency Extension*

| Teacher: | I want you to partner read *The Nest on the Beach* when you leave group today. Make sure that you take turns being the lead reader for each page. |
|---|---|

This ensures that both students read the entire book.

## Word Study

Today, the teacher introduces the focus vowel pattern words for the week that include common *O* patterns (e.g., short *o*: *pot*; long *o*/consonant/silent *e*: *spoke*; *r*-controlled *o*: *or*). These struggling readers may still confuse these vowel patterns in their reading and writing. The teacher begins the lesson with an open sort and allows students the time to look closely at the words for common patterns.

| Teacher: | I'm going to put these cards on the table. I want you to look at these words and see if you can put them into categories based on how they are alike. Talk with each other as you are thinking about how these words might be grouped together. |
|---|---|
| Edward: | Well, I see that some of the words end with an *e*, so that could be one category. |
| Teacher: | All right, go ahead and group those together. |
| Shavon: | Oh, I see some words that all have "or" in them. Can I put those together? |
| Teacher: | What do the rest of you think? |
| Anna: | I think that's right. All we have left are these words that just have one *O*, so I'm going to group those together. |

| Teacher: | Let's look at the first group of words. You said that they all have only one *O* and no other vowels. What else do you notice about the vowel? |
|---|---|
| Edward: | There is a consonant on each side. Is that like the *I* patterns when the vowel was short, and it was closed up on both sides with consonants? |
| Teacher: | Why don't you try it out? Does that work? |
| Anna: | Yes, it does. It is the same thing with all the vowels. |
| Teacher: | We will continue to look at that as we finish up with *U* and *E*. |

The teacher continues leading a discussion of the three vowel patterns.

### *Dictated Sentence*

---

| Teacher: | Take out your word study notebooks for our dictated sentence. Today's sentence has several words with the *O* patterns we talked about today. The sentence is, "Were you born on the west shore?" Listen again: "Were you born on the west shore?" Now, say the sentence with me. |
|---|---|

The students repeat the sentence with the teacher and then write the sentence independently.

### *Word Study Extension*

---

| Teacher: | When you leave group today, I want you to take your own word study cards and sort them into these three categories. Then, I want you to write the sorts in your word study notebooks. I also want you to choose one word from each pattern and write a sentence with each word. |
|---|---|

These students need ample practice both within and outside of the group as they solidify these word study features.

## Comprehension

### *Before Reading*

### Activate and Build Background Knowledge

---

| Teacher: | Today, we are going to read an informational book called *The Dolphins* by Rose Inserra [1999]. I know that you have probably seen dolphins in books or on television. What do you already know about dolphins? |
|---|---|

Juana:      I just saw a show about them on Discovery Channel. They are so cool. I hope that I can go swimming with the dolphins like the people I saw on the show.

Teacher:    That would be a lot of fun!

The teacher and students continue to discuss their knowledge about dolphins.

## Preview Vocabulary

Teacher:    I want to show you some vocabulary words before we start reading the book. There are just a few words that will help us understand the book better. The first word is *breathe*. What do you think this word has to do with a book about dolphins?

Anna:       Well, I know that the dolphin has to breathe, or it couldn't live.

Teacher:    Right, and today we will find out how they do that when they spend most of their time underwater.

The teacher continues to introduce the remaining vocabulary words: *dolphin, smooth, hole, whole,* and *fin.* These words are written on index cards and will be visible during the reading of the story. The words will be reviewed after the story is read.

## Preview Text Features

Teacher:    Based on our discussion so far, we know that this book will be informational. I want to show you some of the book's text features that will be helpful as we read and discuss this book about dolphins.

The teacher shows the students the book's text features, including the glossary and its importance in reading comprehension.

## Set a Purpose

Teacher:    I am going to start today by asking a few questions about dolphins to see who is the expert in the group. When we finish reading the story, we will be able to answer all the questions and see who got the most right. I am going to read four statements. Please write either *fact* or *fib,* based on what you know or what you predict we will find out about dolphins. The first one is: "Dolphins breathe both underwater and above the water."

The teacher quickly reads the four statements, and the students put their answers away to review after reading the text.

_____

Teacher:   As we read the story today, remember all the new things that you learn about dolphins. When you leave group, I want you to create a poster about dolphins.

The teacher does this to set a purpose for reading as well as to prepare students for the extension activity.

## During Reading

### Teacher/Student Questions

_____

Teacher:   Since this is a new book, I am going to be the lead reader on the first page. Remember, when I am the lead reader, all of you will be whisper reading with me. Let's begin on page 2. What do you notice about the picture on this page?

Juana:   It looks like real pictures of dolphins.

Teacher:   That also supports that this is an informational text. Everybody, get ready to whisper read with me.

The teacher reads aloud while the students whisper read along with her for the first three pages. This gives all of the students the chance to read the text with teacher support.

_____

Teacher:   So, we found out the answer to one of the questions that I asked you before reading.

Edward:   Oh, yeah. It told us that the dolphins hold their noses underwater, and they have to go above the water to breathe.

Teacher:   We will find out how many of you got that right when we check our answers. Let's all read the next page chorally.

Shavon:   Wow, I missed that question about the dolphin's teeth. I thought teeth were used to chew the food up, and the book said that the dolphin eats the food whole!

Teacher:   That was new information for me, too! You are really learning some interesting things about dolphins that you can write about. Who would like to be the lead reader on the next page?

Nevah:   I would!

Teacher:   OK, we will all whisper read with you.

The students finish reading the book using a variety of reading comprehension strategies, such as teacher-facilitated discussion, student questioning, and summarizing.

### *After Reading*

### Summarizing

------------

Teacher:     First, let's check the questions that I asked you before reading.

The teacher rereads the questions and confirms the answers with the students.

------------

Teacher:     Let's look at the vocabulary words. Give me a sentence with the word *breathe* that tells something that you learned in the story.

Anna:     Dolphins do not breathe underwater.

The teacher reviews the remaining vocabulary in a similar way.

### *Comprehension Extension*

------------

Teacher:     When you leave group today, I want you to create a poster that lists the top five things you now know about dolphins. You need to think carefully about what we read and decide on the most important things that people should know about dolphins. I want you to share this poster with some students in kindergarten, so make sure that you draw some illustrations.

See Figure 7 for this completed comprehension extension.

## Lesson Summary

These third-grade students are reading two years below grade level and need focused reading instruction that includes fluency practice, word study that focuses on common vowel patterns, and reading and comprehending text at an appropriate level. These students will develop reading vocabulary as the teacher preselects, preteaches, and revisits the words that are critical to understanding. Additionally, these students need support provided by the intervention team, including special education or EL specialists. One 30-minute lesson each day will not be enough time to narrow the enormous gap in reading for these students.

The time that these students spend in independent follow-up activities is critical. The teacher assigns activities to support fluency, word study, and comprehension. The extensions from the small-group work allow the teacher to provide tasks that are

**FIGURE 7**
**Completed Extension Activity for Level 1**

TOP Five Things About...
Dolphins
1. They breathe through a blowhole.
2. Dolphins do not breathe underwater.
3. They do not chew their food.
4. The fin helps it swim.
5. Dolphins are cool!

appropriate and doable for these struggling readers. It is important to hold these students accountable for completing each activity. Obviously, the fluency activity is self-checking: You can count on one partner to tell you if the other fails to partner read the book. Each student should keep a small-group journal for word study assignments and written comprehension extensions. Students can bring these journals to the group daily so that you can monitor completion of assignments. Depending on the word study and comprehension focuses, the following are some additional extensions that could be used with this text.

### Word Study Extensions

- Complete a word hunt in other texts that include words that have the same vowel patterns.
- Complete the Word Study Matrix (discussed in Chapter 7 and available in the Support Materials section of the CD ) to add suffixes to base words as well as to identify appropriate synonyms and antonyms.

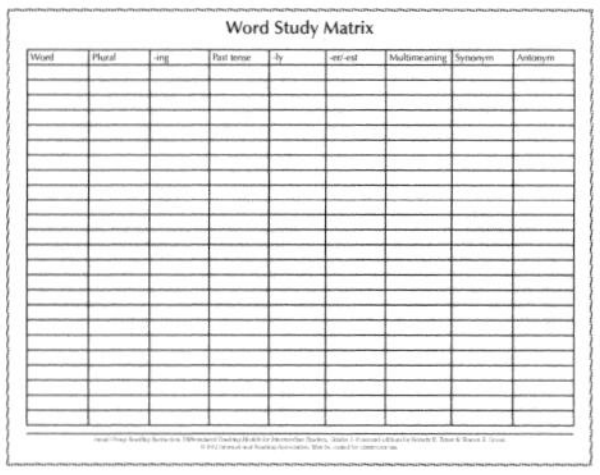

### Comprehension Extensions

- Write a paragraph on dolphins. Include an opening sentence that states the main idea, three things that you learned about dolphins, and a closing sentence.

- Write a sentence with each vocabulary word to tell about something that you read in the story.

- Compare and contrast whales and dolphins using a Venn diagram. Choose three things that are the same and three things that are different for both the whale and the dolphin.
- Draw and label the following parts of a dolphin: blow hole, fins, tail fin, and teeth. List one reason that each part is important to the survival of the dolphin.

# Narrative Lesson Model: Level 3 Intervention

## Description of the Group

This group of struggling fourth-grade students is reading two years below grade level, and spelling assessments confirm that they fall in Intervention level 3. These readers still lack some fluency and need to work on this skill both within and outside of their small groups. The group moves through the word study sequence, focusing on common word features such as compound words, contractions, and simple prefixes and suffixes. Comprehension is a focus both in their groups through in-depth discussions and outside of their groups with written extension activities. As with the level 1 group, this group includes ELs and students with special needs, as well as regular education students who are struggling. Two students from other classrooms are joining the group because there are no other students in their own classrooms who are functioning at the same instructional reading level. Figure 8 shows a completed lesson plan for the group.

## Lesson Goals/Objectives

### Fluency

The fluency goals for this group are to build the speed, accuracy, and expression needed to understand the text message.

### Word Study

The objective in word study is for students to know the meaning of the prefixes *pre-*, *re-*, and *mis-* and then apply this knowledge to new words.

### Comprehension

The comprehension goals include understanding and applying point of view as the reader examines character development.

## Fluency

The teacher has selected a poem (written by Beverly) for fluency practice for the group. This rotates with rereading some of the text both within and outside of the group. Fourth graders may not be fond of rereading, and poetry keeps students motivated. This is the third day that the group has reread the poem:

**FIGURE 8**
**Completed Intervention Reader Lesson Plan for Level 3**

| FLUENCY (REREADING) | FLUENCY EXTENSION(S) |
|---|---|
| ✔ Reread text, selected pages, or poetry<br><br>Text: _"Never Teach Your Dog to Read"_ | _Reread poem with partner_ |

| WORD STUDY | WORD STUDY EXTENSION(S) |
|---|---|
| Level 1 ☐   Level 2 ☐   Week: _____<br>Vowel Pattern Focus: _____<br>☐ Open Sort: (day 1 only)<br>☐ Sound Boxes (day 2)<br>☐ Spelling Sort (days 3–5)<br>☐ Teacher-dictated sentence:<br>_____<br><br>Level 3 ✔  Feature Focus: _Prefixes_<br>☐ Open Sort: (day 1 only)    ☐ Spelling Sort<br>✔ Word Meaning discussion<br>✔ Student-Generated Sentences to show<br>  meaning | _Student will write a sentence with selected words (checking for understanding)_ |

| COMPREHENSION (NARRATIVE TEXT) | COMPREHENSION (INFORMATIONAL TEXT) |
|---|---|
| New text: _The Hare and the Tortoise by Jenny Giles_<br><br>Before Reading<br>✔ Activate and build background knowledge<br>✔ Preview vocabulary: _boasting, meadow, willow tree,_ _plodded_<br>✔ Set a purpose | New text: _____<br><br>Before Reading<br>☐ Activate and build background knowledge<br>☐ Preview text features and structure<br>_____<br>☐ Preview vocabulary: _____<br>_____ |
| During Reading<br>✔ Teacher/student questions: _Encourage students_ _to give evidence to support predictions_<br>✔ Discussion/teaching points: _What is the_ _illustrator trying to show us in this picture?_<br>_____<br>Notes: _Discuss point of view from other characters._ | During Reading<br>☐ Teacher/student questions: _____<br>_____<br>☐ Discussion/teaching points: _____<br>_____<br>_____<br>Notes: |
| After Reading<br>Summarize<br>☐ Plot/story elements<br>✔ Character (traits, motivations, point of view)<br>☐ Setting (mood, importance)<br>☐ Events (sequencing)<br>☐ Conflict and resolution<br>☐ Theme<br>Notes: | After Reading<br>Summarize<br>☐ Main ideas and essential details<br>☐ Compare and contrast<br>☐ Sequence<br>☐ Cause and effect, or problem and solution<br>Notes: |

**WRITTEN COMPREHENSION EXTENSION(S):** _Rewrite the story from the tortoise's point of view._

Notes:

**Never Teach Your Dog to Read**

Never teach your dog to read,
Unless he is a special breed.
One that schools permit inside,
And you can show him off with pride.

Now that you have your dog at school,
He's bound to break most of the rules.
And even though your dog can read,
He'll be sent home with lightning speed!

Teacher:    Please take your fluency folders out and open to the poem that we have been working on this week. Tomorrow, I will have a new poem to share with you. Today, when we read the poem, I want us to really work on the rhythm and flow of the words. Let's tap the rhythm on the table to keep a steady beat while we read.

The teacher and students choral read the poem together.

### Fluency Extension

Teacher:    When you leave group today, please reread this poem one more time with your partner. Then, each of you should select a favorite poem or song in your fluency folder and read those together.

## Word Study

The word study today focuses on simple prefixes. The teacher focuses on the meaning of each prefix and how it assists students in figuring out what the word means. She has also noticed that the students may be able to tell what the word means but are unable to use the words correctly in context. This is the second day focusing on the prefixes *pre-*, *re-*, and *mis-*.

Teacher:    Yesterday, we looked at three prefixes: *pre-*, *re-*, and *mis-*. Who remembers what the prefix *pre-* means?

Laura:      I know. It means *before*. My brother is in preschool, and that means before real school.

Teacher:    Laura, that is a great way to remember the prefix. So, how can that help us if we come to a word that we don't know and it begins with *pre-*?

Jill:       Well, at least we would know that it means before something.

Teacher:    What about the prefix *re-*?

| Mark: | It means to do it again, like *recycle*. When you recycle, you use things again. |
|---|---|
| Teacher: | Great! What about *mis-*? Look at the word *misunderstand*. |
| Kurt: | Oh yeah, now I remember. It means *not*. |
| Teacher: | So, as we are sorting these words, how does *not* relate to *misunderstand* and *misspell*? |
| Monica: | Well, *misunderstand* is like you do not understand, and *misspell* is you do not spell it the right way. |

The teacher finishes the review of prefixes and then explores the meanings of the other words using knowledge about the three prefixes.

### *Word Study Extension*

---

| Teacher: | When you leave group today, I want you to write a sentence using the words *precook*, *prepay*, *reteach*, and *misspell*. I also want you to draw a picture to go with each sentence that gives you something to remind you of the word's meaning. |
|---|---|

## Comprehension

### *Before Reading*

Although these students are reading two years below grade level, the lesson and text supports the fourth-grade Common Core Standards in a mid–second-grade level text. The teacher selected the tale *The Hare and the Tortoise* by Jenny Giles (1998), focusing on the attributes that make the story a fable. Exposing struggling readers to a wide variety of genres is very important. The main comprehension focus for this lesson is point of view and is introduced prior to reading. All appropriate comprehension strategies are weaved throughout the lesson, which extends over a two-day period.

The teacher makes decisions about what to do prior to reading to support the readers in a successful reading and understanding of the text. Included in the book introduction is exposure to important story vocabulary, making connections, and a discussion of the attributes of a fable. Additionally, the teacher establishes a purpose for reading the text with a discussion of point of view. After reading the text, the teacher asks the students to rewrite the fable from the tortoise's point of view.

### Activate and Build Background Knowledge

---

| Teacher: | Today, we are going to start reading a story that most of you are familiar with. (The teacher covers the title of the book on the front |
|---|---|

cover.) Looking at the picture on the front cover, can you guess what the story might be?

Paula: Yeah, it is the story of the turtle and the rabbit.

Teacher: Katrina, do you agree?

Katrina: Yes, I think so, too.

Teacher: How do you know?

Edie: Because there is a turtle and a rabbit, and it looks like they are starting a race.

Carlos: Yeah, but that's not the name of the book. It's called *The Hare and the Tortoise*. Those are other names for a rabbit and a turtle.

Teacher: That's what I always thought, but I wonder if they really are the same? Where could we look to find out?

Angela: Why don't we look on the Internet?

Teacher: Good idea, Angela. Would you and Carlos do some research and report back to the group tomorrow?

The teacher is encouraging students to take responsibility for their own learning. The discussion continues about fables and their characteristics. Then, the teacher introduces important story vocabulary that she feels the students need to be familiar with to comprehend the story.

**Preview Vocabulary**

---

Teacher: Let me show you a few words that you may not be familiar with that we will see in the story today. (The teacher displays all of the preselected vocabulary written on index cards.) Take a look at all of the words. Which word means to brag, like "I made a higher grade on the test than you." Look carefully. Does anyone know? (The teacher waits for a response, but no one answers.) Let me help you out. The word is *boasting*. We don't hear or see that word very often. Can you think of anyone in the story who is boasting? Turn and talk to your partner. How does it make you feel if you are around someone who does a lot of boasting?

The teacher tries to have students make personal connections to the words, knowing that this will increase the probability of them remembering the new vocabulary. She continues the process until all of the vocabulary words have been introduced and discussed.

**Set a Purpose**

_____

Teacher: This story is traditionally told through the eyes of the rabbit, or hare. We call this the hare's point of view. For example, my point of view about missing school all week because of the snow might be different than yours. I was worried that we were missing a lot of time that we could have been learning new things. What was your point of view?

Angela: Well, my point of view was that it was awesome! No school, no homework, and lots of time playing in the snow.

Teacher: As we read the story today, think about what the tortoise might be thinking. What is his point of view about what is happening in the story? When we finish reading, I want you to rewrite the story from the tortoise's point of view. Let's read the story. I am going to give you a reading bookmark to follow along with and a small sticky note.

The bookmark provides student accountability for following along in the text. The teacher will ask the students to use the sticky note to identify a particular word or sentence in the text.

## During Reading

### Teacher/Student Questions

_____

Teacher: Take a look at the illustrations on these two pages. What do you think the illustrator is trying to show us in the pictures? Use what you already know about the story to help you. Turn and talk to your partner about your thoughts.

The teacher allows time for the partners to share and then asks one of the students to share.

_____

Teacher: Carlos, please share your thoughts with us.

Carlos: Well, it looks like the animals all have their backs to the hare. So, I think the illustrator is trying to show us that the animals don't really like the hare. Maybe he is already bragging too much.

Teacher: I am going to be the lead reader on the first two pages. Get your bookmarks ready and whisper read along with me.

The teacher and students complete the reading of the page together. The teacher wants to give the students more support at the beginning of the story by lead reading and will release the reading responsibility gradually as the story unfolds.

---

Teacher: Please take your sticky note and tag the sentence that tells us that the other animals do not like to listen to the hare boasting.

This technique keeps all of the students actively engaged and allows the teacher to note any students who are struggling with the activity.

---

Paula: It says they paid no attention to him. You can see that they all have their backs turned, so they don't have to look at him.

Teacher: Edie, would you please be the lead reader on the next page?

The teacher and the rest of the students whisper read along with Edie.

---

Teacher: Pretend that you are the hare. Get into character and tell us what happened on this page from the hare's point of view.

Beth: Can you believe that the tortoise wants to race? What is he thinking? He already knows that I can beat him!

Teacher: That was really good. Now, who wants to take the tortoise's point of view?

Nick: I am so sick of that hare boasting all the time. I am going to show him once and for all that he is not the best at everything.

Teacher: I wonder how the tortoise knew he could win the race? How did he know that the hare would stop to take a nap?

The teacher and students continue reading and discussing the story until time runs out.

## After Reading

## Summarizing

---

Teacher: Our time is up today. Let's summarize what has happened in the story so far.

The students quickly summarize and sequence the important events.

Teacher:   For this extension activity, you are going to rewrite the story from the tortoise's point of view. Just write to the point that we got to in the story today. When you finish, meet with your sharing partner and read what you have written so far. Write the story in your extension notebook. Remember to look at the rubric in your notebook to make sure you have the correct punctuation and story structure. When you meet with your partner, let him or her give you suggestions on how to make your story better.

See Figure 9 for this completed written extension activity. Extension notebooks are discussed in Chapter 7.

**FIGURE 9**
**Completed Extension Activity for Level 3**

The Tortise

  The tortise said, "I will win the race. The hare is lazy. I can't wait to race! See, he is already sleeping. I will teach him a Lesson. I hope that he is going to be nice to everyone now. I won the race and now everyone is happy. Now we can all be friends."

The END

## Lesson Summary

Many teachers find it difficult to release some of the editing responsibility to other students. Remember, you cannot do everything. Proofreading and discussing ideas are great learning experiences for students.

This lesson focuses on many of the components needed to advance these intervention readers. The students continued to build fluency with the poem in today's lesson. The study of prefixes in word study increases both decoding and vocabulary, which are important as students come across new words with the same prefixes. Finally, the students focused on point of view. Using instructional-level text, the students were able to meet this fourth-grade standard successfully. Depending on the comprehension focus, a variety of written extension activities could have been assigned. The following are additional, appropriate extension activities for word study and comprehension based on this text.

### *Word Study Extensions*

- Complete a word hunt for other words with the prefixes *un-*, *re-*, and *pre-*.
- Find synonyms and antonyms for as many of the words as you can.
- Take the prefix off of each word and add a suffix to each word.
- Add a suffix to each word and use each new word in a sentence.

### *Comprehension Extensions*

- Use each vocabulary word in a sentence that tells something that happened in the story.
- Give a character trait for both the hare and the tortoise. Find two examples of how each character demonstrated this trait in the story.
- What is the theme of this fable? How does the author show theme in the story? What lesson does the author want us to learn?
- Using a timeline, sequence the five most important events in the story.
- Look at the illustration on page __. What is the illustrator trying to tell us about the story? Write a paragraph that explains this illustration.

# Conclusion

These struggling intermediate readers need to meet on a daily basis in their small groups for 30 minutes in the regular classroom setting. These readers also need additional small-group instruction, which can be given by the supplemental teachers (e.g., reading, Title I, EL, special education) while the classroom teacher is continuing to meet with small groups. Please keep in mind that the classroom teacher has already provided the first dose of reading instruction, and these students need multiple doses. Additional instruction is supplemental; it does not take the place of the first dose of instruction by the classroom teacher.

Teachers must attend to all of the components that these struggling readers need: fluency, solid decoding skills, and increased comprehension of various text types. This does not mean that grade-level standards are ignored. Incorporating the grade-level literacy standards should be a regular part of the planning process. These Common Core Standards are taught with readable text, that is, instructional-level text. The question is often asked, "What should intervention look like for struggling students?" The answer is, not something different; the intervention should be increased time and intensity of what you are already doing in small groups during the regular reading block. The intervention should include more fluency practice, more word study, more reading comprehension, and embedded vocabulary development in instructional-level text.

# The Evolving Reader Stage

Evolving readers are best described as readers who have made the transition from learning to read to reading to learn. Instruction for this type of reader must be geared toward continuing to develop fluency, word study skills, and vocabulary that will support these readers as true comprehenders of text. Evolving readers are learning about patterns and word features in multisyllabic words, which are the basis for their journey into the spelling–meaning connection. Students are in the Evolving Reader stage for about two years, typically between grades 2 to 4. This is a critical stage for students' reading development because, in effect, it sets the stage for lifelong learning.

## Characteristics of Evolving Readers in Reading, Writing, and Word Study

### Reading

Evolving readers need time to build and refine fluency. In other words, they need time to develop automatic word recognition. Evolving readers can decode fairly accurately in appropriate text; however, they are refining their automaticity, or ability to decode words automatically. These readers use a variety of word-recognition strategies when decoding unknown words. Further, they use their knowledge of syntax, such as question marks, exclamation points, commas, apostrophes, and hyphens, to understand the author's message. As students' automaticity increases, so does their oral reading fluency. This occurs as a result of being able to focus on the meaning of words rather than on the decoding of words. Thus, when students can focus on the author's meaning, expression naturally follows.

As instruction centers on vocabulary and comprehension, evolving readers determine the meaning of unknown words or phrases using context clues (e.g., definitions, restatements, examples, descriptions, illustrations) and grammatical structure. These readers also are learning to identify and use synonyms, antonyms, homographs, and homophones to determine the meaning of words. Using their knowledge of Greek and Latin prefixes and suffixes that are appropriate for these third- and fourth-grade readers is also important for comprehension.

Evolving readers are exploring new genres in the classroom and in their personal reading. Evolving readers are becoming increasingly familiar with informational text to meet the demands of the curriculum. These students are learning how to differentiate between informational and narrative text structures. They are also beginning to develop comprehension strategies to meet the demands of various text types.

72

## Texts for Evolving Readers

Evolving readers require diversity in the types and complexity of text. Both the grade-level content and the standards dictate that at least half the texts read by students should be informational. Informational text types, such as newspaper articles, biographies, speeches, content-related text, and other nonfiction selections, should be used frequently. Narrative text types should include novels, fables, poetry, myths, and folk tales from varying cultures.

At this stage, evolving readers are still dependent on texts that match their instructional level. Relying solely on leveled text that comes as part of the basal reading series can present problems with quality and content. Schools should consider purchasing quality texts and housing them in a central location for access by all teachers. For teachers using leveled texts as a resource to support small-group differentiated reading instruction, the following book levels are appropriate for evolving readers:

| Leveling System | Book Levels |
|---|---|
| DRA | 20–40 |
| Fountas and Pinnell | K–R |
| Lexile bands | *Grade 3:* 330L–700L, 550L–790L (stretch bands) |
| | *Grade 4:* 445L–810L, 770L–910L (stretch bands) |

## Writing

At the same time that evolving readers develop their reading abilities, they also develop their writing abilities. As they begin to read different genres, these readers also begin to experiment with writing for different purposes. Evolving readers need teacher support to study the various components of the writing process in depth, and then they need time to practice these components independently. Evolving readers are able to write cohesive paragraphs with details and create their own stories, which begin to include character development. In this stage, we often find that students' writing mimics that of their favorite authors. The more proficient these students become as readers, the more they develop as writers.

Writers' workshop, a process-centered approach to writing, is commonly included in the evolving reader's classroom. This approach allows students to work at their own levels and write about topics that interest them. The philosophy guiding this approach is to allow students time and choice: time to practice and choice of format. However, this approach should not be students' only writing instruction; it should be balanced with explicit instruction in the areas of the writing process, types of writing, and grammar.

Evolving readers can demonstrate understanding of text through written comprehension pieces. Early in this stage, the teacher needs to be cognizant of students' abilities in this area and make sure that he or she supports these writers through teacher modeling. If students can orally demonstrate higher level understanding of text, the expectation is that they can do this in writing as well. This kind of in-depth writing requires extensive modeling by the teacher, guided practice, and independent writing opportunities with feedback. We have also seen students fail to reach their writing potential when teachers expect them to write everything by hand. In this digital age, students need to be composing a majority of their pieces on a computer. Technology makes writing much less labor intensive, and students have more energy for their writing tasks.

## Word Study

As mentioned previously, word study involves multiple layers. Evolving readers are typically in the pattern layer of spelling development and are moving into the meaning layer of development. These readers have their phonology in place; they can represent every sound they hear in words. For example, these students recognize that the word *rain* is not spelled *ran*. They realize that the word needs another vowel to make the long *a* sound. Evolving readers should be able to spell most one-syllable words correctly. Word study for these students focuses on the study of multisyllabic words, roots, and affixes. Additionally, common Greek and Latin prefixes and suffixes, needed for decoding, are explored.

As students are completing their study of the pattern layer of the English language, they have built a foundation for the study of syllable patterns and morphology. This foundational knowledge is essential as they progress through the maturing and advanced stages of reading and study morphemic units. Students in the Evolving Reader stage are experimenting with and learning about these spelling features. The features studied during the Evolving Reader stage are outlined in Table 6.

A weekly word study scope and sequence for year 1 and another for year 2 have been provided in the Word Study Materials section on the accompanying CD  . Please note that these are provided only as a guideline. It is crucial for teachers to use assessments to guide their instruction. If students have not mastered a specific list, then they should not move on to study new features. Rather, teachers should reteach and review the features with which students are having difficulty.

# Instructional Components of the Evolving Reader Lesson Plan

The evolving reader lesson plan has three distinct components: (1) fluency, (2) word study, and (3) comprehension (see Figure 10). The top right-hand side allows teachers to plan for quality out-of-group extension activities for developing fluency and word study. Word study will be a consistent lesson component with focused discussion and activities. The comprehension section of the planning model focuses on the strategies that will be used before, during, and after reading. The final part of the lesson plan includes written comprehension responses that students will complete as out-of-group extension activities.

**TABLE 6**
**Word Study Features for the Evolving Reader**

| Feature | Example(s) |
|---|---|
| *R*-controlled vowel patterns (multisyllablic) | *air, ar, are*<br>*ear, eer, er, ere*<br>*ir, ire*<br>*oar, or, ore, our*<br>*ur, ure* |
| Ambiguous vowel patterns (multisyllablic) | *au, aw, ew*<br>*oi, oo, ou, ow, oy* |
| Complex consonants (beginning and ending) | *ge, dge, ge*<br>Triple-letter blends: *shr, thr, scr* |
| Word features: Contractions, homophones, and compound words | Compound words: *any, every, grand, water*<br>All contractions |
| Review suffixes, including plurals and past tense | Doubling: *-ed, -ing*<br>Plurals |
| Syllable patterns | Open syllables ending with long-vowel sound: **open**, **Friday**<br>Closed syllables with short-vowel sound: **think**er, **sip**ping<br>V-C-C-V (vowel-consonant-consonant-vowel): *thu**nd**er* (regular), *fo**ll**ow* (doublet)<br>V-C-V (vowel-consonant-vowel): *ch**ose**n* (open), *R**obe**rt* (closed)<br>V-V (vowel-vowel): *ri**ot**, *l**ia**r* |
| Common prefixes (examples) | *anti-, de-, dis-, em-, en-, fore-, inter-, mid-, mis-, non-, over-, pre-, re-, semi-, super-, trans-, un-, under-* |
| Common suffixes (examples) | Plurals<br>*-ed, -er, -est, -ful, -ing, -ion, -ly, -ness, -or, -y* |
| Number-related prefixes | *mono-, bi-, tri-, quad-* |
| Greek and Latin roots (examples) | *dict* (to say)<br>*scribe* (to write)<br>*tele* (far off) |

# Fluency

Generally, evolving readers need to continue fluency practice both within and outside of the small-group setting. Using poetry or song lyrics for fluency practice serves several purposes. First, poetry is an important genre for evolving readers and can provide valuable vocabulary and comprehension development. Time constraints also make poetry a sensible choice. Beginning the lesson by reading or rereading the poem provides a warm-up and gets the lesson off to a quick start. Evolving readers can sometimes become reluctant when asked to reread longer texts. For these intermediate readers, poetry is motivating, with an endless variety of seasonal, humorous, and serious poems. Song lyrics can also be used (and even sung) as a way to develop fluency.

A variety of out-of-group fluency extensions provides important independent practice. For example, students can build a fluency folder for all of the poems and songs used in their small groups. Then, students can practice the poem or song for the week with a partner or go back and visit favorites. It would also be appropriate to

**FIGURE 10**
**Evolving Reader Lesson Plan**

Narrative Text: _____   Informational text: _____

Text Type: _____   Estimated Length of Time: _____

| FLUENCY | FLUENCY EXTENSION(S) |
|---|---|
| Text: _____ | |

| WORD STUDY | WORD STUDY EXTENSION(S) |
|---|---|
| Features: _____ <br><br> Cycle: _____ Week: _____ <br><br> Word Sort: ☐ Open ☐ Closed <br> ☐ Spelling Sort ☐ Meaning Discussion | |

| COMPREHENSION (NARRATIVE TEXT) | COMPREHENSION (INFORMATIONAL TEXT) |
|---|---|
| Before Reading <br> ☐ Activate and build background knowledge <br><br> ☐ Preview vocabulary: _____ <br> _____ <br> ☐ Set a purpose | Before Reading <br> ☐ Activate and build background knowledge <br> ☐ Preview text features and structure <br> _____ <br> _____ <br> ☐ Preview vocabulary: _____ <br> _____ |
| During Reading <br> ☐ Teacher/student questions: _____ <br> _____ <br> ☐ Discussion/teaching points: _____ <br> _____ <br> _____ <br> Notes: | During Reading <br> ☐ Teacher/student questions: _____ <br> _____ <br> ☐ Discussion/teaching points: _____ <br> _____ <br> _____ <br> Notes: |
| After Reading <br> ☐ Plot/story elements <br> ☐ Character (traits, motivations, point of view) <br> ☐ Setting (mood, importance) <br> ☐ Events (sequencing) <br> ☐ Conflict and resolution <br> ☐ Theme <br> ☐ Summarize: _____ <br> _____ <br> Notes: | After Reading <br> ☐ Review text structure to aid understanding <br> ☐ Author's purpose <br> ☐ Summarize <br>   ☐ Main ideas and essential details <br>   ☐ Compare and contrast <br>   ☐ Sequence <br>   ☐ Cause and effect, or problem and solution <br> _____ <br> _____ <br> Notes: |

**Reading Assignment** (if appropriate)          Read pages: _____

**Written Comprehension Extension(s):** _____

Notes:

ask students to reread a particular text or part of a text with a partner outside of their small groups.

## Word Study

As previously mentioned, the word study component of the small-group model was designed for students to study the same word features for one week. Therefore, teachers would use the first day of the week to introduce and explain the word sort, which typically takes 8–10 minutes. Teachers can choose to use either an open or closed word sort, depending on the features being studied. This introduction should include the meanings of any words that the students are unfamiliar with. (All of the words do not need to be introduced the first day. If you are short on time, you can introduce half of the words on the first day and the second half on the second day.) On the remaining four days, students can complete other word study activities, such as spelling sorts, word hunts, or sentences to show meaning. Students can keep a word study journal as they complete these activities.

## Comprehension

The comprehension section of the lesson plan focuses on the strategies that support students before, during, and after reading. Before reading, the teacher helps build the background knowledge that is necessary for students to understand the book. For example, if the group is getting ready to read a book about a piano recital, and the students are not familiar with the term *recital*, the teacher can explain the concept and give an example that students are familiar with. A teacher might also have students make any personal connections with the text topic prior to reading. Additionally, the teacher should be sure to preselect vocabulary words that are important to the understanding of the story as well as those that students are likely to see in other texts. Making these vocabulary words visual (e.g., writing them on index cards, with pictures if applicable) gives students a concrete aid that they can revisit after they read the text. If an informational text is used, preview the important text features prior to reading the text. This gives teachers the opportunity to make students aware of elements of the text that may help them understand it.

During reading, the teacher not only poses a variety of questions at varying difficulty levels but also encourages students to question the text in the same way. In-depth comprehension conversations during reading are essential in order for teachers to gauge student understanding and help guide further growth. These conversations typically develop out of the discussion points that a teacher has previously identified and recorded on the lesson plan.

After reading, the teacher focuses on a particular strategy to summarize the text. For example, in a text that is read over multiple days, this might include identifying the three most important things that happened in the text for that day. The teacher may choose to use a graphic organizer or visual as the text is discussed. This does not have to be a long, in-depth activity; it is simply a way for students to summarize so that they will remember the text for later discussion. After the text has been introduced, and the first part of the text has been read in the group, the teacher may choose to have the students read the next part of the text with a partner outside of the small group. Using partners gives the teacher a way to hold students accountable and provide assistance with unknown words. Instruct students to stop after each page to question and discuss the text with his or her partner.

Written comprehension as extension activities encourages deeper thinking about the text and helps hone writing skills. This writing assignment may take several days to complete. In our view, it is more effective to have students complete rigorous tasks than numerous worksheets or short-answer assignments.

## Differentiating the Lesson Plan

Because of the differences between narrative and informational text, we adapted the comprehension strategies on the planning template to meet the demands of each text type. The lesson plan is intended for one piece of text. The text might be short and only take a day or two to complete, or it might be part of a lengthier text (e.g., chapter book). We have provided a completed lesson plan for both the narrative and informational lessons discussed in the following section. The students in the narrative lesson are in the beginning of the Evolving Reader stage, and the students in the informational lesson are in year two of the Evolving Reader stage.

# Narrative Lesson Model

## Description of the Group

This group of six third-grade students is in the beginning of the Evolving Reader stage. Fluency skills will be addressed by a new poem introduced at the beginning of the lesson. Word study focuses on adding the suffix -ing to single-syllable words and discovering patterns that require doubling the final consonant prior to adding the suffix. A Japanese folk tale is used for the comprehension portion of the lesson. See Figure 11 for the completed lesson plan.

## Lesson Goals/Objectives

### Fluency

The continuing goal of fluency is to build speed, accuracy, and expression needed to comprehend the text.

### Word Study

For this lesson, the word study goals include being able to verbalize and apply the generalizations for adding the suffix -ing to one-syllable words with short and long vowels.

Narrative Text: _"The One-Inch Boy"_       Informational text: _____

Text Type: _Folk tale_       Estimated Length of Time: _2 days_

| FLUENCY | FLUENCY EXTENSION(S) |
|---|---|
| Text: _"One Inch Tall" poem by Shel Silverstein_ | _Partner read poem_ |

| WORD STUDY | WORD STUDY EXTENSION(S) |
|---|---|
| Features: _-ing_<br><br>Cycle: _1_    Week: _8_<br><br>Word Sort: ☑ Open ☐ Closed<br>☐ Spelling Sort ☐ Meaning Discussion | _Word hunt_ |

| COMPREHENSION (NARRATIVE TEXT) | COMPREHENSION (INFORMATIONAL TEXT) |
|---|---|
| Before Reading<br>☑ Activate and build background knowledge<br>☑ Preview vocabulary: _ancient, persisted,_<br>_miniature, dense, coincidence, fortune_<br>☑ Set a purpose<br>  _Determine important chain of events_ | Before Reading<br>☐ Activate and build background knowledge<br>☐ Preview text features and structure<br>_____<br>_____<br>☐ Preview vocabulary: _____<br>_____ |
| During Reading<br>☑ Teacher/student questions: _How did the boy_<br>_overcome his size? What was the "fortune"?_<br>☑ Discussion/teaching points: _Character traits:_<br>_boy, parents (examples)_<br>_____<br><br>Notes: | During Reading<br>☐ Teacher/student questions: _____<br>_____<br>☐ Discussion/teaching points: _____<br>_____<br><br>Notes: |
| After Reading<br>☐ Plot/story elements<br>☐ Character (traits, motivations, point of view)<br>☐ Setting (mood, importance)<br>☑ Events (sequencing)<br>☐ Conflict and resolution<br>☐ Theme<br>☐ Summarize: _Orally check after reading tomorrow_<br>_____<br>Notes: | After Reading<br>☐ Review text structure to aid understanding<br>☐ Author's purpose<br>☐ Summarize<br>  ☐ Main ideas and essential details<br>  ☐ Compare and contrast<br>  ☐ Sequence<br>  ☐ Cause and effect, or problem and solution<br>_____<br>_____<br>Notes: |

**Reading Assignment** (if appropriate)      Read pages: _Finish story with partner_
**Written Comprehension Extension(s):** _Chain of events_
Notes: _With a partner, determine 6-8 important events in the story that were important to the outcome._

## Comprehension

In comprehension, the overall lesson goals include being able to summarize the story, determine main ideas and essential details, and sequence the events that lead to the story's conclusion.

## Fluency

The lesson begins with the reading of the weekly fluency poem, "One Inch Tall" by Shel Silverstein (2004). The students have read several of his poems and enjoy his humor. Today's poem also ties directly to the comprehension selection. The teacher introduces the poem and models a fluent reading while the students whisper read along with her.

---

Teacher:    Today, we are going to read another one of Shel Silverstein's poems called "One Inch Tall." Based on the other poems we have read by this author, what kind of poem do you think this will be?

Jordan:     Well, it will definitely be funny.

Teacher:    The title of the poem makes me think that, too. What would life be like if you were one inch tall? Turn and talk to your partner about this.

The students discuss with their partners for one minute.

---

Teacher:    Now, I am going to be the lead reader. You can whisper read with me.

The teacher reads aloud while the students whisper read along with her. This allows the teacher to model fluency while the students also participate in the reading process.

### One Inch Tall

If you were only one inch tall, you'd ride a worm to school.
The teardrop of a crying ant would be your swimming pool.
A crumb of cake would be a feast
And last you seven days at least.
A flea would be a frightening beast
If you were one inch tall.

If you were only one inch tall, you'd walk beneath the door,
And it would take about a month to get down to the store.
A bit of fluff would be your bed,
You'd swing upon a spider's thread,
And wear a thimble on your head
If you were one inch tall.

You'd surf across the kitchen sink upon a stick of gum.
You couldn't hug your mama, you'd just have to hug her thumb.
You'd run from people's feet in fright,
To move a pen would take all night,

(This poem took fourteen years to write—
'Cause I'm just one inch tall).

(p. 16)

---

Teacher: Today, we are going to read a folk tale about a boy who is one inch tall. It will be interesting to see if he does some of the same things that the one-inch boy did in the poem.

The students keep the poem in their fluency folders and will practice reading the poem with a partner. The poem will also be revisited in the group during the week as a rereading selection.

### *Fluency Extension*

---

Teacher: When you leave group today, put this poem in your fluency folders. Take turns lead reading the poem with your partner: One partner is the lead reader first, and the other partner will whisper read. The second time you read the poem, be sure to swap responsibilities.

## Word Study

In the following dialogue, the students are starting a new sort. When teachers introduce a new sort, it typically takes about 10 minutes. On subsequent days, however, the time allocated for word study will be less. (This lesson can be broken into two lessons if there is a time constraint.) This will be an open sort; the teacher does not provide the header words or tell the students the pattern they are studying.

The lengthy dialogue that occurs between the teacher and the students is essential in order for students to be able to analyze words using higher level thinking skills.

---

Teacher: Today, we are going to start a new sort. (The teacher lays the words out on cards in front of the group.) Can anyone tell me what you notice about the words?

Carla: All the words have *-ing* at the end of them.

Teacher: Yes, they do. What do we call *-ing*? Try to recall when we learned about *-ing* and *-ed*.

Janette: Those are called suffixes.

Teacher: Right. Now, I think we are ready to start sorting. Who wants to start?

Melody: I'll start. I'm going to put *melting* in a column with words that have a short-vowel sound.

Carla: I'm going to put *snowing* in a column with words that have a long-vowel sound.

Janette: What about *spoiling*? That has an ambiguous vowel sound, so it doesn't fit with the long or the short sounds. Can I make a new column?

Teacher: Yes, you can if you want. What does the rest of the group think?

William: Well, because *spoiling* doesn't have a long or short sound, you have to put it in a different category.

Janette: OK, but what about *scarring*? Scarring has an *r*-controlled pattern. Do we make another category for those?

Teacher: What does the group think?

Melody: We can for now, or we can make this the oddball column and put in words that don't have the long or short sound.

Benjamin: Let's do that because otherwise we may have a lot of columns!

The students continue sorting words into the three categories they determined. The following is their completed sort:

| Short Vowel | Long Vowel | Oddball |
|---|---|---|
| puffing | snowing | spoiling |
| tugging | loading | chewing |
| sprinting | blaming | shouting |
| melting | placing | stirring |
| popping | screaming | blurring |
| quitting | speeding | scarring |
| sobbing | shaping | |
| dragging | driving | |

Teacher: Very good. Now, how else could we sort these?

William: We could sort them by vowel pattern.

Teacher: Let's do that and see what we notice. Let's also write the base words that go along with the words with suffixes on my dry-erase board.

Carla: Where would we put *scarring*? If we look at the pattern of the base word, it's a CVC pattern, but we know that *ar* is an *r*-controlled pattern.

Teacher: What does the group want to do with *scarring*?

Janette: Let's put it in the oddball category for now, and then we can always change it later on.

The students continue sorting the pairs of words. They decide to put additional words in the oddball category as well.

| C-V-C | | C-V-C-C | | C-V-V-C/C-V-V | | C-V-Ce | | Oddball | |
|---|---|---|---|---|---|---|---|---|---|
| tugging | tug | puffing | puff | snowing | snow | blaming | blame | scarring | scar |
| popping | pop | sprinting | sprint | spoiling | spoil | placing | place | stirring | stir |
| quitting | quit | melting | melt | loading | load | shaping | shape | blurring | blur |
| dragging | drag | | | shouting | shout | driving | drive | | |
| | | | | screaming | scream | | | | |
| | | | | speeding | speed | | | | |
| | | | | chewing | chew | | | | |

(Note: Teachers can end the lesson here, if necessary, and continue the lesson the next time the group meets.)

———————————

Teacher: What else do you notice about these words other than they all have *-ing*?

Benjamin: Sometimes you have to add another consonant, but other times you don't.

Melody: And sometimes you have to drop the *e* in order to add the *-ing*.

Teacher: Good! You're both right. Sometimes we have to double the consonant before we add a suffix, sometimes we have to drop the final *e* before we add the suffix, and other times we don't have to do anything.

William: So, we just have to remember that rule?

Teacher: Well, William, we don't just memorize rules when we are learning to spell. What happens to rules?

Group: They get broken!

Teacher: Yes, rules are sometimes broken. This is why we look at patterns and make generalizations, and then when we come across words like this in our reading and writing, we'll know how to read and spell them.

Janette: So, how do we remember when to double the consonant and when not to?

Teacher: Let's look at our words and see if there is another way to sort them.

Carla: Why don't we sort them by what we have to do with them before we add the *-ing*.

Teacher: Let's try that and see what happens.

The students sort the words:

| Double | Nothing | | Drop |
|--------|---------|---------|------|
| tugging | puffing | loading | blaming |
| popping | sprinting | shouting | placing |
| quitting | melting | screaming | shaping |
| dragging | snowing | speeding | driving |
| scarring | spoiling | chewing | |
| stirring | | | |
| blurring | | | |

---

Teacher: What do you notice?

Benjamin: Well, all the words in the "Drop" category are C-V-Ce [consonant-vowel-consonant-silent *e*] pattern words.

Teacher: Yes. What else do you notice?

Carla: The words that we have to double are all short-vowel or *r*-controlled vowel words, but when they are *r*-controlled, they are simple *r*-controlled—not like the more complex *R* patterns, like *eer* in *cheer*.

Teacher: Good observation. How about the words that we don't have to do anything to?

William: Well, they are a combination of long- and short-vowel words, but the short-vowel words all have two consonants after the vowel. See, like *melt*. It has the *lt* after the *e*, but the other words that we have to double the consonant don't, like *tug*.

Teacher: Good! The reason that we have to double the consonant for the words in the first column is to protect the short-vowel sound. If we don't double the consonant, then we would have *pō/ping* rather than *pop/ping*. This aspect of protecting the short-vowel sound will become more important as we keep learning about different types of syllables. The *r*-controlled words are a bit less common, but I wanted to include them, so you could analyze them as well. What about the long-vowel words? What do you notice with these words?

Melody: Well, with the words that have the C-V-Ce pattern, you have to drop the *e* before you add -*ing*, but for the words with the C-V-V-C or C-V-V pattern, you don't have to drop anything.

Teacher: You're right! This is because the words that have the C-V-V-C pattern already have another vowel there to protect the long-vowel sound. The words that have the C-V-Ce pattern don't need the *e* because the *i* in -*ing* acts as another vowel for the word. If we didn't drop the *e*, we would be adding another vowel pattern between the juncture of the base word and the suffix, and they are different parts of the word.

Look at this in *driveing*. This is why we have to drop the *e*. Here's a way for you to decide if you have to double the consonant. Ask yourselves the following 1-1-1 check [Ganske, 2000]. Remember, this is only a generalization.

- Does the word have one syllable?
- Does the word have one vowel?
- Does the word end with one consonant?

## Word Study Extension

Teacher:    During your independent work time, I want you to do a word hunt and look for other words that have the features we're studying. Look through some of the books that you have read. Next week, we are going to look at these words again when we talk about open and closed syllables.

Figure 12 demonstrates students working together on a sort.

**FIGURE 12**
**Students Completing a Word Sort**

*Note.* Photo courtesy of Heather Hughes.

# Comprehension

*Before Reading*

## Activate and Build Background Knowledge

In the following dialogue, the group is reading a Japanese folk tale called "The One-Inch Boy." The teacher introduces the story and encourages the students to make connections to other folk tales that the group has read.

---

| | |
|---|---|
| Teacher: | Today, we are going to read another folk tale. This time it is from Japan. What do we already know about folk tales? |
| Melody: | Folk tales are stories that have been told over and over. We often don't know who really wrote them. |
| Teacher: | Good. Is there anything you want to add? |
| Carla: | Well, they usually have some sort of lesson we can learn from, and they come from all around the world. |
| Teacher: | I wonder if the one-inch boy in the folk tale will have some of the same situations as the one-inch boy in the poem by Shel Silverstein had. |

## Preview Vocabulary

---

| | |
|---|---|
| Teacher: | Let's look at some words that we will be seeing in the folk tale that we read today. |

The teacher introduces preselected vocabulary that she thinks is important for the students to know before they read the story: *ancient, persisted, miniature, dense, coincidence,* and *fortune.* The teacher also writes the vocabulary words on index cards so that they can be used in a review after the story is read.

---

| | |
|---|---|
| Teacher: | Take a look at these words that we will read in the story today. Find the word that means something that is very old. |
| Janette: | Oh, that's *ancient.* It means really old things. |
| Teacher: | Yes. I wonder what that will have to do with the story? |
| Benjamin: | It is an ancient folk tale because it has been told for many years over and over again. |
| Teacher: | We'll find out how all of these words are used in the story as we read today. |

**Set a Purpose**

_____

Teacher: As we read the story, think about the important events that lead up to the conclusion. When we finish reading, I am going to ask you to determine the chain of events that were the most important.

*During Reading*

**Teacher/Student Questions**

_____

Teacher: Take a look at the picture. How does the author show us in the illustration how small the baby really is?

Janette: The illustrator drew a person's hand, and then you can really see how small the baby is in the basket.

Teacher: Let's read the first part together and find out where this very small baby came from.

The teacher and students choral read the first two paragraphs.

_____

Teacher: So, what questions do you have about what has happened so far?

Benjamin: I don't understand why he doesn't grow any bigger. He'll probably have a hard life if he doesn't grow any more.

Teacher: I really don't think we will find out why he didn't grow, but we'll find out how he was able to adjust to his small size. Who would like to be the lead reader for the next paragraph? (Several students raise their hands.) OK, Jordon. You read out loud, and we will all whisper read with you.

Jordon reads aloud while everyone else whisper reads along with him.

_____

Teacher: So, how is the one-inch boy able to be helpful to his family?

Jordon: Even though he's small, he's helping around the house and not just being lazy.

Teacher: The boy has now told his parents that he wants to go and "find his fortune." What do you think he means by that?

William: I think it means that he wants to go off on his own and work and have his own life.

Teacher:    Why do you think that his parents are so worried? Turn and talk to the person beside you about what you are thinking.

The students discuss with their partners for one minute.

———————

Teacher:    How did the one-inch boy demonstrate his respect for his parents? Find the sentence that gives us that information.

The group continues to read and discuss the story until the group time is finished.

### After Reading

———————

Teacher:    Our time is almost up, so let's take a few minutes to talk about what we've read so far. What are the most important events that have happened so far?

William:    Well, it would have to start with the couple adopting the one-inch boy.

Benjamin:    And then next, I think it would be how he overcame his size to be helpful at home.

The discussion is completed with the discussion of key events. (Note: Even if you have not finished the selection, it is important to recap the information from the text.)

### Comprehension Extension

———————

Teacher:    We have finished the first half of this story. Your group won't meet tomorrow, so here's what I want you to do. First, finish reading the story with your partner. Take turns lead reading and don't forget to ask your partner questions after they lead read. Remember what we have talked about regarding types of questions. Be sure to ask different types. Don't just ask the easy ones where you can find the answer right in the text.

    When you finish, I want you to create a chain of events map that shows the important events leading to the one-inch boy reaching his fortune. You must have at least five events in the chain, so you and your partner need to agree on the events before you create the map. You can decide how you want to illustrate the chain of events with your partner.

See Figure 13 for this completed extension activity.

FIGURE 13
Completed Extension Activity for Narrative Text

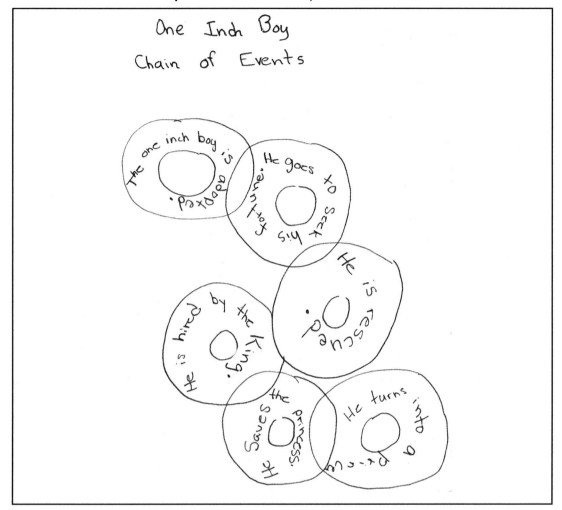

## Lesson Summary

The evolving reader lesson plan gives teachers a concrete structure for planning comprehensive reading instruction. The poem was selected for fluency practice as well as the connection that it had with the text selection. Rereading the poem is the only fluency extension appropriate for this lesson. Word study introduced these evolving readers to a simple suffix and word structures that required modification of the word before adding the suffix. This knowledge is crucial as these readers add more complex suffixes to their word knowledge.

The selection of the Japanese folk tale was aligned to genres suggested in the Common Core Standards. Folk tales from various cultures provide rich content as these evolving readers navigate varied text genres. There are numerous choices when deciding the comprehension focuses.

The following are additional extension activities that would also be appropriate for this lesson.

### Word Study Extensions

- Complete parts of the Word Study Matrix that are appropriate. (The matrix is discussed in Chapter 7 and available in the Support Materials section of the CD 🔘.)
- Create sentences for specified words.
- Write what you learned about what to look for when adding *-ing* to a word.

### Comprehension Extensions

- Use each story's vocabulary word in a sentence to tell something that happened in the story. (summarizing and vocabulary development)
- The one-inch boy was very persistent. Find three examples that show how he demonstrated his persistence and how it affected the outcome of the story. Write a paragraph that includes this information. The paragraph should be at least eight sentences in length. (character traits)
- What is the overall theme in this folk tale? What was the author trying to tell us? Write a paragraph that identifies the theme and how it was supported in the story. (theme)
- With a partner, identify the 10 most important (key) sentences in this folk tale. After the two of you agree, each partner needs to write the 10 sentences in the correct sequence from the story. (main ideas and details)

The quality of the written assignment is critical. This includes holding students accountable for length, depth, spelling, and grammar conventions, as well as appropriate sentence structure, word choice, and voice. The assignment needs to focus on the comprehension of the text. For example, asking students to write about what they would do if they were one-inch tall is a creative writing activity instead of a comprehension-focused activity. The extension activities that we offer in this book are meant to deepen comprehension. Combining both comprehension and writing goals allows teachers to save time in the classroom: working smarter not harder.

# Informational Lesson Model

## Description of the Group

In science, these fourth-grade evolving readers are studying pollution and its effects on the environment. The teacher has selected a poem about the water cycle to support the content area focus as well as to develop fluency. Contractions are the word study feature focus. The study of contractions will assist students in both their reading and writing development. The group reads an informational article and discusses the causes of water pollution as well as ways to prevent it. See Figure 14 for this completed lesson plan.

## Lesson Goals/Objectives

### *Fluency*

Students will continue to increase speed, accuracy, and expression to increase their ability to comprehend text.

### *Word Study*

Students will be able to identify the two words that make up the contraction as well as to use the contractions correctly in writing.

### *Comprehension*

In this lesson, the overall comprehension objectives include identifying important cause-and-effect relationships and determining essential main ideas and details.

## Fluency

This lesson begins with an introduction of a poem by Helen H. Moore (1997) entitled "The Water Cycle."

---

Teacher: Let's start today by rereading "The Water Cycle" poem. Since we've practiced it already, let's read it with a partner. Each of you read every other line.

The students read the poem while the teacher listens in on partners.

**The Water Cycle**

When I was young, I used to think
that water came from the kitchen sink.
But now I'm older, and I know,
that water comes from rain and snow.
It stays there, waiting, in the sky,
in clouds above our world so high.
And when it falls, it flows along,
and splashes out a watery song.
As each raindrop is joined by more
and rushes to the ocean shore,
or to a lake, a brook, a stream,
from which it rises, just like steam.
But while it's down here what do you think?
Some DOES go to the kitchen sink!

(p. 8)

From A POEM A DAY by Helen H. Moore. Copyright © 1997 by Helen H. Moore. Reprinted by permission of Scholastic, Inc.

**Completed Evolving Reader Informational Lesson Plan**

Narrative Text: _____    Informational text: _Water pollution_____

Text Type: _Science article_____    Estimated Length of Time: _2 days_____

| **FLUENCY** | **FLUENCY EXTENSION(S)** |
|---|---|
| Text: _"The Water Cycle" poem by Helen H. Moore_ | Reread with partner |

| **WORD STUDY** | **WORD STUDY EXTENSION(S)** |
|---|---|
| Features: _contractions_____ <br><br> Cycle: ____4____    Week: ____3_____ <br><br> Word Sort:  ☐ Open  ☑ Closed <br> ☐ Spelling Sort   ☐ Meaning Discussion | Partner spelling sort in word study notebook |

| **COMPREHENSION (NARRATIVE TEXT)** | **COMPREHENSION (INFORMATIONAL TEXT)** |
|---|---|
| Before Reading <br> ☐ Activate and build background knowledge <br><br> ☐ Preview vocabulary: _____ <br><br><br> ☐ Set a purpose | Before Reading <br> ☑ Activate and build background knowledge <br> ☑ Preview text features and structure <br> _____ <br><br> ☑ Preview vocabulary: _wastewater, agriculture,_ <br> _pollution, livestock, water treatment plant_ |
| During Reading <br> ☐ Teacher/student questions: _____ <br><br> ☐ Discussion/teaching points: _____ <br> _____ <br> _____ <br> Notes: | During Reading <br> ☑ Teacher/student questions: _How is agriculture_ <br> _affected by water pollution? How are water and air_ <br> _pollution the same?_ <br> ☑ Discussion/teaching points: _Ways to save_ <br> _clean water, cause-and-effect relationships_ <br> _____ <br> Notes: |
| After Reading <br> ☐ Plot/story elements <br> ☐ Character (traits, motivations, point of view) <br> ☐ Setting (mood, importance) <br> ☐ Events (sequencing) <br> ☐ Conflict and resolution <br> ☐ Theme <br> ☐ Summarize: _____ <br> _____ <br> Notes: | After Reading <br> ☐ Review text structure to aid understanding <br> ☐ Author's purpose <br> ☐ Summarize <br>    ☑ Main ideas and essential details <br>    ☐ Compare and contrast <br>    ☐ Sequence <br>    ☑ Cause and effect, or problem and solution <br> _____ <br> Notes: |

**Reading Assignment** (if appropriate)          Read pages: _Complete article_____
**Written Comprehension Extension(s):** _Design poster: "Ways to Save Clean Water"_____
Notes:

---

Teacher: Please put this poem in your poetry folder and read this poem with your partner today.

These students have developed an extensive fluency folder of both songs and poems. Students reread these poems with partners as a way to increase reading fluency.

## Word Study

In the following dialogue, the students are beginning a new sort. It is an open sort: The students must decide on categories in which to place the words they are studying. The teacher asks the students to justify their reasons for sorting. The students will need a full week to study these new features.

---

Teacher: This week, we will be looking at contractions. Does anyone know or remember what a contraction is?

Helen: A contraction is like a compound word. You put two words together and come up with a new word.

Teacher: It is kind of like a compound word; however, it is different in one distinctive way. Does anyone know what that is?

Clint: In a contraction, you have to take out a letter and put an apostrophe in its place.

Teacher: Right, we use apostrophes as a placeholder. Let's look at our words. Can you think of a couple of categories?

Mary: Well, we could use *have, not,* and *will.*

Teacher: How did Mary come up with those categories, Adam?

Adam: Because this way all the words that have something to do with the words *have, not,* or *will* can go in the same category.

Teacher: OK, let's try Mary's way. I'll pass out the words, and you can take turns reading them and decide which category to put them in. (The teacher passes out the cards.) Who would like to start?

Katie: I'll start. I have the word *they've.* I think it goes in the "have" category.

Teacher: Why do you think that, Katie?

Katie: Because *they've* is made up of *they* and *have.*

Teacher: Right, Katie. What word do you have, Clint?

Clint: I have *couldn't.* It goes in the *not* category because it means *could not.*

Teacher: Good, Clint!

The students continue to sort based on the identified categories.

| have | not | will |
|------|-----|------|
| they've | couldn't | we'll |
| would've | won't | that'll |
| you've | doesn't | she'll |
| should've | haven't | you'll |
| we've | isn't | it'll |
| could've | wouldn't | that'll |

---

Teacher: What do you notice about the words in the "not" category?

David: The apostrophe takes the place of only one letter.

Teacher: What does David mean, Clint?

Clint: Well, in the word *couldn't*, the apostrophe takes the place of the *o*. But, in the "have" category, the apostrophe takes the place of two letters: the *h* and the *a*.

Teacher: Clint is right, and he brings up a good point. Does anyone notice anything else about the words in the "not" category? Think about what you know about parts of speech.

Helen: All the words are verbs?

Mary: *Could* is not a verb, and neither is *would*.

Helen: Yes, it is. We could go to the zoo if we want to see the elephants.

Teacher: Let's look it up and see what we find.

The students look up *could* in the dictionary.

---

Teacher: What did you find out?

Mary: The definition reads "past tense of can."

Teacher: So, Helen was right. All of the "not" words are verbs. How about the words in the "have" category? What type of words are those?

The teacher continues to discuss the parts of speech for the categorized words.

## *Word Study Extension*

---

Teacher: OK, when you get back to your seats, you are going to do a spelling sort with your partner in your word study notebook. For this sort, you have to write the contraction under the category that shows the word that the apostrophe stands for.

These students have completed spelling sorts in their groups, so they are very familiar with this concept. The students will take turns calling out contractions while the partner writes the word under the correct category. This independent practice with contractions will help students solidify and apply this word feature.

## Comprehension

*Before Reading*

**Activate and Build Background Knowledge**

Teacher: Today, we are going to read a short article about water pollution. We have talked a lot about air pollution, but today we are going to learn about water pollution. In what ways do you think they will be the same?

Katie: They are both going to ruin our world. Pollution can make our air dirty and our water dirty.

Teacher: Good point. Based on what you know, what things do you think pollute our water?

Clint: What about the oil spill in the Gulf? That really caused water pollution.

Teacher: So, what have been the effects of that oil spill?

The teacher and students continue the discussion.

**Set a Purpose**
The teacher uses the Fact or Fib? activity (see the Support Materials section on the CD  ) to provide a purpose for reading the article as well as to motivate students to want to find out the answers.

Teacher: Before we begin, let's see how much you already know about the subject. I am going to read statements about water pollution. Some are actual facts and some are fibs.

   1. People can live for weeks without water.

   2. Dirty water is treated with chemicals to clean it, and then we can drink it again.

   3. To save water, you should stop brushing your teeth so often.

   4. You should take short showers to save clean water.

   5. You can play an important part in preventing water pollution.

Now, put your answers away, and we will check them again when we finish reading the article.

## Preview Vocabulary

---

Teacher: Let's look at some vocabulary words that will be important to know as we read the article.

The teacher introduces the following vocabulary: *wastewater, agriculture, pollution, petroleum, livestock,* and *water treatment plant*. The teacher has the terms written on index cards along with a picture for each word that was obtained from the Internet. These visuals will assist students as they add new words to their reading and expressive vocabulary.

---

Teacher: First, I want you to take a look at these six pictures. As I show you each vocabulary term, see if you can identify the picture that represents it. My first word is *agriculture*. Do you know what that means?

Helen: I've heard of it before, but I'm not sure what it means.

Teacher: Does anyone else know? *Agriculture* means farming and growing things to sell.

Clint: Oh, I know. It's the picture of the corn growing in the field.

Teacher: Right. What other things could the farmer grow that he could sell to make money?

Adam: Farmers could also sell their animals.

Teacher: Good point. How might water pollution be harmful to agriculture?

Katie: Well, if the water was dirty, it wouldn't be good for the plants or the animals.

The discussion continues as each vocabulary term is introduced.

---

Teacher: As we read the article, think about how we can reuse, recycle, and reduce the amount of clean water we waste.

## *During Reading*

## Teacher/Student Questions

---

Teacher: Let's read the first paragraph together. I think that we may confirm one of the answers to the questions I asked you.

The teacher and students read the first paragraph together.

_____

Paul:      Oh, yeah, I got that one right. You can't live for weeks without water, but you can live for weeks without food.

Teacher:   I want everyone to whisper read the next paragraph. When you finish, be ready to retell how a used paper bag and recycling are related.

All of the students whisper read the next paragraph while the teacher monitors.

_____

Teacher:   Please turn to your talking partner and discuss the relationship between the used paper bag and recycling.

The teacher listens in to the conversations between students.

_____

Teacher:   In the next paragraph, we are going to learn more about the term *wastewater*. Remember, *wastewater* is one word. It is a noun, a thing, not like you were wasting water. Katie, will you be the lead reader for this part? We will all whisper read along with Katie.

The teacher and students all whisper read together while Katie reads aloud.

_____

Teacher:   So, where does the wastewater go, and what is it used for?

Clint:     The wastewater goes to the water treatment plant.

Mary:      Thank goodness we don't have to drink it. I thought that if you put chemicals in the water, it would pollute it, and this says the chemicals can clean it.

Teacher:   It depends on what kind of chemicals they are talking about. Some chemicals, as we will read later in the article, can pollute the water. Based on what we have read so far, what do you think the author's purpose is for writing this article?

Clint:     I think that the author is writing to tell us about water pollution and what we should do to prevent it.

The teacher and students continue reading and discussing until the time is up.

*After Reading*

---

Teacher: So, what have we learned about the effects of water pollution?

The teacher records the students' responses on a Cause and Effect chart.

---

Adam: Well, we've learned that it can harm the environment in a lot of ways, like it can hurt animals when the water they drink is polluted.

Paul: Yeah, and it can also make the food we eat dangerous if the dirty water gets into the soil that plants grow in.

Teacher: Anything else?

Katie: Well, it can also hurt animals that live in the water, like the oil spill harmed a lot of animals.

*Comprehension Extension*

---

Teacher: When you leave your group today, I want you to finish reading the article with your partner. After that, I want you to create a poster that tells five ways to save and protect clean water. I have some poster board on the back table that you can use. Plan to spend the next two days working on your posters. You can post them around school when you finish. I won't meet with your group tomorrow, so I want you to take each vocabulary term from the article and write a sentence that tells something that you learned. We will share those when we meet next time.

See Figure 15 for this completed extension activity.

## Lesson Summary

This small-group lesson served several important purposes. Fluency was addressed by reading and rereading a poem. Additionally, these students focused on contractions in word study that they need in their reading and writing. The teacher selected a text piece that supported the science content standards of the fourth-grade curriculum at an appropriate reading level. These students were supported as they read an informational article on water pollution. Again, it is important to combine instructional objectives whenever possible, given the limited time in the classroom.

**FIGURE 15**
**Completed Extension Activity for Informational Text**

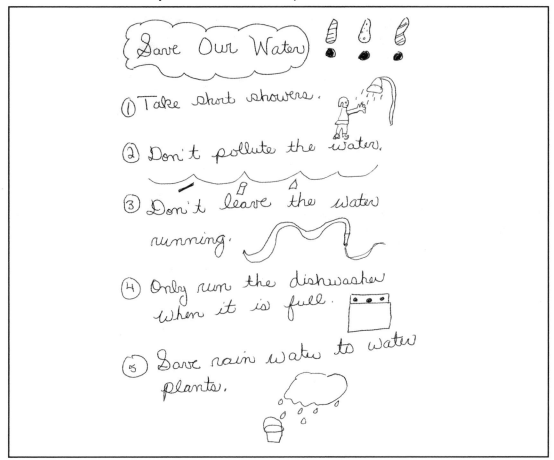

## Word Study Extensions

The following are some other extension activities that are appropriate for this word study focus:

- Conduct a word hunt for other contractions with the same pattern.
- Write the two words that stand for each contraction.

## Comprehension Extensions

Written comprehension extensions will vary depending on the comprehension focus. The following are some additional written extension activities that are appropriate for this article:

- Identify three important cause-and-effect relationships that contribute to water pollution.
- Write an article for the school newspaper on how to recycle, reuse, and reduce to save clean water.

- Compare and contrast water pollution and air pollution. (The Compare and Contrast With Meaning activity is discussed in Chapter 2 and a reproducible is in the Support Materials section on the CD 💿.)
- Describe some different ways that agriculture can be harmed by water pollution.

# Conclusion

Evolving readers continue to need both teacher and text support to achieve success. We began the chapter by describing each component of the lesson plan as it relates to the evolving reader. In addition, we provided teacher–student dialogue to guide you through actual lesson plans. As evidenced throughout the dialogue, evolving readers require the appropriate amount of teacher scaffolding as they move through this stage. This will help them develop independent strategies as they focus on gaining information from text rather than decoding it.

# CHAPTER 5

# The Maturing Reader Stage

The expectations for intermediate readers have risen dramatically over the past few years. The Common Core Standards have increased the rigor required for these readers, particularly those in the Maturing Reader and Advanced Reader stages. The texts that students are required to read in college and in their future careers demand a sophistication for which many students today are not prepared. Maturing readers are able to read to learn; however, they need support to fully engage with complex texts. Both in their classrooms and in everyday life, students are immersed in different types of text, including novels, textbooks, reference materials, magazines, newspapers, and many forms of digital literacy. Exposure to these types of texts challenges maturing readers to fine-tune their thinking about and comprehension of a given text. Thus, maturing readers must learn to adapt their thinking to promote understanding. This is especially true with regard to digital literacy. As maturing readers continue to use digital media to access information, they need to be able to sift through this information in an effective, efficient manner.

In this book, all of the extension activities are directly tied to the Common Core Standards. We explicitly demonstrate instructional ideas that will help teachers differentiate their instruction while meeting the required standards.

## Characteristics of Maturing Readers in Reading, Writing, and Word Study

### Reading

Maturing readers have developed their fluency in oral reading. They can read expressively with the appropriate pace, phrasing, intonation, and rhythm of speech. However, fluency is a skill that needs to be continually practiced. Although fluency is not part of the maturing reader's small-group lesson plan, we have provided examples of appropriate independent activities to promote fluency in Chapter 7.

Maturing readers understand the differences between the characteristics of narrative and informational text, including technical and persuasive. Further, they understand the purposes of text features such as graphs, charts, maps, tables of contents, pictures and illustrations, headings and subheadings, glossaries, and indexes. Maturing readers use these features to locate information in the text and gain meaning from them. Additionally, these students are continuing to develop their digital literacy skills. Although there are varying definitions of *digital literacy*, it is not simply the ability to read online. It requires one to locate, organize, understand, and critique/analyze information (and verify trustworthiness of source) using some form of digital media, including but not limited to a computer, smartphones, and other digital devices. Some researchers also include interpreting media types, such as text, sound, and images, and the ability to digitally manipulate the media as well as applying knowledge to future digital experiences (Jones-Kavalier & Flannigan, 2006).

While reading, maturing readers are learning to generate and respond to literal, inferential, and application questions before, during, and after reading. Thus, these readers begin to use this information to make inferences and draw conclusions about a given text. They compare and contrast varying elements of text, including topics, character traits, and themes, and identify problems and solutions and cause-and-effect relationships. Maturing readers are able to retell main ideas or events as well as provide supporting details about both narrative and informational text.

In the classroom, there is an emphasis on content area knowledge. As a result, maturing readers are expected to know and be able to use technical vocabulary associated with each specific content area. Consequently, they use their knowledge of word structure, such as syllable patterns, contractions, root words, prefixes, and suffixes, when faced with an unknown word.

Maturing readers also are beginning to learn about the meaning and elements of figurative language, such as similes, metaphors, analogies, personification, and symbolism. In addition, these readers are learning about the relationship between an author's use of literary devices in a text (e.g., foreshadowing, flashback, irony) and his or her purpose for writing the text or the bias that an author has.

Finally, maturing readers are developing their abilities to make inferences, synthesize, and evaluate information; therefore, comprehension is the main focus of instruction for maturing readers. These higher level thinking skills will continue to be fine-tuned well into adulthood.

## Texts for Maturing Readers

Maturing readers should read silently from a variety of genres; however, they will continue to need explicit comprehension instruction to fully understand the author's meaning. Text selections for maturing readers should consist of novels, magazines, poetry, newspaper articles, and informational pieces that support content area standards. Traditionally, chapter books have been the genre of choice for maturing readers; however, instruction should not be limited to these texts. Although we understand that many teachers are constrained by available resources, many free online resources are available to support teachers in their quest for additional reading materials.

Some examples of appropriate chapter books for maturing readers include *Bridge to Terabithia* by Katherine Paterson, *A Wrinkle in Time* by Madeleine L'Engle, *Holes* by Louis Sachar, and *Maniac Magee* by Jerry Spinelli. Although some of the novels read during this stage may not be very challenging with regard to word recognition, the content is meant for mature audiences who can conceptualize more difficult topics such as death, racism, time travel, and freedom.

For those using leveled texts as a resource to support small-group differentiated reading instruction, the following book levels are appropriate for maturing readers:

| Leveling System | Book Levels |
|---|---|
| DRA | 40–44+ |
| Fountas and Pinnell | S–W |
| Lexile bands | *Grade 5:* 565L–910L, 860L–980L (stretch bands) |
| | *Grade 6:* 665L–1000L, 950L–1040L (stretch bands) |

## Writing

At the same time that maturing readers are fine-tuning their reading abilities, they are also fine-tuning their writing skills. These students are familiar with the steps of the writing process, but many may need additional instruction with particular aspects of writing to achieve proficiency. Maturing readers need to write a variety of different narrative (e.g., creative pieces, poetry, autobiographies, memoirs), informative (e.g., research, explain concepts), and persuasive (also known as arguments; i.e., attempting to change an opinion) pieces. Please note that small-group reading time is not the time to give writing instruction. Rather, a teacher should consider separate whole-group writing instruction time to address different types of writing.

Maturing readers also are able to express themselves in their writing, which they no longer view as a laborious process because of the breadth of their word knowledge. Students are not limited by the number of words that they can spell automatically; therefore, they have more mental energy to expend on their ideas. Nurturing the link between reading and writing is essential at this stage. Although writing instruction is not the focus of this book, we would be remiss if we did not provide teachers with meaningful writing extensions based on their small-group reading. As outlined in Chapter 7, there are many follow-up writing extensions that can be completed outside of small-group instruction. The ideas presented are written comprehension *extensions* rather than writing *instruction*. The extension activities that students do outside of their small groups are directly connected to their in-group instruction; thus, the connection is seamless.

In our classroom observations, we have seen teachers become proficient with teaching their students simple reader-response types of writing. Although these are valid and worthwhile activities, intermediate students need to spend time developing critical thinking skills in their writing. For example, with narrative text, rather than writing a new ending to a story, take it one step further and have students write a new ending, then compare their ending to the author's ending and explain why theirs is more creative. Using this approach, the students complete two forms of writing, narrative and persuasive. Another example in informational text would be to have students search online for three additional sources of information about a particular topic. After analyzing all the data, have them write a 10-sentence summary to present to the class covering the three important points and explain why they chose those particular aspects. This allows students to practice writing informational pieces. With the shortage of instructional time, it is crucial for teachers to find ways to maximize student learning.

## Word Study

Maturing readers are typically in the meaning layer of spelling development and encounter multisyllabic words in their daily reading. They are continuing to learn about the spelling–meaning connection, particularly with regard to content-specific vocabulary, and they are becoming adept with morphemes. As students study the meaning layer of the English language, they are able to make spelling–meaning connections. The focus for these students is primarily on complex syllabication and Latin and Greek roots. A weekly word study scope and sequence for year 1 and another for year 2 have been provided in the Word Study Materials section on the accompanying CD and is provided only as a guideline. It is crucial for teachers to use assessment to guide their instruction. If students have not mastered particular features, it is best to solidify those features before teaching something new. It will be worth the time to reteach and review the features that students are confusing. The features studied during the Maturing Reader stage are outlined in Table 7.

# Instructional Components of the Maturing Reader Lesson Plan

There are two components for the lesson plan for maturing readers (see Figure 16). For the first component, word study, the teacher records the current word study feature on

### TABLE 7
#### Word Study Features for the Maturing Reader

| Feature | Example(s) |
| --- | --- |
| Adding /shən/ with and without other predictable changes and spelling changes | *ct + ion*, ending blends + *ion* |
| Assimilated prefixes | *ad-* (to, toward), *com-* (with, together) |
| Consonant/vowel alternations | *cave/cavity, sign/signal* |
| Doubling and no doubling with polysyllabic base words | *-ed, -ing* |
| Final *K* sound | *c, ck, k, que* |
| Greek and Latin root words and prefixes | *Greek: cat-, circum-, hyper, hyp/hypo, peri-*<br>*Latin: aud* (to hear), *spec/spect/spic* (to see, to look) |
| Latin suffixes | *-ant/-ent, -able/-ible* |
| Number-related prefixes and root words | *dec-/deca-, oct-/octa-/octo-, pent-, quad-/quadri-, uni-* |
| Polysyllabic homographs | *graduate, separate* |
| Plurals | *-sis/-ses, -um/-a* |
| Spelling patterns at the end of words | *al, el, il, ile, le* |
| Vowel patterns in stressed/unstressed syllables | *al, el, le*, the unaccented vowel sound or schwa, schwa+*n* |

104

# FIGURE 16
## Maturing Reader Lesson Plan

Text type: _____     Narrative text: _____

Estimated length of time: _____     Informational text: _____

| WORD STUDY | WORD STUDY EXTENSION(S) |
|---|---|

**WORD STUDY**

Features: _____

Cycle: _____     Week: _____

Word Sort:  ☐ Open  ☐ Closed
☐ Spelling Sort  ☐ Meaning Discussion

**WORD STUDY EXTENSION(S)**

---

**COMPREHENSION (NARRATIVE TEXT)**

Before Reading
☐ Activate and build background knowledge
☐ Preview vocabulary: _____

☐ Set a purpose

**COMPREHENSION (INFORMATIONAL TEXT)**

Before Reading
☐ Activate and build background knowledge
☐ Preview text features and structure
_____
_____

☐ Preview vocabulary: _____
_____

---

During Reading
☐ Teacher/student questions: _____
_____
_____
_____

☐ Discussion/teaching points: _____
_____
_____

Notes:

During Reading
☐ Teacher/student questions: _____
_____
_____
_____

☐ Discussion/teaching points: _____
_____
_____

Notes:

---

After Reading
☐ Plot/story line
  ☐ Character Development (traits, motivation,
    point of view)
  ☐ Setting (mood, importance)
  ☐ Conflicts
  ☐ Resolutions
  ☐ Theme
☐ Summarize: _____
_____

Notes:

After Reading
☐ Review text structure to aid understanding
☐ Author's purpose
☐ Summarize
  ☐ Main ideas and essential details
  ☐ Compare and contrast
  ☐ Sequence
  ☐ Cause and effect, or problem and solution
_____
_____

Notes:

---

**Reading Assignment** (if appropriate)          Read pages: _____

**Written Comprehension Extension(s):** _____

Notes:

the lesson plan and determines whether the students will be completing a word sort, completing a spelling sort, or having a meaning discussion. Additionally, the teacher decides which extension activity is most appropriate for the features studied.

For the second component, comprehension, students focus on more challenging aspects of text. Since the lesson plan is designed to be used for one piece of text, a teacher can decide which aspects of comprehension will need the most attention. We want to again emphasize the importance of classroom discussion—critical not only to students' understanding but also for application of the information learned. It is during this time that teachers can extend students' knowledge. Rich discussion is achieved through in-depth questioning on the part of the teacher and, more important, on the part of the students.

## Differentiating the Lesson Plan

Again, we present one lesson plan to support both narrative and informational text. Similar to the evolving reader, we adapted the comprehension strategies on the planning template to meet the demands of each text type. We also provide a completed lesson plan for both narrative and informational text.

Please note that for consistency purposes, the word study sequence for the maturing reader remains the same regardless of the type of text used. We provide in-depth classroom dialogue to guide readers through each lesson plan. The lesson plans follow two different groups of students. You will notice that not every element on the lesson template is covered in the example lessons. Realistically, it is not appropriate or feasible to incorporate all parts of the template into every small-group lesson.

# Narrative Lesson Model

## Description of the Group

This group of six students is in the beginning of the Maturing Reader stage. In word study, they are just starting to study the *-ible/-able* suffixes. In the reading portion of the lesson plan, the students are reading the poem "Casey at the Bat" by Ernest Thayer (1888). You will notice that the teacher reads the first three stanzas with the students before they go off and read the rest of the poem on their own. The teacher embeds discussion points (i.e., figurative language, plot of the poem) throughout the comprehension section. See Figure 17 for a completed lesson plan.

## Lesson Goals/Objectives

### Word Study

For this lesson, the word study goals include being able to verbalize a generalization about the *-ible/-able* suffix and finding at least five words that follow this pattern. Students will also learn how the suffixes alter the meaning of the words.

## FIGURE 17
## Completed Maturing Lesson Plan for Narrative Text

Text type: _Poetry_       Narrative text: _"Casey at the Bat" by Ernest Thayer_

Estimated length of time: _2-3 days_       Informational text: _____

| WORD STUDY | WORD STUDY EXTENSION(S) |
|---|---|
| Features: _-able/-ible_ <br><br> Cycle: ___3___     Week: ___5___ <br><br> Word Sort: ☑ Open   ☐ Closed <br> ☐ Spelling Sort   ☑ Meaning Discussion <br> _Base/root words_ | _Word hunt_ |

| COMPREHENSION (NARRATIVE TEXT) | COMPREHENSION (INFORMATIONAL TEXT) |
|---|---|
| Before Reading <br> ☐ Activate and build background knowledge <br> ☑ Preview vocabulary: _melancholy, haughty,_ _grandeur, and multitude_ <br> ☐ Set a purpose | Before Reading <br> ☐ Activate and build background knowledge <br> ☐ Preview text features and structure <br> _____ <br> _____ <br><br> ☐ Preview vocabulary: _____ <br> _____ |
| During Reading <br> ☑ Teacher/student questions: • _What do we know so_ _far about the setting of the poem? How do we know this?_ <br> • _What else does the author tell us in the first three_ _stanzas?_ <br> • _What is something that we can infer from the poem?_ <br> ☑ Discussion/teaching points: _____ <br> • _Figurative language (examples)_ <br> • _Story in the poem: What does it tell us?_ <br> Notes: _Students need to back up their thinking and_ _provide examples._ | During Reading <br> ☐ Teacher/student questions: _____ <br> _____ <br> _____ <br> _____ <br> ☐ Discussion/teaching points: _____ <br> _____ <br> _____ <br> Notes: |
| After Reading <br> ☐ Plot/story line <br>    ☐ Character Development (traits, motivation, <br>      point of view) <br>    ☐ Setting (mood, importance) <br>    ☐ Conflicts <br>    ☐ Resolutions <br>    ☐ Theme <br> ☑ Summarize: • _Main points of story_ <br> • _Casey character: Why do people need heroes? Is_ _this related to the theme?_ <br> Notes: <br> • _When students bring back their answer sheets, be_ _sure that they used multiple sources._ <br> • _Students need to say why they would ask the_ _question they chose._ | After Reading <br> ☐ Review text structure to aid understanding <br> ☐ Author's purpose <br> ☐ Summarize <br>    ☐ Main ideas and essential details <br>    ☐ Compare and contrast <br>    ☐ Sequence <br>    ☐ Cause and effect, or problem and solution <br> _____ <br> _____ <br> Notes: |

**Reading Assignment** (if appropriate)      Read pages: _Remainder of poem_

**Written Comprehension Extension(s):** _Question/answer sheet_

Notes: • _Students will find answers on their own, using other resources._
      • _Students will also bring in one question that they would ask the author._

*Comprehension*

In comprehension, the overall lesson goals include being able to identify and understand specific parts where the author uses figurative language in poetry, creating one question to ask the author related to students' opinions of the poem, and locating additional information about the poem and/or author using online resources.

## Word Study: Day 1

In the following dialogue, the students are starting a new sort. When teachers introduce a new sort, it will typically take about 10 minutes, although at times there will need to be substantial discussions about word meaning, which will take more time. Again, this meaning discussion is crucial to students' development of vocabulary knowledge. The example below is an open sort; thus, the teacher does not provide the header words or tell the students the pattern they are studying. Additionally, all students have their own word cards to sort.

———————————

Teacher:     Today, we are going to start a new sort. Here are your words. Take a look and then sort the words by yourself.

The teacher gives about two or three minutes to sort.

———————————

Teacher:        Can anyone tell me what you notice about the words and how you sorted them?

Carla:          All the words have either *-able* or *-ible* at the end.

Teacher:        Yes, they do. So, how did you sort them?

Thomas:         That's easy...by *-able* or *-ible*. See, I have two columns.

Teacher:        Does everyone have two columns?

All students:  Yes.

Teacher:        What do you notice about the words other than the ending they have?

Melody:         The words with *-ible* seem to be shorter.

Carla:          I agree. They have fewer letters.

Teacher:        Let's look a bit more closely. What else do you notice?

Thomas:         I don't know.

Melody:         Neither do I.

Harrison:       Is *aud* a word?

Thomas:         A real word?

Harrison:       Yes, a real word by itself, without the *-ible*.

Teacher:        What do the rest of you think?

Melody:         No, it's not a real word.

| Thomas: | No, I don't think so. |
|---|---|
| Teacher: | Why do you ask that, Harrison? |
| Harrison: | Well, because I was going to say that most of the *-ible* words are not real words—by themselves, I mean, without the suffix. But, the words with *-able* are all words by themselves. |
| Teacher: | What do the rest of you think of Harrison's observation? |
| Carla: | He's right, except for *access* and *assess*. |
| Teacher: | How about if we put those two words aside for a moment. Now what do you see? |
| Melody: | Well, now Harrison is right. All of the words in the *-ible* column are not words by themselves. |
| Teacher: | Who remembers what we call words that can stand alone and those that cannot? |
| Thomas: | Words that can stand alone are called base words. They have a base that you can add on to. |
| Carla: | The other ones are called root words. I remember that because they have to be rooted in something—like they need something else to hold onto to make them a word. |
| Teacher: | You are both right! Now, what conclusions can we come to based on what we know about these words? |
| Harrison: | You could say that words with root words use *-ible,* and base words use *-able.* |
| Carla: | What about *access* and *assess*? They don't fit that. |
| Melody: | But they both end with two *S*s. What about that? Is that the trick? |
| Teacher: | Let's see if we can find more words that end in double *S* and what we find. Now, how can we sort these? |

The students continue sorting the words into the three categories that they have determined. Additionally, the teacher discusses how the suffix changes the meaning of the words. See the following completed sort:

| *-able* | *-ible* | *ss + -ible* |
|---|---|---|
| agreeable | audible | accessible |
| breakable | edible | assessible |
| dependable | visible | |
| laughable | horrible | |
| perishable | tangible | |
| predictable | legible | |
| profitable | terrible | |
| remarkable | | |
| transferable | | |

*Word Study Extension*

---

Teacher:    During your independent work time, I want you to do a word hunt and look for other words that fit the *-ible* and *-able* patterns. Tomorrow, we'll take a quick look to see what you found.

## Comprehension: Day 1

*Before Reading*

### Activate and Build Background Knowledge

---

Teacher:    Who has heard of the poem "Casey at the Bat"?

Harrison:    Isn't that a baseball story? I thought it was a book, though, not a poem.

Melody:    I've never heard of it.

Carla:    Neither have I.

Thomas:    I think my dad might have read it to me when I was younger.

The teacher quickly finishes the discussion.

### Set a Purpose

---

Teacher:    Today, you are going to read the poem. It was written by Ernest Thayer in 1888. It is considered the most famous baseball poem ever written. We are going to do things a bit differently with this poem. We'll review some vocabulary words that you might not be familiar with before you read it. Then, you are going to read through the poem a few times. As you read it, you are going to use sticky notes to track two different things: Use the pink one to identify where or if your meaning gets lost. Use the blue one to identify where the author uses figurative language. On the blue sticky note, I want you to write what you think the author really means.

### Preview Vocabulary

---

Teacher:    First, let's take a look at some of the words that you will encounter in the poem. Who knows what the word *melancholy* means?

No one answers within about 30 seconds, and the teacher continues.

| Teacher: | Let's break the word into chunks. How do you think the word is broken up? |
| --- | --- |
| Khyati: | I think *-oly* is a suffix, so maybe *melanch* is the root. |
| Carla: | Would it just be the *melan* part? |
| Teacher: | Where can we go to find out that information? |
| Kate: | Let's just google it. |

The teacher leads the search and goes to the Root Word Dictionary (www.macro evolution.net/root-word-dictionary.html) and Merriam-Webster (www.merriam-webster.com/dictionary/melancholy) websites.

| Teacher: | We learned that *melan* is a Greek root meaning dark, black, or murky. The online dictionary defines *melancholy* as "1 *a*: an abnormal state attributed to an excess of black bile and characterized by irascibility or depression; *b*: black bile; *c*: melancholia; 2.*a*: depression of spirits: dejection; *b*: a pensive mood." So, we know that *melancholy* has something to do with depression or being in a black mood. We can see how the root is linked to the word's meaning. Who would like to summarize for the group? |
| --- | --- |
| Kate: | It means to be depressed or sad. |

The group continues to discuss the following words: *haughty, grandeur,* and *multitude.*

## *During Reading*

## Teacher/Student Questions

| Teacher: | We have a few more minutes for today, so let's start reading the first few stanzas of the poem. Then, after group, you will read the rest of the poem on your own. I'll read the first three stanzas today, and you can read the rest of the poem. |
| --- | --- |

> **Casey at the Bat**
>
> The outlook wasn't brilliant for the Mudville Nine that day:
> The score stood four to two, with but one inning more to play,
> And then when Cooney died at first, and Barrows did the same,
> A sickly silence fell upon the patrons of the game.
>
> A straggling few got up to go in deep despair. The rest
> Clung to that hope which springs eternal in the human breast;
> They thought, if only Casey could get but a whack at that—
> We'd put up even money, now, with Casey at the bat.

But Flynn preceded Casey, as did also Jimmy Blake,
And the former was a lulu and the latter was a cake;
So upon that stricken multitude grim melancholy sat,
For there seemed but little chance of Casey's getting to the bat.

The teacher decided to read to the students to model fluency and increase their motivation. Kids at any age like to listen to their teacher read.

---

| | |
|---|---|
| Teacher: | What do we know so far about the setting of the poem? (literal) |
| Thomas: | It takes place at a baseball game. |
| Teacher: | How do we know that? (inferential) |
| Melody: | Because it says here, "with but one inning more to play." Only baseball uses innings. |
| Teacher: | What else does the author tell us in the first three stanzas? (literal) |
| Carla: | Well, we know they are losing, and the game is almost over. |
| Teacher: | True, what else? Think about something that the author is not explicitly stating but we can infer from the poem. (inferential) |
| Harrison: | I think the team's best player is coming up to bat. |
| Teacher: | Why do you think that? (metacognitive: explaining thought process) |
| Harrison: | Because the author says, "We'd put up even money, now, with Casey at the bat." This guy Casey is at the bat, and they think they can win. |
| Teacher: | It does say that, but let's look at the lines before and after it. When we read those, what else can we infer? (inferential) |
| Khyati: | I don't think he is up to bat yet. I think the audience is hoping he will get a turn, but the last line of the third stanza says, "For there seemed but little chance of Casey's getting to the bat." That makes us believe that he isn't up to bat, but they want him to be. |
| Teacher: | Good point, Khyati. While you are all reading this poem, we are going to use your sticky notes to identify where the author uses figurative language. Who remembers what figurative language is? |
| Kate: | It's when an author describes something by comparing it to something else, like if I said I was so hungry I could eat a horse. |

### Comprehension Extension

---

| | |
|---|---|
| Teacher: | Right. Good job, Kate! So, while you are reading, you are going to put a pink sticky note where you see the author do what Kate just described. You can use the blue ones to track where you are not sure |

what is going on. Be sure that you are specific about what you don't understand, so you will remember for tomorrow. I also want you to think of one question that you would ask the author if you could. This must be an inferential or application-level question. I do not want to see any literal-level questions.

The teacher dismisses the students to complete their reading for the next day.

## Comprehension: Day 2
### *After Reading*

### Summarizing
The teacher uses open-ended questions to summarize the plot.

---

| | |
|---|---|
| Teacher: | Let's talk about the story that took place in the poem. Who wants to start? |
| Melody: | There was this baseball game, and the one team—what was it called again? |
| Thomas: | Mudville, I think. |
| Melody: | Yep, that was it. So, the Mudville team was down two runs, and they only had one more inning to play. |
| Teacher: | Good. Who wants to pick it up from there? |
| Carla: | Well, the crowd wanted this guy Casey to get up to bat, and at first it didn't look like he was going to get the chance, but then he did. |
| Teacher: | Yes, and then what happens? |
| Harrison: | Well, basically, he strikes out, and they lose, and everyone is upset. |
| Teacher: | In a nutshell, yes, Harrison, that's what happens. Who wants to share one of the places in the text where they found the author using figurative language? |
| Melody: | In the third line of the first stanza, the author wrote, "And then when Cooney died at first, and Barrows did the same." |
| Teacher: | Why is that an example of figurative language? |
| Melody: | Because the players didn't die, they just struck out. The author compared their striking out to dying. |
| Teacher: | Good. Who has another example that they would like to share? |
| Khyati: | I have a question. I put one of my sticky notes here. I didn't understand what the author was talking about in the third stanza. What does he |

mean with these two lines, "But Flynn preceded Casey, as did also Jimmy Blake / And the former was a lulu and the latter was a cake"?

Teacher:    Who can help Khyati out?

Thomas:    I was confused by that one, too. Last night, I asked my dad, and he wasn't sure either. He thought that it was referring to pitches, but that wasn't right. We looked it up. I wrote it down here: "A lulu" is talking about a guy who is sort of a wimp, and "a cake" refers to someone who is not very good.

Teacher:    Thomas, good idea to look it up. Let's keep looking at where Thayer uses figurative language along with any other parts that confused you.

The group continues to clarify parts and review figurative language.

### Comprehension Extension

--------------------

Teacher:    For our extension activity today, we are going to brainstorm some questions about other information that we can find about this poem. For example, let's see if we can find what the author's purpose was in writing the poem. Who has an idea? Use this sheet to track your questions.

The teacher distributes a chart with the column headings "Questions," "Sources," and "Answers."

--------------------

Melody:    How about if we try to see if he wrote it about a particular person?

Teacher:    Good. Who else?

Carla:    What else was happening in the world when he wrote it?

Thomas:    How did it become so famous?

The group continues to brainstorm until they have five or six questions.

--------------------

Teacher:    OK, now that you have your list, don't forget to cite your sources, so we can find the information again. Bring it back to group by the day after tomorrow.

See Figure 18 for this completed extension activity.

114

**FIGURE 18**
**Completed Extension Activity for Narrative Text**

| Question | Answer | Source |
|---|---|---|
| Did he write it about a particular person? | I couldn't find it exactly, but there was a player named Mike Kelly who played for Boston and people from the East Coast thought it was about him. | Joslin Hall Company (www.joslin hall.com/casey_at_the_bat.htm) |
| What else was happening in the world when he wrote it? | There was nothing special that was going on as a reason for him writing it. | Wikipedia (en.wikipedia.org/wiki/ Casey_at_the_Bat) |
| How did it become so famous? | There was a writer who gave it to De Wolf Hopper, a singer from New York, to recite it on stage in front of the NY, and Chicago baseball groups and he made it famous. It had already been published in the paper. | Liben Music Publishers (www .liben.com/caseyhistory.html) and Baseball Almanac (www.baseball-almanac.com/poetry/po_case .shtml) |
| How old was he when he wrote the poem? | It was published on Sunday, June 3rd, 1888. He was only 24, he was almost 25. It was read by Hopper on his 25th birthday, not on purpose. | Joslin Hall Company (www.joslin hall.com/casey_at_the_bat.htm) |
| Is Mudville a real place? | There is a neighborhood in MA called Mudville and Stockton, CA, was known as Mudville for a little while. | Wikipedia (en.wikipedia.org/wiki/ Casey_at_the_Bat) |

## Lesson Summary

As you can see, the narrative lesson plan for the maturing reader requires careful teacher planning to ensure that students are being challenged at an appropriate level. For example, this text was chosen because the fifth-grade Common Core Standards require students to understand figurative language as well as read a variety of text types and complexity. Because poetry lends itself to this particular feature, "Casey at the Bat" was a natural fit. Additionally, this is a well-known poem, and the teacher wanted to expose her students to it.

The goals for comprehension are always about a student's ability to understand the text. Thus, the students not only need to locate figurative language, but also they need to be able to verbalize what they believe the author means. To generate a question related to their opinion, the students must first understand the poem, and the teacher gauges understanding based on their questions. Students who understand the poem on a deeper level will ask higher level questions.

You will also notice that the teacher asked the students a few times to explain their thinking. To develop students' metacognitive skills, this type of questioning is essential. As students engage in reading and discussing more complex story lines, teachers need to scaffold the maturing readers' instruction to enhance their critical thinking, a skill that is necessary throughout this stage.

We must always keep our student goals in mind when creating a lesson plan and extension activities. The following are other examples of appropriate extension activities for this lesson.

### Word Study Extensions

- Create a crossword puzzle.
- Do a spelling sort with a partner (students need to decide if the word has a base or root word before adding the suffix).
- Pick six words (three of each) and complete the Vocabulary Word Map. (See the Support Materials section on the CD 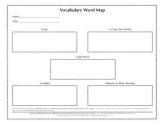.)

### Comprehension Extensions

- Write a five-stanza poem using at least five examples of figurative language.
- Create eight different questions about the poem, using various question types. Switch with a partner and answer each other's questions.
- Write a letter to the author questioning his use of figurative language and vocabulary choices.

# Informational Lesson Model

## Description of the Group

This group of six students is in the mid– to late Maturing Reader stage. In word study, they are studying multisyllabic homographs. For the comprehension aspect of the lesson, you will notice that the students read the text outside of their groups. This is because the text is short, and the teacher knows her students will not have difficulty reading it on their own. Further, time in the small groups is spent prepping the students for the information that they are going to read and following up after they have read. The students are reading an informational piece on Sir Isaac Newton. (See Figure 19 for a completed lesson plan.)

## Lesson Goals/Objectives

### Word Study

For this lesson, the word study goals include being able to understand the relationship between syllabication stress and part of speech.

### Comprehension

In comprehension, the overall lesson goals include being able to differentiate essential and nonessential details, developing an overall general understanding of the

## FIGURE 19
### Completed Maturing Reader Lesson Plan for Informational Text

Text type: _Descriptive, short essay_  Narrative text: _____

Estimated length of time: _2–3 days_  Informational text: _"Isaac Newton" from LessonSnips_

| WORD STUDY | WORD STUDY EXTENSION(S) |
|---|---|
| Features: _Homographs_ <br><br> Cycle: ___1___  Week: ___2___ <br><br> Word Sort: ☑Open  ☐Closed <br> ☑Spelling Sort  ☑Meaning Discussion <br> _Stress and part of speech_ | Student-created sentences: Students need to show the difference between noun and verb use. |

| COMPREHENSION (NARRATIVE TEXT) | COMPREHENSION (INFORMATIONAL TEXT) |
|---|---|
| Before Reading <br> ☐ Activate and build background knowledge <br> ☐ Preview vocabulary: _____ <br> _____ <br> ☐ Set a purpose | Before Reading <br> ☑Activate and build background knowledge <br> ☑Preview text features and structure _(use I-chart)_ <br> _Students identify structure and tell why they think that_ <br> _____ <br> ☑Preview vocabulary: _Bubonic plague_ <br> _Students can identify others as they read._ |
| During Reading <br> ☐ Teacher/student questions: _____ <br> _____ <br> _____ <br> _____ <br> ☐ Discussion/teaching points: _____ <br> _____ <br> _____ <br> Notes: | During Reading <br> ☑Teacher/student questions: _____ <br> _Will focus on information from before reading_ <br> _____ <br> _____ <br> ☐ Discussion/teaching points: _____ <br> _____ <br> _____ <br> Notes: Students list ideas about Newton on their <br> I-charts and use their list as they are reading. |
| After Reading <br> ☐ Plot/story line <br>  ☐ Character Development (traits, motivation, point of view) <br>  ☐ Setting (mood, importance) <br>  ☐ Conflicts <br>  ☐ Resolutions <br>  ☐ Theme <br> ☐ Summarize: _____ <br> _____ <br> Notes: | After Reading <br> ☐ Review text structure to aid understanding <br> ☐ Author's purpose <br> ☐ Summarize <br>  ☑Main ideas and essential details <br>  ☐ Compare and contrast <br>  ☐ Sequence <br>  ☐ Cause and effect, or problem and solution <br> _Go over descriptive text structure, and facts and_ <br> _essential details about his life. Summarize the three_ <br> _most essential: Why are they the most important?_ <br> Notes: <br> _Essential vs. important: Have students identify the_ <br> _difference and why_ |

**Reading Assignment**  Read pages: _Read article_

**Written Comprehension Extension(s):** _I-charts for Newton_

Notes: • Students need to find support from different sources.

 • Students will come up with one question that they would ask Newton and explain why.

importance of Sir Isaac Newton's work, and finding additional support for information about him.

## Word Study

The following dialogue focuses on students who are continuing to learn about the connections between stress, meaning, and parts of speech. This exchange takes place on the second day of the sort as students study two-syllable homographs.

---

Teacher: Today, we are going to do a spelling sort. I am going to say the homographs that we learned yesterday in a sentence, and I want you to place each word in one of two columns, depending on whether the stress is on the first or second syllable.

After the students complete the spelling sort, the teacher leads the discussion.

---

Teacher: OK, let's take a look at the first word, *reCORD*. What syllable is stressed?

Pete: I have it in the second-syllable column.

Teacher: How about *CONduct*?

Glenn: That word is stressed in the first syllable.

The students continue to go through the words and discuss each word as the stress changes from the first to the second syllable.

---

Teacher: OK, let's review our homographs and their parts of speech.

Dyanne: When the stress is on the first syllable, the word is a noun.

Susanna: And when the stress is on the second syllable, the word is a verb.

The teacher repeats the sentence, and then the students say it chorally. The teacher then monitors while the students complete their sentences.

### Word Study Extension

---

Teacher: Today, for your extension, you will create two sentences for each word: one when the word is used as a verb and one when the word is used as a noun.

# Comprehension

The comprehension portion of the lesson plan is based on the following short text (LessonSnips, 2009):

**Isaac Newton**

Sir Isaac Newton was an English physicist, mathematician, astronomer, and natural philosopher. He is considered one of the most important scientists of all time. He was born in January 1643 in Woolsthorpe in Lincolnshire, England. At the age of 18, Newton went to Cambridge to study mathematics. However, in 1665, the university shut down because of the bubonic plague and he returned home to continue his studies.

It is said that one day while he was in his garden at Woolsthorpe, he saw an apple drop from a tree. This made him start thinking why the apple should fall downwards instead of any other direction. He came to the conclusion that the downward fall of the apple must be because the Earth attracted the apple and this resulted in him working out the theory of gravitation.

It was also during this same time that Newton started to examine the nature of white light by passing a beam of sunlight through a prism. He noticed that passing a beam of sunlight through a prism spread out into a colored band of light, which is known as a spectrum. These colors are the same colors as the ones in a rainbow. By conducting many experiments, he reached the conclusion that sunlight is a combination of all the colors of the spectrum and that sunlight separates when passed through a prism because of [*sic*] each color in the spectrum has a different refrangibility property. The refrangibility property is the ability of light rays to be refracted or bent by a substance.

He also started developing his ideas on calculus. In 1667, he returned to the University of Cambridge and in 1669, he became a professor of mathematics. In 1668, his work on light resulted in Newton building the first reflecting telescope, which was the basis for many modern large telescopes. In 1672, Newton became a Fellow of the Royal Society. In 1687, he published his most famous work called the "Mathematical Principles of Natural Philosophy." This book, known as the Principia, is one of the most influential books in the history of science and contains his work on the laws of motion, the theory of tides, and gravitation.

In 1707, he published another work called "Opticks" that discussed his theory of light. He also published other works on history, theology, and alchemy.

Newton was in charge of the Royal Mint for a few years, where he carried out some reforms in coinage. He was also twice a member of parliament, though it is said that he was not interested much in politics. In 1705, he was knighted by Queen Anne.

He died in March 1727 and is buried in Westminster Abbey in England.

## *Before Reading*

## Activate and Build Background Knowledge

_____

Teacher:    Today, after meeting in your small group, you are going to read a short piece on Sir Isaac Newton. First, we are going to brainstorm some things that we know or think we know about him. You will be using an Inquiry Chart (I-chart) to keep track of the ideas we come up with. Then, we'll take a look at the text and skim it for any vocabulary words that we might not know as well as looking at the way the text is organized—the *structure* of the text. After you read the short passage, you will also look for the answers from some other sources. That will be your extension activity. Who can tell me something that they know or think they know about Sir Isaac Newton? As we think of things, keep track of them on your Inquiry Chart. You need to have at least four things listed at the top. They don't have to be all your ideas, but at the end of our discussion, you need to have at least four.

Dyanne: So, we won't all have the same four things?

Teacher: No, you won't. Everyone can pick four things that they want to study about him. Who's ready?

Beth: I am! Is he the guy that studied the theory of relativity?

Bill: I think he's the guy that did gravity.

Ginny: I want to know where he went to college.

Teacher: Ginny, you are giving me something that you want to know, but what we are doing is creating a list of what we know or think we know. How can you rephrase that?

Ginny: I think he went to college in America.

Teacher: Good. Who else wants to add something? Who haven't we heard from?

Susanna: Did he study electricity? I think he did.

Pete: I think he got interested in science because his brothers were scientists as well.

Teacher: OK, now we have some ideas for guiding questions as you are reading.

## Preview Text Features and Structure

Teacher: In looking at this one-page article, what do you notice about the way it is laid out?

Pete: It looks like there are a few paragraphs that will tell us about him.

Brian: They only give us the title, and the article isn't separated in any way to point out different sections.

Teacher: In thinking about the way it is set up, what would you guess would be the structure?

Glenn: I bet it'll be the description one we've learned about.

Teacher: Why do you think that?

Glenn: Because it doesn't have anything else that would give us a hint that it's going to add something other than telling us about him.

## Preview Vocabulary

_____

| | |
|---|---|
| Teacher: | Let's look at some words that might be important to understand as we read this article. The first term is *bubonic plague*. Does anyone know what the bubonic plague was? |
| Ginny: | Well, it must have been some sort of really bad disease. |
| Teacher: | It was. Can anyone add to Ginny's description? |
| Brian: | It was a really long time ago, though—I think like a couple hundred years. |
| Teacher: | You're right. It was back in the 1300s, and it was a bacterial infection. Many people died because we didn't have antibiotics back then. OK, I don't see any other terms that you might need help with. If you come across other terms while you're reading, be sure to write them down, so we can go over them tomorrow. |

## *During Reading*

Note: Because the students already had guiding ideas to focus on while they were reading, and the selection was short, the discussion and questions can be found in the following section.

## *After Reading: Day 2*

## Summarizing

_____

| | |
|---|---|
| Teacher: | First, let's take a look at some of the information that you learned about Sir Isaac Newton from the guiding ideas you had on your I-charts. Then, we'll talk about the essential details about his life. Who wants to start? |
| Beth: | I found out he was the guy who studied gravity, not electricity. |
| Teacher: | True! What else did you find out? |
| Pete: | He also went to college in Europe, not the United States. |
| Susanna: | I'm not sure about his family, though, or how he got interested in science. There must be more to that apple falling from the tree story! |
| Teacher: | I agree. You can search for more about that story when you find your other sources. Is there anything else on your I-charts that you want to share? |

When no one has anything new to add, the teacher moves on.

| Teacher: | OK, if you had to pick the three most essential details about Newton's life that were shared in the article, what would they be? |
|---|---|
| Brian: | One would definitely be about his theory of gravity. |
| Dyanne: | Another would be about the work he did with light. What was it called again? |
| Teacher: | Let's go back in the text and see if we can find out. Let me know when you've found it. |
| Bill: | Here it is. It's in the third paragraph. It tells about the refrangibility of light. |
| Glenn: | I always thought it was the *refractability* of light. I was confused when I first read this. |
| Teacher: | How did you clarify it for yourself? |
| Glenn: | The last sentence in that paragraph actually gives the definition for *refrangibility*. It basically means that light rays can be refracted or bent. |
| Teacher: | So, we now have two essential details, his theory of gravity and his work with the properties of light. We need one more. What are some other thoughts? |
| Susanna: | I think that it's important that he was a professor. |
| Teacher: | Why do you think that is an essential detail rather than just a fact? |
| Susanna: | Because he taught other people about his knowledge, and that's important. |
| Bill: | It might be important, but I don't think it's essential. I think the fact he wrote a book that is one of the most important science books ever is essential. |
| Teacher: | What do the rest of you think? |
| Beth: | I agree with Bill. Sir Isaac Newton being a professor is important, but it's not an essential detail to this text. |

The teacher and students wrap up the discussion.

### Comprehension Extension

| Teacher: | Remember that I told you yesterday that you were going to use your I-Charts to track your guiding ideas and find additional sources to support them. I want you to start doing this today, and we can continue into tomorrow if you need extra time. You can use the computers or any other text you find. If you use the Internet, be sure you cite your |
|---|---|

**FIGURE 20**
**Completed Extension Activity for Informational Text**

| Things We Think We Know: | He invented the theory of relativity. | He invented the theory of gravity. | He went to college in the United States. | He studied science because someone in his family was a scientist as well. |
|---|---|---|---|---|
| Source 1:<br>Article from class | No, that was Einstein. | Yes | No | Didn't say |
| Source 2:<br>Science Kids (www.science kids.co.nz/sciencefacts/ scientists/isaacnewton.html) | No | Yes | No | Didn't say |
| Source 3:<br>BBC (www.bbc.co.uk/history/ historic_figures/newton_ isaac.shtml) | No | Yes | No, he went to Cambridge University. | No, unhappy childhood |
| Source 4:<br>School of Mathematics and Statistics, University of St. Andrews, Scotland (www .history.mcs.st-andrews .ac.uk/Biographies/Newton .html) | No | Yes | No | No, his family was awful and he had a very sad childhood. |

**My Question:** Was there something special he was thinking about the day the apple fell?

source correctly, so we can find it again. Also, I want you to create one question that you would ask Sir Isaac Newton if you saw him today. I want you to also explain why you came up with the question you did.

See Figure 20 for this completed extension activity.

## Lesson Summary

This lesson focused on differentiating between essential and nonessential details of content area material as well as summarizing information. Again, teacher preparation is key to students' success because as students navigate difficult text, the teacher provides them with the supportive environment necessary to guide their understanding.

You will notice that the teacher spent time reviewing the structure of the text and one vocabulary term that the students would encounter. Because the text did not have many unknown words and was short, the teacher knew that the students would not have difficulty completing the reading on their own. As the students read the short piece, they had guiding ideas to help keep them focused. The teacher also had them use the

I-Chart (see the Inquiry Chart in the Support Materials section on the CD  ) as a way for them to keep track of what they were learning. It is important for students to have a way to remember what they learn from day to day. The teacher also chose the extension activity based on the fact that she wanted them to be able to search for additional sources of information to back up their ideas.

Teachers must always keep instructional goals in mind when creating lesson plans and extension activities. The following are other examples of appropriate extension activities for this informational lesson plan.

## Word Study Extensions

- Write a two-stanza humorous lyric.
- **Teach Me:** Each partner takes two pairs of homographs and comes up with a creative way to teach them to someone else.

## Comprehension Extensions

- **ABC Brainstorm/Summary:** What did they learn that is related to Sir Isaac Newton? (See Chapter 7.)

- Write an informative speech/talk about Sir Isaac Newton that discusses his most famous works. Create a visual support (e.g., a PowerPoint presentation) for your speech/ talk.
- **Question Maker:** (See Chapter 7.)

# Conclusion

Maturing readers are developing their skills as critical readers and writers. Although they do the majority of their reading silently and independently, the teacher needs to provide explicit instruction, particularly in the area of comprehension with complex texts in both narrative and informational genres. Strengthening the connection between in-group and extension activities is vital as students take more responsibility for their own understanding of texts. Scaffolded instruction is essential for maturing readers as they move toward the Advanced Reader stage.

# CHAPTER 6

# The Advanced Reader Stage

Advanced readers can read and understand text on their own on both a literal and critical level. However, these students still require teacher guidance to develop their higher level thinking skills, particularly with regard to evaluating and critiquing texts. The goal for the advanced reader is to be able to read and understand a variety of complex texts beyond a surface level. They also are learning to form an opinion about what they read.

The main difference between maturing readers and advanced readers is that advanced readers read the majority of their texts independently, outside of small-group instruction. Therefore, the lesson plan for advanced readers does not include a During Reading section. However, to accommodate these readers, we have moved the Before Reading section to the end of the lesson plan to help prepare students for their reading. During their reading time, students need to have a clear purpose. They can have guiding questions or open-ended prompts to help focus their reading. Reading without a specific purpose often leaves readers unfocused, which causes them to miss important information. During their reading time, they also need something to help them remember what they have read from one day to the next. For example, they can keep track of their questions (about the text or to the author), opinions, and information learned by using different-colored sticky notes. As they are reading, they place the sticky notes in the appropriate place in the text. The teacher's role with advanced readers is to guide their higher level thinking about text rather than their actual reading of text.

As with the other readers, the extension activities presented in this chapter directly relate to the Common Core Standards. Again, we want to demonstrate how teachers can meet the standards while still providing differentiated instruction.

## Characteristics of Advanced Readers in Reading, Writing, and Word Study

### Reading

Most students in the Advanced Reading stage are fervent readers. If they have had proper modeling, they are able to use their metacognitive skills to monitor, regulate, and repair their learning when needed. If they have not had guided instruction in using these skills, they must be taught how to use them appropriately. Advanced readers are learning how to critically evaluate text and combine their learning from multiple sources to make an informed conclusion or opinion. They are also learning how to justify their opinions when appropriate, based on fact rather than feeling. They can take what they have learned and apply this knowledge to new situations.

Advanced readers continue to learn about the meaning and elements of figurative language, including analogies, hyperbole, idioms, and imagery. They are also learning about the relationship between an author's use of literary devices in a text (e.g., irony, symbolism, tone, mood) and his or her purpose for writing the text, as well as how to recognize any bias on the part of an author.

These students are taught how to identify an author's position in persuasive text and describe techniques that the author uses to support that position. These techniques may include testimonials, statistics, and other methods that appeal to reason or emotion. In addition, students can distinguish between fact and opinion and recognize propaganda (e.g., advertising, media, politics) and stereotypes in various types of texts.

Advanced readers form and revise questions for investigations, including questions arising from readings, assignments, and units of study. Students can use this information to create a hypothesis statement. They also create literal, inferential, and application questions as they read to clarify the text's message. They can locate appropriate print and nonprint information using texts and technical resources, including databases. Finally, they are learning to distinguish between accurate and inaccurate or misleading information. This is particularly important when reading information online. As they become proficient with digital literacy, advanced readers learn to skim and scan the Web for the information they are seeking. They read and use hyperlinks quickly and efficiently. Further, they are able to follow the links that they have opened and refer back to previous information with ease.

## Texts for Advanced Readers

Advanced readers need a variety of challenging material to further advance their critical reading skills. They continue to read from a variety of genres as they automatically incorporate a wide variety of comprehension strategies. Appropriate texts are rich in vocabulary and provide a variety of the aforementioned language elements. Poetry, magazine articles, and documents, as well as award-winning and classic literary pieces, should all be part of advanced readers' reading experience. Comprehension instruction focuses on crucial thinking skills as students become more responsible for reading text independently. Texts commonly used with advanced readers include titles such as *Narrative of the Life of Frederick Douglass: An American Slave* by Frederick Douglass, *Johnny Tremain* by Esther Forbes, *A Christmas Carol* by Charles Dickens, the Harry Potter series by J.K. Rowling, The Chronicles of Narnia series by C.S. Lewis, *Anne Frank: The Diary of a Young Girl* by Anne Frank, and *Charles and Emma: The Darwins' Leap of Faith* by Deborah Heiligman.

For teachers who continue to use leveled books as a part of their literacy program, the following book levels are appropriate for advanced readers:

| Leveling System | Book Levels |
| --- | --- |
| Fountas and Pinnell | U–Z |
| Lexile bands | *Grade 7:* 880L–960L, 1000L–1090L (stretch bands) |
| | *Grade 8:* 900L–1010L, 1040L–1160L (stretch bands) |

## Writing

In addition to being avid readers, students in the advanced stage of reading are often avid writers. They write in a variety of forms, including descriptive, narrative, informational, and persuasive (arguments). They research different sources to critically analyze information and make informed judgments. Advanced readers are fine-tuning their ability to express themselves in a clear, concise manner.

Students in the Advanced Reader stage continue to learn how to use specialized vocabulary and tend to do a lot of informational writing. They attempt to choose words and phrases appropriate for specific purposes and various audiences. In addition, they use more precise words such as powerful verbs, specific nouns, and vivid adjectives and adverbs to help create images in the reader's mind. They also use these words to convey mood and develop characters. Students in the Advanced Reader stage continue to develop the use of voice that is appropriate to the purpose of the piece.

Advanced readers must be challenged as writers. They would greatly benefit from teacher writing conferences to receive specific, constructive feedback about their writing. Again, small-group reading time is not the time for writing instruction. Teachers should plan a separate time for their writing instruction. That said, the extension activities in this book are a great way for students to practice the writing skills previously taught. Advanced readers also are able to use the writing process effectively to publish final copies of various writing formats.

## Word Study

Advanced readers have mastered issues related to syllable patterns. Students in this stage are continuing to learn about the spelling–meaning connection, particularly with regard to content-specific vocabulary. They are proficient with structural analysis; that is, they recognize meaningful word parts such as base words, root words, prefixes, and suffixes.

In order for students to understand the spelling–meaning connection, words in the meaning layer of spelling development are often presented in derivationally related pairs, such as *prescribe* and *prescription*. Students are able to detect the relationship between these two words based on the Latin root *scrib*, which means to write. Because of the significant number of Latin and Greek roots in the English language and their relation to the spelling–meaning connection, students should continue studying them throughout the Advanced Reader stage.

It is best to begin word study at this stage with words that have obvious connections, such as those with Greek roots or the most common pairs that students encounter. Once students have established a foundation of these common derivationally related words, then they will be ready to study the less frequent pairs and morphemes. When students study one Latin or Greek root per week, a word sort or spelling sort is not an appropriate word study activity. Rather, they need instructional activities focused on the meaning of the words. For example, using a root web in which they have to find and identify the given root and how it is used in a variety of different words (e.g., *bio*: *biology, biography, biogeny*).

During the word study component of the lesson plan, students should be actively engaged in a discussion of the meaning of the root word and the meaning connection to the list of words. For example, students can use a dictionary or online resources to find out if the root has a Latin or Greek origin. Further, students can complete other vocabulary activities, such as the Vocabulary Word Map or Root Web, so students can focus on the spelling–meaning connection of the words.

A weekly word study scope and sequence has been provided on the CD  to assist teachers as they plan for and teach the word study component of the lesson. The foundation for the scope and sequence is based on the work of Bear et al. (2007) in *Words Their Way: Word Study for Phonics, Vocabulary, and Spelling Instruction* and Ganske's (2000) *Word Journeys: Assessment-Guided Phonics, Spelling, and Vocabulary Instruction*. The features studied during the Advanced Reader stage are shown in Table 8. You will notice that the scope and sequence consists of Greek and Latin roots. Because these readers focus on meaning only, they do not have pre-, post-, or cycle spelling assessments. Rather, after the students finish the Maturing Reader cycle, they should begin with year 1 cycle 1 for the advanced reader.

### TABLE 8
### Word Study Features for the Advanced Reader

| Root Word(s) | Greek or Latin | Definition |
|---|---|---|
| aer | Greek | air |
| arch | Greek | chief, ruler |
| aster, astr | Greek | star |
| aud | Latin | to hear |
| aut, auto | Greek | self, directed from within |
| avi | Latin | bird |
| ben, bene, bon, boun | Latin | good, well |
| bi, bio | Greek | life |
| centr | Greek | center |
| cephal, cephalo | Greek | head |
| chron | Greek | time |
| cide | Latin | to kill, to cut |
| cosm | Greek | universe, world |
| cracy, crat | Greek | government, rule, authority |
| cris, crit | Greek | to judge, to separate |
| dem | Greek | people |
| derm | Greek | skin |
| dic, dict | Latin | to speak |

*(continued)*

## TABLE 8
### Word Study Features for the Advanced Reader (Continued)

| Root Word(s) | Greek or Latin | Definition |
| --- | --- | --- |
| dom | Latin | lord, master, building |
| equa, equi | Latin | even |
| forc, fort | Latin | strong |
| grad, gred, gress | Latin | to step, to go, to walk |
| graph | Greek | to write |
| hydr | Greek | water |
| ject | Latin | to throw |
| jud | Latin | a judge |
| jur, jus, just | Latin | right, upright, law |
| kine | Greek | movement, motion |
| lingu | Latin | language, tongue |
| log, logue | Latin | thought |
| log, ology | Greek | discourse, study of |
| mal, male, mali | Latin | bad |
| mis, miss, mit | Latin | to send |
| mob, mot | Latin | to move |
| morph | Greek | to form, to shape |
| omn, omni | Latin | all, every |
| ped | Greek | child |
| ped | Latin | foot |
| pel, puls | Latin | to push, to drive |
| pend, pens, pense | Latin | to hang, to weigh |
| phob, phobia | Greek | fear |
| phon | Greek | sound |
| phos, phot, photo | Greek | light |
| pon, pone, pos | Greek | to put, to place |
| port | Latin | to carry |
| prim, princ | Latin | first |
| retr, retro | Latin | backward, behind |
| scop | Greek | to see, to view |
| scribe, script | Latin | to write |
| sens, sent | Latin | to feel |
| spec, spect, spic | Latin | to see, to look |
| spir | Latin | to breathe |
| sum, sume, sumpt | Latin | to take, to use, to waste |
| tele | Greek | far off |
| tempo, tempor | Latin | time |
| terr, terra, terri | Latin | earth |
| tract | Latin | to pull, to drag, to draw |
| vac | Latin | empty |
| vers, vert | Latin | to turn |
| vid, vis | Latin | to see |
| voc, voca | Latin | to call, to talk, to speak, voice |

# Instructional Components of the Advanced Reader Lesson Plan

The lesson plan for the advanced reader (see Figure 21) begins with the word study component. Because word study for the advanced reader is focused on vocabulary development, there is much discussion about the words. Additionally, the in-group and extension activities should all be related to the spelling–meaning connection. You will notice in the lesson plans that vocabulary instruction is embedded in both word study and comprehension.

The comprehension component is the focus of this lesson plan as students refine their critical reading skills. The Before Reading and After Reading sections have been transposed in this plan to accommodate the reading that students do independently. Therefore, the comprehension component within the small group begins with after-reading activities as the group discusses the text they previously read. The lesson concludes with before-reading activities, so the teacher can prepare the students for their next reading assignment. You will notice a lot of dialogue in the lesson plans. This is essential for the students to develop their critical thinking skills. Similar to the lesson plans for evolving and maturing readers, all of the elements listed in the lesson plan template for advanced readers are not appropriate for every small-group lesson and must be adapted accordingly.

## Differentiating the Lesson Plans

Advanced readers can successfully read (i.e., decode) most narrative and informational pieces with ease. Again, we present one lesson plan to accommodate both narrative and informational texts. Although the word study component is the same for both, the narrative section of the plan focuses on strategies used with narrative text, whereas the informational section focuses on strategies specific to that type of text. The lesson plan addresses the need for advanced readers to read independently, allowing for more small-group instructional time to discuss, analyze, and share ideas that students have about the text.

# Narrative Lesson Model

## Description of the Group

This group of six students is in the middle of the Advanced Reader stage. In word study, they are just starting to study the Greek root *hydr*. In the reading portion of the lesson plan, the students are reading a Greek myth. On the first day, the teacher spends her small-group time introducing the myth genre and reviewing vocabulary that the students will encounter when they are reading the myth on their own. (See Figure 22 for a completed lesson plan for narrative text.)

**F I G U R E   2 1**
**Advanced Reader Lesson Plan**

Text type: _____  Narrative text: _____

Estimated length of time: _____  Informational text: _____

| WORD STUDY | WORD STUDY EXTENSION(S) |
|---|---|
| Features: _____<br><br>Cycle: _____  Week: _____<br><br>Word Sort:  ☐ Open   ☐ Closed<br>☐ Spelling Sort   ☐ Meaning Discussion | |
| **COMPREHENSION (NARRATIVE TEXT)**<br>After Reading<br>☐ Plot/story line<br>  ☐ Character development<br>  ☐ Conflicts<br>  ☐ Resolutions<br>  ☐ Theme<br>☐ Summarize<br>☐ Teacher/student questions: _____<br>_____<br>☐ Discussion/teaching points: _____<br>_____<br>_____<br>Notes: | **COMPREHENSION (INFORMATIONAL TEXT)**<br>After Reading<br>☐ Review text structure to aid understanding<br>☐ Author's purpose<br>☐ Summarize<br>  ☐ Main ideas and essential details<br>  ☐ Compare and contrast<br>  ☐ Sequence<br>  ☐ Cause and effect, or problem and solution<br>☐ Teacher/student questions: _____<br>_____<br>☐ Discussion/teaching points: _____<br>_____<br>_____<br>Notes: |
| Before Reading<br>☐ Activate and build background knowledge<br>☐ Preview vocabulary: _____<br>_____<br>☐ Set a purpose<br>Notes: | Before Reading<br>☐ Activate and build background knowledge<br>☐ Preview text features and structure<br>☐ Preview vocabulary: _____<br>_____<br>☐ Set a purpose<br>Notes: |

**Reading Extension**          Read pages: _____
**Written Comprehension Extension(s):** _____
Notes:

**FIGURE 22**
**Completed Advanced Reader Lesson Plan for Narrative Text**

Text type: _Myth_        Narrative text: _"Hercules: The Labors of Heracles From Greek Mythology" by Joel Skidmore_

Estimated length of time: _2-3 days_        Informational text: _____

| **WORD STUDY** | **WORD STUDY EXTENSION(S)** |
|---|---|
| Features: _hydr_ <br><br> Cycle: ___4___    Week: ___6___ <br><br> Word Sort: ☐ Open   ☐ Closed <br> ☐ Spelling Sort   ☑ Meaning Discussion <br>       _with example words_ | Find other words with the _hydr_ root and complete a root web. |

| **COMPREHENSION (NARRATIVE TEXT)** | **COMPREHENSION (INFORMATIONAL TEXT)** |
|---|---|
| After Reading _Day 2_ <br> ☐ Plot/story line <br>    ☐ Character development <br>    ☐ Conflicts <br>    ☐ Resolutions <br>    ☐ Theme <br> ☑ Summarize _Day 3_ <br> ☑ Teacher/student questions: _• Recap the story_ <br> _• Do you think his story is tragic? Why?_ <br> ☑ Discussion/teaching points: _Heroic qualities_ <br><br><br> Notes: <br> Students create their own questions to ask, as if they were the teacher. <br> Day 3: Students ask, analyze type of question and answer the questions they came up with. | After Reading <br> ☐ Review text structure to aid understanding <br> ☐ Author's purpose <br> ☐ Summarize <br>    ☐ Main ideas and essential details <br>    ☐ Compare and contrast <br>    ☐ Sequence <br>    ☐ Cause and effect, or problem and solution <br> ☐ Teacher/student questions: _____ <br> _____ <br> ☐ Discussion/teaching points: _____ <br> _____ <br><br> Notes: |
| Before Reading _Day 1_ <br> ☐ Activate and build background knowledge <br> ☑ Preview vocabulary: _unerring, atone, parentage, fray, wrath, impenetrable, and demise_ <br> ☐ Set a purpose <br> Notes: <br> Need to discuss myths as a genre: What makes a story a myth? Link to Greek mythology. <br> Go over distinction and connection between Hercules and Heracles so students understand. | Before Reading <br> ☐ Activate and build background knowledge <br> ☐ Preview text features and structure <br> ☐ Preview vocabulary: _____ <br> _____ <br> ☐ Set a purpose <br> Notes: |

**Reading Extension** _Read the Heracles myth_ Read pages: _All_

**Written Comprehension Extension(s):** _Heroic characteristics chart_

Notes: _Students also need to have evidence to support their claims._

## Lesson Goals/Objectives

### Word Study

For this lesson, the word study goals include being able to understand the meaning of the Greek root *hydr*, using this knowledge to find other words with the same root, and being able to identify similarities and differences in the meaning of the identified words.

### Comprehension

In comprehension, the overall lesson goals include being able to identify aspects of myths that are different from other narratives that the students have read, identifying and justifying heroic character traits that Heracles exhibited, and demonstrating understanding of the myth by creating questions (literal, inferential, and application) to ask a peer.

## Word Study: Day 1

The students are beginning to study a new Greek root, *hydr*. The teacher introduces the root and then asks the students to define new words based on their common feature. Because the students are studying one root this week, the focus is vocabulary building; therefore, word sorting and spelling sorting are not appropriate activities.

---

Teacher:    Today, we are going to continue our study of Latin and Greek root words. Let's take a look at a few of the words for this week. You will notice that I only gave you three. This is because you are going to find others on your own.

The teacher lays out the word cards for *hydroplane*, *hydrate*, and *hydrant*.

---

Tom:    Well, they all begin with the letters *H, Y, D, R*.

Teacher:    Are you familiar with any of these words?

Victoria:    The only ones I recognize are *hydrant* and *hydroplane*.

Teacher:    What do those two words mean?

Maggie:    I know that you get water from a hydrant, and when your car hydroplanes, it slides on water.

Teacher:    So, we know that both words have something to do with water. What about *hydrate*?

Michael:    I know that when we are playing football, our coaches constantly tell us to drink water to hydrate our bodies.

## Word Study Extension

Teacher: Yes, it's important to do that! Now that we know that all our words have something to do with water, I want you to work with your partner today to search for other words that have the root *hydr*. You will each create your own vocabulary root web. Additionally, because we are studying Greek mythology, I want you to see if you can find any connection between *hydr* and mythology. Be sure you add in a few words describing what each word means—in your own words. (See the Support Materials section on the CD for a Root Web sheet, and Figure 23 for a completed root web.)

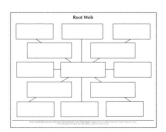

**FIGURE 23**
**Completed Word Study Extension Activity**

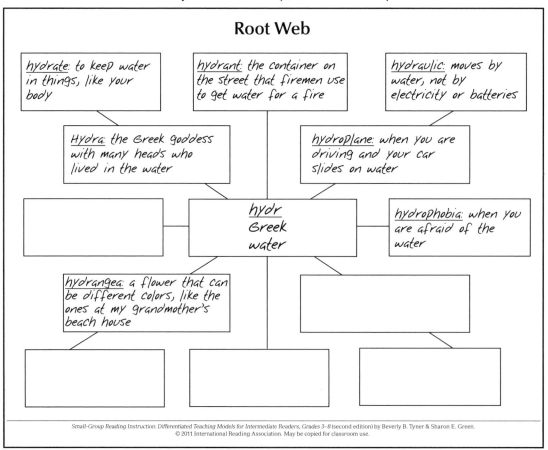

# Comprehension

*Before Reading: Day 1*

## Activate and Build Background Knowledge

_____

Teacher: Today, we are going to look at a new genre that we have not yet studied in depth. We are going to be reading a Greek myth. Have you ever heard of a myth?

Nicole: When I hear the word *myth*, it makes me think of something that's not true, like when someone says, "That's just a myth!"

Teacher: OK, how about someone else? What do you think of when you hear the word *myth*?

Maggie: Myths are made-up stories.

Teacher: You are both right. Myths are stories that are not true, but they are different from a run-of-the-mill story with a beginning, middle, and end. A myth often tries to explain something in life. We are going to be looking at a particular myth that focuses on one character who you have probably heard of—Hercules. Hercules is actually the Roman name for Heracles. He was known as a great hero in Greek mythology.

Michael: Is that He-Man? I had a He-Man action figure when I was a kid, and I love that show!

Teacher: I'm not sure if he is He-Man, but I'm sure that we could find out if He-Man was based on the story of Heracles. The story that we are going to read is a Greek myth, meaning that this story came out of Greek mythology. Myths were often a way to explain the relationship between the gods and humans. Do you know any other Greek mythology figures?

Kevin: Everyone's heard of Zeus. He was the leader of the gods, right?

Teacher: Yes, Zeus was the most powerful Greek god who ruled over Mount Olympus. There are many famous Greek gods and goddesses. Heracles was actually the son of Zeus and a mortal, or human, woman. Zeus's queen, Hera, did not like this at all and was very jealous of Heracles.

## Preview Vocabulary

_____

Teacher: There are a few words that we need to look at before you begin to read the story. Let's take a look at the word *unerring*. Has anyone ever seen this word?

| Michael: | I'm not sure, but I think it has something to do with not doing something. See, it has the *un-* prefix at the beginning, and that means not. |
|---|---|
| Teacher: | Good job, Michael! What else can you learn about the word by looking at it? |
| Maggie: | The *-ing* at the end tells us that the word is a verb, right? |
| Teacher: | Explain what you mean, Maggie. |
| Maggie: | Well, *-ing* is always added to a verb to change the tense. When we add *-ing* to a verb like *run,* you get *running.* You can't add *-ing* to a noun or adjective because the words wouldn't make sense. |
| Teacher: | Let's look at the word in context and see if we can get any other ideas. The sentence begins, "When he had come of age and already proved himself an unerring marksman with a bow and arrow." Any thoughts? |
| Kevin: | It really doesn't sound like a verb. It seems like an adjective because it is before the noun *marksman.* When you read the rest of the sentence, you get the idea that he was a really good marksman who didn't make any mistakes. |
| Teacher: | Let's look it up and see what we find out. |

The teacher uses the computer to quickly look up the word *unerring.*

———————————

| Maggie: | The definition says that *unerring* is an adjective that means committing no errors, faultless. I thought *-ing* couldn't be added to adjectives. |
|---|---|
| Teacher: | Let's also look at the derivation of the word and see what we find. |

The teacher and students continue to analyze the word and review others, including *atone, parentage, fray, wrath, impenetrable,* and *demise.*

### Comprehension Extension
The teacher ends the lesson by asking students to read the story of Heracles that she handed out, which was written by Joel Skidmore (1997). Additionally, the students need to come up with a list of heroic characteristics that Heracles demonstrated and need to show evidence of their decisions. (See Figure 24 for the completed activity.)

### *After Reading: Day 2*

### Plot and Story Line

———————————

| Teacher: | Let's take our Heracles myth and talk about what you wrote. Let's start by recapping his story. Who wants to start? |
|---|---|

## FIGURE 24
### Completed Extension Activity for Narrative Text

| My Heracles Chart | |
| --- | --- |
| **Heroic Characteristics** | **Proof** |
| Brave | He killed the lion in his first labor with his bare hands. |
| Strong | He carried the Erymanthian Boar back to his cousin on his shoulder. The boar was still alive but couldn't move. |
| Caring | He was able to pin down the Cerynitian hind without wounding it. He knew that Artemis would be angry if he hurt the deer. |
| Smart | He figured out a way to clean out years of manure piled up without getting dirty. He moved 2 rivers through the stableyard. |
| Fearless | He took on every single challenge that he was given. He never said no and always did his best. |

Kevin: Well, he sort of had a horrible life. I mean, he came into the world as an illegitimate child whose stepmother tried to kill him.

Nicole: Yeah, that was really awful. She put snakes in his crib!

Teacher: Yes, but let's remember that it is a myth, so the story is not true.

Nicole: I know, but who thinks of things like that? Then, she drove him crazy until he killed his own kids!

Teacher: Would you say that his story is somewhat tragic?

Maggie: I think so, although he didn't give up. He kept trying through a lot of challenges that were really hard.

Michael: No kidding! Especially with Hydra. It was funny that we just learned that root in word study, and then she was in the story as the water monster with all the heads. Now I get the connection between the Greek root and the meaning. Interesting!

Teacher: Now, let's take a look at your list of heroic qualities and talk about why you chose those qualities.

The teacher leads a group discussion of the heroic qualities and asks the students to provide evidence of their identified qualities in the text. They brainstorm some questions that they would ask if they were the teacher. Each student needs to come up with two of each type of question: literal, inferential, and application.

*Summarize: Day 3*

**Discussion Points**

_____

Teacher:     Today, we are going to continue to work with the Heracles myth. What questions did you come up with?

Michael:     Why did Heracles have to perform the labors?

Teacher:     What type of question is that?

Maggie:      Literal. You can find the answer directly in the text.

Teacher:     Who would like to share the answer and one of their own questions?

Kevin:       Heracles had to do the labors because he killed his kids. That was how he made up for his crime, so it was his punishment. I guess they didn't have any jails! My question is, If Heracles was so physically powerful, why didn't he just overtake his cousin, King Eurystheus?

Teacher:     Who would like to tell us what type of question that is, *and* who knows the answer?

Nicole:      I think it is an application question, but I'm not sure.

Teacher:     Why do you think it is an application question?

Nicole:      I was up in the air between inferential and application, but it doesn't ask us to infer anything from the text. It is asking us to use what we know about Heracles and then make a decision.

Teacher:     What do the rest of you think?

Maggie:      I agree with Nicole. Kevin's question is not asking us to use any actual information in the myth. We need to use our own thoughts and decide our opinion.

For the remainder of the lesson, the students continue to share their questions while others determine the type of question along with the answers.

The following is a list of other discussion points. Add to this list as you come up with additional areas for discussion.

- Compare and contrast myths, legends, folk tales, and fairy tales.
- Review the essential components of myths.
- Look at example lists that students generate of myths they know and the real-life scenarios the myths attempt to explain.

*Comprehension Extension*

_____

Teacher:     For your extension activity today, you will decide which of the 12 labors were the most interesting and/or challenging and why. Then, write a three-paragraph essay describing why you think this. This is going to prepare you for the next thing we are going to do: writing your own myth.

## Lesson Summary

Similar to the lesson plans for evolving and maturing readers, instructional decisions about word study and text types for advanced readers were made with the Common Core Standards in mind. To reiterate, our hope is that we can help teachers teach what is required while still meeting the needs of all of the students in their classrooms. The advanced lesson plan also requires teacher preparation and scaffolding in order to help students solidify their independent critical thinking skills. In word study, the teacher made the decision to have the students find more words with the Greek root on their own. This was done because it is easy to give students the words to study, and they get used to this type of support. When they have to search for words on their own, they must make some decisions along the way about which words they should choose. Additionally, they have some choice and control over their own learning. This is important for an advanced reader.

In comprehension, because the students read the text outside of their small groups, the teacher prepared them for the type of text they are reading. Because they have never before read a myth in her class, she wanted to make sure that they knew what it was. There was much discussion about the vocabulary, particularly about the word *unerring*. This is the type of word that is perfect for the group to discuss because of its features and meaning. The teacher was secretly hoping that one of the students would think the word was a verb, and the rich discussion that took place as a result is critical for advanced readers. They need to use all of the tools they have when reading, so they can truly understand and not simply read to read. In order to gauge understanding, the teacher had them come up with different questions. One cannot create higher level thinking questions without a solid understanding of the text.

The following are other examples of appropriate extension activities for this lesson.

### *Word Study Extensions*

- **Context Poem:** Using at least three *hydr* words, write a four-line lyrical poem that demonstrates understanding of the root word. The poem can be humorous if you would like.
- **Hink Pink:** (See Chapter 7 for a description of this extension activity.)
- **Challenge Me:** Divide the words among the small-group members. Students are then given the responsibility to come up with a creative way to teach their small-group mates about their given words.

*Comprehension Extensions*

- **Interview a Character:** In partner pairs, the students take turns being interviewed as if they were one of the characters in the story. The interviewer creates a list of 10–15 questions. Then, the students look for themes in the data that they collected and write a synthesis of the identified themes.

- **Character Analysis:** Come up with a list of eight adjectives that describe your character. Then, write a character analysis describing why you chose those adjectives and support your choices with evidence from the story. Evidence that can be used includes the character's behavior, words, feelings, actions, and thoughts.

- **Change My Story:** Choose a character from the story and decide what his or her role is in the story: protagonist or hero, antagonist or villain, supporting player (a helpmate of either the hero or villain, or a catalyst, also known as an agent for change; usually this character is not directly in the action but inspires the lead character in some way).

# Informational Lesson Model

## Description of the Group

This group of six students is in the beginning of the Advanced Reader stage. In word study, they are studying three number-related roots: *quad, pent,* and *uni.* In the reading portion of the lesson plan, the students are reading the Bliss version of the Gettysburg Address (Lincoln, 1863). On the first day, the teacher spends small-group time building the students' background knowledge and introducing the anticipatory set for the text. On the second day, the teacher focuses comprehension instruction on prepared directed questions that revolve around the main points and issues related to equality and the impact of speech. (See Figure 25 for a completed lesson plan for informational text.)

## Lesson Goals/Objectives

### Word Study

For this lesson, the word study goals include being able to understand the meaning of the three number-related roots and demonstrating understanding by using the words to create analogies.

### Comprehension

In comprehension, the overall lesson goals include being able to separate myths from facts about the Gettysburg Address, researching additional sources of information about the speech to gain a deeper understanding, and being able to answer questions related to speaker, audience, tone, theme, and so forth.

# FIGURE 25
## Completed Advanced Reader Lesson Plan for Informational Text

Text type: _Speech_      Narrative text: _____

Estimated length of time: _2-3 days_      Informational text: _The Gettysburg Address_

| WORD STUDY | WORD STUDY EXTENSION(S) |
|---|---|
| Features: _quad, pent, and uni_<br><br>Cycle: ___2___    Week: ___5___<br><br>Word Sort: ☐ Open ☐ Closed<br>☐ Spelling Sort ☐ Meaning Discussion | Create analogies and solve each other's |

| COMPREHENSION (NARRATIVE TEXT) | COMPREHENSION (INFORMATIONAL TEXT) |
|---|---|
| After Reading<br>☐ Plot/story line<br>    ☐ Character development<br>    ☐ Conflicts<br>    ☐ Resolutions<br>    ☐ Theme<br>☐ Summarize<br><br>☐ Teacher/student questions: _____<br>_____<br><br>☐ Discussion/teaching points: _____<br>_____<br>_____<br><br><br>Notes: | After Reading Day 2<br>☐ Review text structure to aid understanding<br>☑ Author's purpose<br>☐ Summarize<br>    ☐ Main ideas and essential details<br>    ☐ Compare and contrast<br>    ☐ Sequence<br>    ☐ Cause and effect, or problem and solution<br>☑ Teacher/student questions: • How did Abraham Lincoln describe the United States in his speech?<br>• Do you think that he meant to forget everything that was done thus far and start fresh?<br>• Why do you think this speech is so revered?<br>☑ Discussion/teaching points: length of speech, impact on those listening, equality<br>Notes: |
| Before Reading<br>☐ Activate and build background knowledge<br><br>☐ Preview vocabulary: _____<br>_____<br><br>☐ Set a purpose<br>Notes: | Before Reading Day 1<br>☑ Activate and build background knowledge<br>☑ Preview text features and structure<br><br>☐ Preview vocabulary: No vocab<br>_____<br>☑ Set a purpose<br>Notes:<br>• See what students know about the speech: importance of battle to Civil War<br>• Talk about primary documents<br>• Do anticipatory set: 5 myths sheet |

**Reading Extension**      Read pages: _Entire speech_

**Written Comprehension Extension(s):** _Finish the 5 myths sheet and complete the SOAPSTone (plus Theme) sheet_

Notes:

## Word Study

The students in this lesson are learning the spelling–meaning connection as they explore number-related root words. During this week, the students are sorting three different root words: *pent*, *quad*, and *uni*. They are studying three because the words are related in meaning, and the students more than likely have some familiarity with some of the words on their list. In this exchange, the students are starting a new sort. It is an open sort; therefore, the teacher will not provide students with the header words or show the students the pattern they are studying. Teachers should allow students a full week to study the new features. Again, students should prepare their individual word study cards before coming to their small groups to save valuable instructional time.

---

| | |
|---|---|
| Teacher: | Today, we are going to start a new sort. [The teacher lays the words cards in front of the group.] What do you notice about the words in this week's sort? |
| Michael: | Well, they have similar beginnings. |
| Teacher: | What do you mean? |
| Michael: | Well, the words all begin with *pent-*, *quad-*, or *uni-*. |
| Teacher: | Does anyone remember what we call a group of letters that has direct meaning? |
| Nicole: | It's either a prefix or a root word. |
| Teacher: | Right, Nicole. It's one of those. Can anyone help her out? |
| Kevin: | It's a root word. A prefix can be added onto a root word or base word, but they both have specific meanings and cannot stand alone as a real word. |
| Teacher: | Good. You remembered a lot about root words and prefixes. Let's start sorting the words and see what we come up with. |

The teacher guides the sort, then the students discuss the words *square* and *reunion* because they are not sure why these two words might be included in this sort or where they go.

| pent | quad | | uni | |
|---|---|---|---|---|
| pentadactyl | quadrangle | quadruple | unicycle | unity |
| pentagon | quadrant | quadruplets | unicorn | universal |
| pentameter | quadriceps | squad | uniform | universe |
| pentathlon | quadrilateral | square | unify | unique |
| pentatonic | | | unilateral | reunion |
| | | | unison | |

142

| | |
|---|---|
| Teacher: | Who thinks they know what the root words mean? Let's go online and see what we come up with for our three root words. |
| Nicole: | These are easy. *Uni* means one. I know that because a unicycle only has one wheel, and a unicorn has one horn on the top of its head. |
| Teacher: | Good. Who else wants to try? |
| Michael: | I think *pent* means six. I think I remember seeing something about the Pentagon building in Washington, DC, having six sides. I'm not sure of the other words, though. |
| Teacher: | Let's think about a pentagon. Who can draw it? |
| Maggie: | I can. Here's one. |
| Teacher: | Let's all look. How many sides does it have? |
| Michael: | Oh, it's only five sides, not six. |
| Teacher: | Right, so what do you think *pent* means now? |
| Michael: | It means five. |
| Kevin: | Well, I think that *quad* means four because we put *square* in that category, and a square has four sides. |

Using an online dictionary and other word origin resources, the students discover the correct spelling of the root words and the correct meaning of each word. Then, the students discuss each word in their sort and how it is related in meaning to other words and the root words.

### *Word Study Extension*

| | |
|---|---|
| Teacher: | When you go back to your seats, I'd like you to work with a partner and choose five words from each category to create analogies. Tomorrow, you will switch with another group and discuss each other's analogies. Be sure to write them in your word study notebooks, so we can share them on Friday when we have group again. |

## Comprehension

This lesson uses the text of the Gettysburg Address. The first day for this lesson is discussed in the Before Reading: Day 1 section, and the second day in the After Reading: Day 2 section.

## Activate and Build Background Knowledge

—————————————

Teacher:     For today, you are going to read the Gettysburg Address. Who can tell me what they know about this speech?

Abigail:     I know that Abraham Lincoln gave the address, but I'm not sure when or where.

Paul:        He gave the speech during the Civil War, I think.

Teacher:     You are correct, Paul. President Lincoln gave the speech during the Civil War on November 19, 1863. He gave the speech at the dedication of the Soldiers National Cemetery in Gettysburg, Pennsylvania, four and a half months after the Battle of Gettysburg. Who knows why the Battle of Gettysburg is so important to Civil War history?

Bernice:     We went to Gettysburg this summer, and I learned that more people died in that battle than any other of the other battles in the Civil War.

Teacher:     Absolutely right, Bernice! It was also the battle that some historians say redefined the war. There are some historians who believe that if the Confederacy had won that battle, they could have continued on and won the Civil War. The United States would be a very different country if that had happened.

Tom:         Why? I don't understand.

Teacher:     Who can explain this for Tom? Why would the United States be a different country today if the South had won the Civil War?

Abigail:     Well, one of the major issues in the Civil War was slavery. The North didn't want it, and the South wanted to keep it. So, if the South had won the war, there is no telling when slavery would have been abolished or if it would have ever been abolished.

Teacher:     Good point, Abigail. Does that make sense, Tom?

## Set a Purpose (through the Anticipatory Set extension activity)

—————————————

Teacher:     Before you read this speech, I want you to take a look at five statements and decide if you think they are myths or truths.

  1. President Lincoln wrote the speech on the back of an envelope.

  2. President Lincoln wrote the speech on the train from Washington, DC, to Gettysburg.

  3. The cemetery was complete when the dedication took place.

4. President Lincoln thought his speech was a failure.

5. The audience at Gettysburg was disappointed by the short speech.

Then, after you read it, you can partner up and see what each of you thought and discuss why you thought that.

The teacher continues to discuss the speech as a primary document and clarifies any other confusing points before the students read.

## Preview Vocabulary

Teacher:     I don't think you will have any difficulty with the words in the speech, but you might have questions about the language or the way it is written. If so, write your questions in the margins as you are reading, so we can discuss them the next time we are in our groups.

## After Reading: Day 2

## Summarizing: Main Ideas and Essential Details

Teacher:     Let's take a look at the myth sheets that you did. Then, we will discuss Abraham Lincoln's speech.

The students share their decisions and the thought processes behind their decisions, and the teacher leads the discussion.

## Teacher/Student Questions

Teacher:     How does Lincoln describe the United States in his speech? (inferential)

Paul:        He sort of says that with this war, we need to start a new country.

Bernice:     I agree. He says in the beginning that the country is now at war with itself, and at the end, he talks about "birthing" a new country.

Teacher:     Do you think he means to forget everything that has been done thus far and start fresh? (application)

Tom:         No, I think he just means that the country can't go on fighting or it won't survive, so they needed to do something to come together as one again.

More discussion on this topic ensues.

| Teacher: | Why do you think his speech is so revered? (application) |
|---|---|
| Abigail: | When you read it, his message is one of equality. He believed that everyone was created equal. |
| Paul: | The United States is still battling issues of equality. We seem to still be fighting over certain people getting certain things. |
| Tom: | It's ironic that he said, "The world will little note, nor long remember what we say here," yet here we are over a hundred and fifty years later still studying what he said. |

The discussion continues and is primarily led by the teacher. Discussion points include length of speech, impact on those listening, and issues of equality.

### Comprehension Extension

| Teacher: | For your extension activity today, I want you to take your myths sheet and find out if they are fact or fiction. You can use the online resources that we discussed, but be sure to cite correctly! Then, you are going to use the SOAPSTone [originally developed by Ogden Morse (2007)] + Theme organizer and complete it for the Gettysburg Address. Bring this back to group when we meet again. You might need to use the additional information that you found to help support your answers. (See Figure 26 for this completed extension activity, and the Support Materials section of the accompanying CD  for the blank SOAPSTone + Theme sheet and the instructions.) |
|---|---|

## Lesson Summary

The instructional decisions that were made in this lesson were based on both individual and group needs. In word study, the students had studied number-related roots and thus were well equipped to be able to understand the words and create analogies with the words. Creating analogies is a more difficult word study extension activity and thus is best used with words with which the students have some familiarity.

In comprehension, knowing that the students had some basic knowledge about the Gettysburg Address, the teacher wanted to deepen their understanding of the significance of the speech and the events happening in the nation at the time Lincoln delivered it. The teacher gave the students the anticipatory set of statements to help them focus their thinking as they were reading. Additionally, the teacher asked them to locate other sources of information to help sort myths versus truths. Students in the Advanced Reading stage need to be able to pull together information from different sources.

**FIGURE 26**
**Completed Extension Activity for Informational Text**

# SOAPSTone + Theme

for _The Gettysburg Address_

Speaker: _Abraham Lincoln. He was the 16th President of the United States._

Occasion: _He was giving the speech at the dedication of the Soldiers National Cemetery on November 18, 1863._

Audience: _He gave the speech to the people who attended the ceremony. 15,000 people were there. Many were the families of the 7,500 people who were buried there._

Purpose: _Lincoln wanted to see the fighting end. He was trying to get everyone to realize that if we continued to fight, we would not be one country anymore and both the North and South needed each other._

Subject: _He talked about how all people should be equal and reminded people about the ideas that the United States was founded on._

Tone: _Sadness but at the same time, he gently reminded people what was important but not in a lecture type of way._

Theme: _We need to change. Lincoln made it clear without directly saying that the Civil War had to end in order for the United States to survive._

_Note._ Adapted from _SOAPSTone: A Strategy for Reading_ and _Writing,_ by O. Morse, 2007, retrieved May 17, 2011, from apcentral.collegeboard.com/apc/public/preap/teachers_corner/45200.html.

Additionally, the text allowed for a rich discussion of history, bridging language arts with the content areas.

Again, choosing appropriate extension activities depends on the teacher's goals and the individual students in the group. The following are other examples of appropriate extension activities for this lesson.

### Word Study Extensions

- Make a matching pair. Divide up words between two students. Each student must create a picture definition of the words that he or she is given. The students can then play a memory game, matching the word with the picture definition.
- Create two synonyms and two antonyms for each word. Then, decide which words would not work with a synonym or antonym and explain why.
- **Vocabulary Fact or Fib?:** In groups of two, have students each create three sentences that define their words, where only one of the sentences is true. They then switch with their partner, who must choose which one is the actual definition.

### Comprehension Extensions

- Pick out at least two things that you would change about Abraham Lincoln's speech and create your own verbiage within the speech. Then, discuss why you made those changes.
- Design your own assessment for the Gettysburg Address. If you were the teacher, what are the most important aspects of the address, and how would you make sure that your students knew them? The students can also swap assessments and have students complete each other's.

# Conclusion

Advanced readers are able to draw from experience and knowledge while comprehending the text that they read. They assume more responsibility for their learning; however, they still require teacher direction as they learn to critically evaluate text and formulate opinions. Advanced readers have reached a level of literacy expertise that allows them to access and apply their own knowledge and relate it to the text. They understand the structure of the English language and can apply this understanding when faced with challenging vocabulary and texts. The journey of reading and learning never ends, but advanced readers are well equipped for their future reading endeavors.

# CHAPTER 7

# Extending and Managing Small-Group Reading Instruction

One of the most common questions that we are asked is, What are the other students doing while I am teaching small groups? The management aspect of small-group differentiated instruction is the most critical and often the most difficult part of implementation for many teachers. The management aspect requires appropriate text and meaningful extension activities that support students' learning outside of their small-group work. Therefore, as the teacher is providing small-group instruction, the other students are engaged in these extension activities. The extensions that we provide in this book are designed to keep students occupied in learning activities that will continue to develop them as readers and writers rather than simply keep them busy. Keeping students busy is keeping the teachers even busier. Our goal is to help teachers work smarter not harder. The extension activities empower teachers to do just that.

This chapter is divided into two sections. First, we provide extension activities for each component of the small-group lesson plan models. Second, we examine the two most common intermediate classroom configurations: (1) the self-contained classroom, most frequently seen in grades 3–5, and (2) the departmentalized model, used in many upper elementary and middle school classrooms. Each of these configurations can be adapted to include small-group differentiated instruction, although the organization and management will probably look different to maximize the instructional efficiency of each environment.

## Extension Activities

The extension activities listed in this chapter provide additional practice with materials that students have been working with in their small groups. Thus, a teacher could have all of the small groups completing the same extension activity but with material that is on each student's independent level. Additionally, there are some extension activities that could be used in either small-group or whole-group settings. For example, a teacher could decide to do a whole-group lesson on a particular Latin or Greek root. The Root Web activity is appropriate for this purpose.

We have added a substantial number of writing extension activities in this section because we recognize the importance of purposeful writing exercises that demonstrate student comprehension. Please keep in mind that students need uninterrupted time to write; thus, writing is completed *outside* of small-group work rather than within. The extension activities allow for meaningful learning while the teacher is working with other small groups.

As with other curricular activities, teachers should plan first to model and discuss the expectations for each activity. This can be easily accomplished with a modeled or shared writing activity after completing a read-aloud during whole-group instruction. It is essential that teachers model and practice with students before asking them to complete any of these activities on their own.

**Extension Notebook:** This notebook is a tool to write and keep track of all the students' written extension work. If students are using the computer, they can print their documents and insert them into their notebook or loose-leaf binder.

**Fluency Folder:** Each student creates a folder to hold all of his or her fluency reading material. The students can three-hole punch their poems, Readers Theatre scripts, song lyrics, repeated reading charts, and so forth and keep them all in one place. Shared reading pieces from the students' small groups can also be housed in their fluency folders. This will make finding their fluency materials easier as well.

## Extension Activities That Support Fluency

Reading fluency can best be developed by reading and rereading independent-level texts. The evolving readers will reread texts in their small groups, whereas the maturing and advanced readers may either be assigned or independently choose material to practice outside of their small groups. For example, these readers might choose a poem that they are preparing to present to the class. The following are suggested extension activities that support continued fluency practice.

**Readers Theatre:** Students use a script in a minimalistic theater. Lines are not memorized, and props are not used; this activity is simply a group of students practicing a script. Each student plays a specific part, including a narrator. Students can also play more than one part if necessary. The script is read multiple times in order to perfect speed, accuracy, and expression. Students can also perform their script for the teacher and/or class.

**Poetry Alive!:** This individual or choral reading activity provides students the chance to practice their intonation, use of voice, pitch, and stress using dramatic presentations.

**Record and Self-Reflect:** This activity uses a fluency rating scale (see the Support Materials section on the CD ). Students record themselves reading a short passage (no more than 150 words) and then reflect on their own fluency ability. Students then listen to themselves and record their own performance on the rating scale. This should be repeated two or three times.

**Read With Me:** This activity allows students to choose different partners three times per week who will listen to them read the same short passage. The listening partner uses the Read With Me rating scale (see the Support Materials section on the CD 💿 ) to rate his or her partner's oral reading.

**Karaoke Lyrics:** With the use of technology (e.g., computers, iPads, smartphones), students can sing or speak along with karaoke prompts. This engaging activity is best used with song lyrics that students are unfamiliar with at first, as the purpose is to practice their speed and word recognition.

**Reading Buddies:** Upper grade students partner up with lower grade students and read to each other. In this activity, the students each read aloud their respective independent-leveled texts.

**Partner Reading:** Students who are reading material at the same level can partner up and practice from their fluency folders or reread a text that was used during small-group time.

### Web Resources for Fluency

Many are available, but here are some of our favorites:

- Readers Theatre
  - Author Online! Aaron Shepard's Home Page: www.aaronshep.com
  - Timeless Teacher Stuff: www.timelessteacherstuff.com
  - Web English Teacher: www.webenglishteacher.com/rt.html
- Poetry
  - Giggle Poetry: www.gigglepoetry.com
  - Kenn Nesbitt's Poetry4kids.com: www.poetry4kids.com/
  - Poetry 180: www.loc.gov/poetry/180
- Song Lyrics
  - A–Z Lyrics Universe: www.azlyrics.com
  - eLyrics.net: www.elyrics.net
  - SongLyrics: www.songlyrics.com

## Extension Activities That Support Word Study

The following activities are designed to support the word study component of small-group instruction. These extensions allow students experience with the focus features in multiple contexts. Students need continuous opportunities to manipulate new words and apply their knowledge in order for the words to become part of their daily conversations.

**Word Hunt:** Students are asked to find words in independent- or instructional-level text that have the same features that the students are currently focusing on in their small groups. It would be appropriate to use texts in their fluency folders as well as texts that they have or are currently reading in their small groups. Students can write these words in their word study notebooks. This activity allows students to make the connection between studying words in isolation and recognizing generalizations in context (see Figure 27).

**Partner Spelling Sort:** Students partner up with another student from their small group and take turns calling out the words and completing the spelling sort.

**Analogies:** Having students create their own analogies is a purposeful instructional activity that naturally incorporates higher level thinking skills. A teacher will want to give a minilesson that explicitly describes an analogy, being sure to walk students through the thought process involved in creating one. Having them create their own analogies will also help prepare them for future standardized tests.

**Root Web:** This activity is appropriate for evolving, maturing, and advanced readers who are studying Latin or Greek root words. Students write the root that they are studying in the center of their root web (see the Support Materials section on the CD 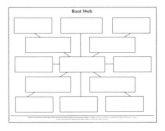 ) and words containing the same root in the boxes around the center. Then, the students discuss how all of the words are related in meaning.

**Root of the Day:** Using the Root Web format, Root of the Day can be a whole-class activity or individual extension. When students enter the classroom in the morning, the

**FIGURE 27**
**Student Completing a Word Hunt**

*Note.* Photo courtesy of Heather Hughes.

152

teacher provides a root word to study that day. Each student brainstorms as many words as he or she can think of with that particular root. Later in the day, the students discuss the words they found and how the meanings are related.

**Vocabulary Word Map:** This activity allows students to use a graphic organizer (see the Support Materials section on the CD 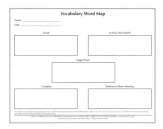 ) to visually define a given word using examples, illustrations, sentences, and student-generated definitions that demonstrate their understanding.

**Visualizing Vocabulary:** Students create a picture or other visual aid that helps solidify the meaning of a vocabulary word. They also write a sentence about the visual to put the word in context.

**Word Study Matrix:** This activity (see the Support Materials section on the CD  ) can have multiple uses. Students can use the matrix to build new words by adding suffixes and/or prefixes. They can also use it to explore synonyms, antonyms, and multimeaning words.

**Hink Pink:** This activity is best used with partners to help get students' creative juices flowing. Students can use the identified vocabulary word that appears either in the riddle or in the answer of the "hink pinks." This is not always easy, but students like the challenge! Hink pinks are one-syllable words that rhyme, hinky pinkies are two-syllable words that rhyme, and hinkety pinketies are three-syllable words that rhyme. For example, what's a hinky pinky for a humorous animal with long ears? The answer is a funny bunny, of course! Here are some other examples of questions and their answers for this activity:

- What's a hink pink for an obese feline? (fat cat)
- What's a hinky pinky for an improved written communication? (better letter)
- What's a hinkety pinkety for a believable food? (credible edible)
- What's a hinky pinky for a turbulent sauce? (wavy gravy)
- What's a hink pink for something you see that glows? (bright sight)

**Extension Games:** Teachers can create their own word study games, such as Suffix Rummy and Homophone Rummy, using a simple game board and word cards.

## Extension Activities That Support Comprehension

The following activities are direct extensions of small-group instruction for both narrative and informational text. We have expanded the extension activities to meet the rigor needed for intermediate students to be successful in meeting grade-level standards. As such, many of the extensions are writing pieces that require depth, critical thinking, and time. That said, teachers need to consider quality over the quantity of assignments given, depth versus breadth. These comprehension extension activities support both research-based comprehension instruction and the Common Core Standards. As the teacher, you are the most important decision maker, so you should choose extensions that you think best meet the needs of your students.

## Character

**Character Counts:** For this activity (see the Support Materials section on the CD  ), students identify a particular character trait of one of the main characters in a story. Students also have to provide evidence (at least two examples) of where the trait is exhibited in the story. For example, in *The Wizard of Oz* (Baum, 1900/1993), when the Wicked Witch of the West melts away after being splashed with water, Dorothy seems somewhat sad. Additionally, when the wizard is revealed to be a regular man hiding behind curtains pretending to be something that he is not, Dorothy displays a caring attitude for the man even though he deceived her.

**Character Traits:** Select a character from the story. What character trait did he or she exhibit? (Keep a list of character traits posted in the classroom.) How did the character exhibit this trait in the story? Have you read a book with another character who exhibited this character trait? How did that character show the trait?

**Character Timeline:** Pick a character and describe how that character changes from the beginning of the story to the end. Develop a timeline that shows the important events that led to the changes.

**Bio-Poem:** This activity can be used after reading a narrative text or biography. Students contribute pertinent attributes about a character in the form of poetry. The poem follows an established, free verse pattern (see the Support Materials section on the CD ).

Here are some additional ideas for extension activities:

- Write a letter of advice to a character from your perspective.

- Rewrite the story (or chapter) from the point of view of another character.

- Write a letter to a character in the story relating the experiences of the character to an experience that you have had.

- Create an emotion map that indicates the high and low points in the character's life. Support your thinking with examples from the story.

- Create a two-sided mask that shows a character at the beginning of the story on one side and the same character at the conclusion of the story on the other side. The mask should demonstrate the character's emotions and/or traits.

- Create an acrostic poem about one of the characters.

- Imagine that you are one of the characters in the story. Use that character's voice to explain your role in a diary entry. (Be sure to review voice before you assign this activity.)

- Create a dialogue journal between two characters. (Be sure to specify how long the journal should be, which depends on the students' stage of development.)

- Show how two minor characters felt and reacted to each other in the book. Explain how you think these characters contribute to the overall story.

- Imagine that you are one of the characters in the story and you drop a note out of your pocket. What would it say?

- If you (from the perspective of another character) could give one piece of advice to another principal character, who would you select, and what advice would you give? At what point in the story would you have said it? How do you think that would have changed the story's outcome?

- If you could delete a character, who would it be? Why and how would it affect the story?

- Select the character you admire most and explain why.

### Illustrations

**Picture Power:** Look at the illustration on a particular page of a book. What is the illustrator trying to communicate to the reader? Write a paragraph to discuss this and provide evidence to support your thoughts.

**You Are the Illustrator:** Students can add an illustration to a book. Their illustration should demonstrate a point in the story that they think was significant. Students can also follow up with a written paragraph describing their illustration and its connection to the story.

### Main Idea and Details

**What's the Big Idea?:** This activity (see the Support Materials section on the CD  ) can be used during or after reading as students summarize key points from the text. Students use this strategy to identify the main and supporting ideas in informational text.

**What's Important?:** Choose the five most important events in the story (or chapter). Write them in the order that they happened in the story.

**Top 10 List:** Using the graphic organizer as a guide (see the Support Materials section on the CD  ), make a poster listing the top 10 things you learned about the topic (informational text). Draw an illustration for the poster that shows some of the key points.

**Let Me Advise You:** Use an advice column format to describe the problem or conflict in the story and assume the advice columnist role to write a response.

**I-Prompts:** Choose something from the text to complete an I-prompt, such as "I think…," "I feel…," "I don't understand…," or "I was surprised…."

## Point of View

**What Really Happened?:** Select a major event from the story. Next, choose two characters who were part of the event. Write a summary of the event from each character's point of view. Include dialogue for each character.

**Same Story, Different Version:** Retell the story from the point of view of another character, either a main or supporting character. Students should also write why they chose the characters they did.

## Prediction

**Story Impression:** Give students a handful of main words from the story and have them write a prediction using those words in the order you gave them. After reading, have them write a summary of what really happened using the same words in the same order. (This activity is provided courtesy of Jennifer Krause, a teacher at Mt. Olive Lutheran School in Overland Park, Kansas.)

**Book Bits:** Read little snippets from a book (e.g., exciting parts, climax, character development) and have students write predictions or questions. They can answer their questions or respond to their predictions while reading the text in entirety. (This activity is provided courtesy of Jennifer Krause, a teacher at Mt. Olive Lutheran School in Overland Park, Kansas.)

**What Happens Next?:** Write a paragraph that tells what you predict will happen in the next part of the text. Make at least three predictions and give reasons for your predictions.

## Questioning

**Question Maker:** After small-group instruction, students make up their own questions in each of the three following categories: literal, inferential, and application (see the Support Materials section on the CD  ). Students write one question for each category. Then, they exchange questions with a partner and answer their partner's questions.

**Questions, Questions:** Write three questions that you have about what you have read in the text so far. With a partner, have a written conversation as you exchange the questions with each other for written responses (thoughts rather than specific answers). (Each student will create three original questions and respond to his or her partner's three questions.)

**The 5 Ws:** This is another type of questioning activity that promotes identifying the main idea from a text; it can be done before, during, or after reading a text. Each student selects a card on which is written one of five question words: *who, what, where, when,* or *why.* Students are asked to use their words as a stem for a question that they generate as they read the next section of the text. Then, students pose their questions to the group to generate discussion about the reading.

## Sequencing

**Secret Sequence:** As a follow-up to small-group instruction, this activity (see the Support Materials section on the CD  ) calls for students to write a list of five events in the story in random order and create an answer key. Each student exchanges his or her list of events with a partner and then places the partner's events in the proper sequence. Then, the partners check their final products against their answer keys.

**Five Important Events:** Determine the five most important events in the story. List them in order in a summary paragraph, using at least four transitional words (related to sequence).

**Timeline:** This graphic organizer (see the Support Materials section on the CD  ) helps students recall important events and place the events in the order in which they occurred in the story.

## Setting

**The Perfect Setting:** In this activity (see the Support Materials section on the CD  ), students write a descriptive paragraph of the setting of the story. The description must include the time, place, and three descriptive details. Students also should include a drawing of the setting on the back of their sheet.

## Summarizing

**Sum It Up:** This strategy (adapted from an activity on the ReadingQuest website, www.readingquest.org) can be started in small-groups sessions and extended outside of group. Sum It Up helps students write concise summaries that focus on the main idea of a text. Students imagine that they are placing a classified ad or sending a telegram, and every word costs them a certain amount of money. (This activity is also great for teaching math!) The teacher determines how much each word will cost and how much students can spend. For example, a teacher might determine that students have $5 to spend and that each word costs 10 cents. Then, students have to write a summary using 50 words or fewer. Teachers can also have students write multiple summaries, in which case, they are given successively less money to spend. For example, after students write their 50-word summaries, the teacher can reduce their spending money to $3, so students have to cut out 20 words. (See the Support Materials section on the CD .)

**ABC Brainstorm/Summary:** This activity (adapted from an activity on the ReadingQuest website, www.readingquest.org) can be used to either activate or assess prior knowledge, or summarize/assess what has been learned. This strategy (see the

Support Materials section on the CD  ) also helps students brainstorm and summarize the key ideas associated with a given concept by thinking of words or phrases associated with that concept; each concept begins with a letter of the alphabet.

**The Essentials:** After reading a piece of text or a text in its entirety, students are asked to individually identify the essential details from the text, which can be done outside of their groups. Then, in  their small groups, the teacher leads a discussion of common essential details and common interesting facts. The group moves on to discuss differing details. During the discussion, students need to be able to justify why they think their details are essential rather than interesting facts, and vice versa. (See the Support Materials section on the CD .)

**You're the Reporter:** In this activity (see the Support Materials section on the CD  ), students write a summary of a story for a newspaper article. The summary must address who, what, when, where, and why.

**Fact or Fib?:** For this activity (see the Support Materials section on the CD  ),  students write three facts and one fib about information they learned while listening to or reading a text. Students exchange this information with one another and see if they can trick their friends. The student who tricks the most people is the winner.

**Top 10 List:** For this activity (see the Support Materials section on the CD  ), students listen to or read a selection independently. Then, they create their own top 10 lists about the reading, such as the 10 most important details of the story or the 10 most important facts about a given topic.

**Summarize With Vocabulary:** Summarize the story (or chapter) using the story's vocabulary. (Note: Students should use the vocabulary words that the teacher taught with the particular text.) Include at least three sentences that tell what happened at the beginning, middle, and end of the story (or chapter). For each vocabulary word, write a sentence that tells something that happened in the text.

**RAFT:** RAFT (adapted from an activity on the ReadingQuest website, readingquest.org) is a writing prompt (see the Support Materials section on the CD  ) that helps students understand and focus their role as a writer and understand the audience they are addressing, various formats for writing, and the topic they are writing about. By using this strategy, teachers encourage students to write creatively while still incorporating content. Additionally, students must consider a topic from a different perspective and gain practice writing for different audiences and in different formats.

**SOAPSTone + Theme:** This strategy (adapted from Morse, 2007) helps students think about the important aspects of text. (See the Support Materials section on the CD .)

**Inquiry Chart:** Originally developed by James Hoffman in 1992, this activity requires students to identify ideas that they know or think they know about a particular topic. Then, the students are

required to find evidence supporting their hypotheses from at least three different sources. Teachers can use this as a guide and tweak the activity in order to meet their own instructional goals. (See the Support Materials section on the CD .)

## Text Structures

**Story Map:** This graphic organizer (adapted from Beck et al., 1979; see the Support Materials section on the CD ) is a visual aid that represents the elements of narrative.

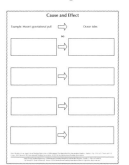

**Cause and Effect:** This graphic organizer (see the Support Materials section on the CD ) helps students collaborate and discuss examples of cause and effect in narrative and informational text. Typically, we find cause and effect both difficult to teach and difficult for students to learn. An important thing to emphasize when teaching should be to allow the students to describe why they think the outcome (effect) was caused by a particular event.

**Problem–Solution:** This organizer (see the Support Materials section on the CD ) allows students to list the particular problems in a text and the solution that solved the problem. A teacher should be sure to discuss how this text type is different from cause and effect. In a problem–solution scenario, the reader can find an answer to the issue rather than a causal relationship.

**Compare and Contrast With Meaning:** This graphic organizer (see the Support Materials section on the CD ) is used by students to compare and contrast characteristics of given topics. Adapted from an activity on the ReadingQuest website (readingquest.org), this activity requires students to think about how given aspects are related or different.

**Transitions:** How does the author show transitions in the story? Select words, phrases, or sentences that are important in these transitions.

**Table of Contents:** Look at the table of contents. How did the author organize the information in this text? Do you think this organization helped you understand the text? Why, or why not? (This activity should be used with informational text.)

### Theme

**Examining Theme:** What is the overall theme for the story, such as friendship, perseverance, or rewards for helping someone. How is the theme shown in the story?

**Theme Poetry:** Write a poem that addresses the theme of the story.

### Vocabulary

**Vocabulary Cards:** For this activity, students (or the teacher) write each of the story's vocabulary words or content-specific words on index cards. Then, students line up while the teacher tapes a word to each student's back. Each student creates a list of questions that have a yes or no answer, such as "Is the word a noun?" or "Does the word have anything to do with losing sleep?" Students go around the room and ask their classmates their questions (students will inevitably have to create more questions as they go). Students keep rotating around the classroom until they guess the word they are wearing. This activity can be completed as a review (then you would have many words) or, if using this with a particular story or unit of study, simply double up on the words (they are taped to students' backs, and they will not know that words have been used twice).

**Class Libs:** Using newly acquired vocabulary, students use the words to create a Mad Libs–type activity for their partners. Class Libs is best described as a game in which one player prompts another for a list of words to substitute for blanks in a story, usually with funny results.

**Vocabulary Word Map:** Using this graphic organizer (see the Support Materials section on the CD ), students create ways to make their own meaning of a word by writing a definition in their own words, writing a sentence that demonstrates the word's meaning, drawing a visual image, and providing examples.

## Managing Small-Group Differentiated Instruction

This section examines the two most common intermediate classroom configurations: (1) the self-contained classroom, most frequently seen in grades 3–5, and (2) the departmentalized model, used in many upper elementary and middle school grades. Each of these classroom configurations can be adapted to include small-group differentiated instruction, although the organization and management will probably look different to maximize the instructional efficiency of each environment.

160

**FIGURE 28**
**Sample Daily Schedule for a Fourth-Grade Self-Contained Classroom**

| Time | Curricular Area | Details |
|---|---|---|
| 8:00–8:15 (15 minutes) | Students arrive | • Morning announcements and classroom business (lunch choices, attendance, and homework collection)<br>• Students read independently leveled text to promote fluency. |
| 8:15–10:15 (120 minutes) | Language arts block | • Whole-group instruction<br>• Small-group instruction (basal text: read-aloud and shared reading) |
| 10:15–11:00 (45 minutes) | Special classes | • Art, music, physical education, computer, or library |
| 11:00–12:00 (60 minutes) | Math | |
| 12:00–12:30 (30 minutes) | Lunch | |
| 12:30–1:00 (30 minutes) | Recess | • Bathroom, water, etc. |
| 1:00–1:45 (45 minutes) | Continuation of language arts block | • Process writing and grammar |
| 1:45–2:45 (60 minutes) | Social studies or science | • Rotate depending on the unit of study |
| 2:45–3:00 (15 minutes) | Wrap-up | • Prepare for dismissal (homework reminders and classroom business reminders, e.g., field trips, library books) |

*Note.* Modified from *Small-Group Reading Instruction: A Differentiated Teaching Model for Intermediate Readers, Grades 3–8* (p. 112), by B. Tyner and S.E. Green, 2005, Newark, DE: International Reading Association. Copyright 2005 by the International Reading Association.

## The Self-Contained Classroom

The self-contained classroom that is subsequently discussed is one in which the classroom teacher is primarily responsible for teaching all of the subject areas. This does not preclude students who may be pulled out to receive services, such as speech and language, special education, Title I, English as a second language, or other specialized instructional programs. This self-contained classroom allows teachers the flexibility to plan for and implement both whole- and small-group instruction in a manner that maximizes instructional time for both the teacher and the students.

Typically, self-contained classrooms are organized in blocks of time, especially with regard to reading and math instruction. Figure 28 is an example of a fourth-grade self-contained classroom's daily schedule. We have also taken into consideration general curricular guidelines as they pertain to time allocations for each subject area.

### Planning for the Reading Block

A two-hour literacy block is common in many upper elementary classrooms. It also is quite common to have four reading groups at various instructional levels in any given classroom. This is particularly widespread in classrooms with 25 or more students. In this fourth-grade classroom (see Figure 29), there are four different groups of readers within the class, each of which is included in a rotational model that reflects more support for the readers who are below grade level and more independent work time for readers who are at or above grade level. This independent work time is reflected in the extension activities previously discussed.

All groups do not meet with the teacher every day. In our experience, we have found that it is unrealistic for an intermediate teacher to provide quality, small-group reading instruction to 25 students per day. Therefore, a rotating schedule is necessary (see Figure 30) and must be driven by the classroom assessment data. For example, the students who are

**FIGURE 29**
**Sample Daily Reading Block Schedule for a Fourth-Grade Self-Contained Classroom**

| Time | Grouping Configuration | Details |
|---|---|---|
| 8:15–8:55 (40 minutes) Monday–Wednesday<br><br>8:15–8:45 (30 minutes) Thursday and Friday | Whole class | • Read-aloud and shared reading (with basal if district mandated or use content-related text)<br>• During this time, instruction will focus on specific comprehension strategy instruction and vocabulary development. |
| 8:55–9:25 (30 minutes) | Small group A (two years below grade level) | • Complete small-group lesson plan |
| 9:25–9:55 (30 minutes) | Small group B (one year below grade level) | • Complete small-group lesson plan |
| 9:55–10:15 (20 minutes) | Small group C (at grade level) | • Word study only |
| | Small group D (above grade level) | • Independent work day |

*Note.* Modified from *Small-Group Reading Instruction: A Differentiated Teaching Model for Intermediate Readers, Grades 3–8* (p. 112), by B. Tyner and S.E. Green, 2005, Newark, DE: International Reading Association. Copyright 2005 by the International Reading Association.

**FIGURE 30**
**Sample Weekly Schedule for Small-Group Reading Instruction in a Fourth-Grade Self-Contained Classroom**

| Monday | Tuesday | Wednesday | Thursday | Friday |
|---|---|---|---|---|
| 80 minutes for small-group reading:<br>8:55–9:25 (30 minutes)<br>9:25–9:55 (30 minutes)<br>9:55–10:15 (20 minutes) | | | 90 minutes for small-group reading:<br>8:55–9:25 (30 minutes)<br>9:25–9:55 (30 minutes)<br>9:55–10:25 (30 minutes) | |
| A | C | D | C | A |
| B | A | B | B | C |
| D<br>(reading only)<br>Word study activities completed outside of group. | B<br>(reading only)<br>Word study activities completed outside of group. | A<br>(reading only)<br>Word study activities completed outside of group. | A | D |

*Note.* Modified from *Small-Group Reading Instruction: A Differentiated Teaching Model for Intermediate Readers, Grades 3–8* (p. 113), by B. Tyner and S.E. Green, 2005, Newark, DE: International Reading Association. Copyright 2005 by the International Reading Association.

performing two grade levels below average in reading must receive small-group instruction at least four times per week in the regular classroom, whereas the readers who are above grade level may meet for small-group instruction only two or three times per week.

In some schools, readers who are below grade level are often pulled from the classroom for their primary reading instruction. More often than not, this instruction consists of a scripted reading program that does not support the developmental reading process. There is little attention given to the literacy needs of the individual student, so the first line of defense for these students is the instruction that they must receive from the regular classroom teacher. Any additional reading support should supplement what the classroom teacher is providing rather than supplant it.

## *Description of the Groups*

### Group A
This group consists of six students who are transitioning into the Evolving Reader stage. As such, they are currently reading about two years below grade-level expectations. These students meet with the teacher four times per week for small-group reading instruction and an additional 20 minutes on the remaining day for just the comprehension portion of the lesson plan.

### Group B
This group consists of seven students who are in the middle of the Evolving Reader stage. They are currently performing about one year below grade level. This group of students meets with the teacher three times per week for small-group reading instruction and an additional 20 minutes on another day to focus on the comprehension portion of the lesson plan.

### Group C
This group consists of seven students who are currently at the end of the Evolving Reader stage. These students are able to read grade-level material. They meet with the teacher three times per week for small-group instruction.

### Group D
This group consists of five students who are currently at the beginning of the Maturing Reader stage. These students are reading material that is above grade level; therefore, the teacher meets with these students two times per week for a complete lesson and an additional 15 minutes on another day for word study (if necessary).

Although we strongly advocate for at least a 90–120-minute reading block, we realize that many teachers are working under time constraints that limit the amount of time devoted to small-group instruction. However, when we consider the reading-level diversity in any given intermediate classroom, this time allocation needs to be seriously reconsidered. Much of the controversy about spending more time in small-group instruction has focused on the amount of time that students spend working independently. This is why we developed the extension activities that provide meaningful independent work time. This allows for students to build stamina with extended reading and provides time to create in-depth writing pieces. When you assign an in-depth writing piece, be sure to model and have specific expectations of what you want the students to do. If you expect a three-paragraph essay that compares character traits, do not accept four sentences. Training students to be held accountable may take time, but it is time well spent.

### Additional Support Personnel

This reading block configuration does not take into consideration the supplemental reading instruction that must be provided for the students who are reading below grade level. These students need an extra dose of reading instruction that is consistent with the instruction that the classroom teacher is providing. In most schools, this extra instruction is very different from the classroom teacher's instruction. This often results in the already struggling reader feeling more confused and frustrated with the reading process. A true double dose of reading instruction involves the classroom teacher and the additional support teacher (e.g., Title I teacher) focusing on the same skills simultaneously. For example, if the students are reading a level 21 text and working on long *A* vowel patterns in their small-group instruction in the classroom, they should be reading a different text at a comparable instructional level and working on long *A* vowel patterns with the additional support teacher. This allows students to read another instructionally appropriate text. It is really quite simple: More time with instructionally appropriate material yields better readers.

### Whole-Group Instruction

Although the focus of this book is to provide guidance for small-group reading instruction, we cannot ignore the usefulness of whole-group instruction with the intermediate reader. Whole-group instruction allows the opportunity for teacher read-alouds and shared readings. Both of these activities are rich experiences for all students to build and increase vocabulary and comprehension skills. So, how can the teacher provide meaningful instruction in the context of the whole group? This question becomes more complex when coupled with district mandates for basal instruction. Thus, we have included information about basal reading instruction because we recognize that many school districts mandate the use of these basal programs.

### What About the Basal Program?

Because the basal story for the week is not an appropriate leveled text for all of the students in the class, it is best used as a shared reading, in which the teacher is primarily responsible for reading the story while the students follow along in their own books. The teacher uses this shared reading as a way to guide comprehension instruction through modeling his or her thought processes and monitoring students' understanding by engaging them in meaningful questioning activities that focus on literal, inferential, and application questions.

Although the basal format is specific with regard to weekly lesson plans, many of the suggested activities are not appropriate for all students in a given classroom.

Therefore, the basal activities must be modified. For example, the excessive workbook pages that many basal reading programs include do not give students an opportunity to express themselves in writing; filling in the blanks on a worksheet will not help develop students' critical thinking or writing skills. Teachers must pick and choose the basal activities that hold the most value for whole-group student learning. (See Table 9 for

**TABLE 9**
**Suggested Basal Program Modifications**

| Day | Required Basal Program Activities | Alternate Activities |
|-----|-----------------------------------|----------------------|
| Monday | • Build background knowledge<br>• Preview story vocabulary<br>• Predict<br>• Focus skill in phonics and comprehension<br>• Workbook pages | **Keep**<br>• Build background knowledge<br>• Preview story vocabulary<br>• Predict<br>**Modify**<br>• Substitute workbook with varied vocabulary and comprehension activities<br>• Omit phonics focus skill, which is taught systematically and explicitly in the word study portion of the small-group lesson plan |
| Tuesday | • Review story vocabulary<br>• Reading of the story (may include independent, partner, or shared reading)<br>• Workbook pages | **Keep**<br>• Review story vocabulary<br>**Modify**<br>• Shared reading in a whole-group setting (The teacher is responsible for the majority of the reading.)<br>• Substitute workbook pages with varied vocabulary and comprehension activities |
| Wednesday | • Book on tape<br>• Use leveled reader to support higher/lower readers<br>• Workbook pages | **Keep**<br>• Use leveled book if appropriate<br>**Modify**<br>• Use book on tape as a literacy center activity<br>• Follow up with a comprehension activity<br>• Substitute workbook for partner discussion or an authentic writing activity |
| Thursday | • Partner read the story for fluency<br>• Workbook pages | **Modify**<br>• Reread other appropriate leveled text for fluency practice with a partner<br>• Partners complete a common comprehension activity based on fluency read<br>**or**<br>• Shared reading or teacher read-aloud of informational text to support content area standards<br>• Engage students in meaningful comprehension and vocabulary activities |
| Friday | • Selection assessment | **Modify**<br>• Shared reading or teacher read-aloud of informational text to support content area standards<br>• Engage students in meaningful comprehension and vocabulary activities |

*Note.* Modified from *Small-Group Reading Instruction: A Differentiated Teaching Model for Intermediate Readers, Grades 3–8* (p. 116), by B. Tyner and S.E. Green, 2005, Newark, DE: International Reading Association. Copyright 2005 by the International Reading Association.

suggested modifications of basal program activities.) This discrimination process frees up more time for small-group instruction as well as focused content area instruction during the reading block.

You will notice on the sample daily reading block schedule (Figure 29) that we have provided more time in the beginning of the week for whole-group basal instruction so that the text can be introduced and read together. Although the basal might suggest that the text be read two or three times during the week, this is probably not the best use of instructional time. Rather, this time can be used engaging students in grade-level content information that meets the required curricular standards. This can also be time allotted for student reading in independent-leveled text to build fluency (see Figure 31). Rereading the basal text numerous times over the course of the week will not increase fluency for those students who are reading below grade level. The text is simply too difficult. Further, although many basal reading programs are accompanied by one lower level and one higher level book to supplement weekly instruction, these books may or may not be at the students' instructional reading level. Clearly, a wider variety of text selections is critical to the overall reading program in any given classroom.

**FIGURE 31**
**Students Reading Independently in a Self-Contained Classroom**

*Note.* Photo courtesy of Heather Hughes.

FIGURE 32
**Sample Daily Schedule for a Middle School Classroom**

| Time | Curricular Area | Details |
|------|-----------------|---------|
| 8:00–8:15 (15 minutes) | Homeroom | • Morning announcements<br>• Classroom business (lunch choices and attendance) |
| 8:15–9:45 (90 minutes) | Language arts block | • Whole-group instruction<br>• Small-group instruction |
| 9:50–11:20 (90 minutes) | Math block | |
| 11:20–12:00 (40 minutes) | Lunch | |
| 12:00–1:30 (90 minutes) | Social studies or science | • Rotate, depending on the unit of study |
| 1:30–2:15 (45 minutes) | Elective class | • Art, music, physical education, or theater<br>• Rotational |
| 2:15–3:00 (45 minutes) | Elective class | • Health or computer<br>• Rotational |

*Note.* Modified from *Small-Group Reading Instruction: A Differentiated Teaching Model for Intermediate Readers, Grades 3–8* (p. 118), by B. Tyner and S.E. Green, 2005, Newark, DE: International Reading Association. Copyright 2005 by the International Reading Association.

## The Departmentalized Classroom

As students transition from upper elementary to middle school, the complexities in teaching reading become even greater. In most middle schools, there is a 90-minute block of time dedicated to literature, writing, and grammar instruction in the departmentalized classroom. *Departmentalized* refers to an organizational structure whereby teachers are assigned to teach specific subject areas (e.g., language arts, math, science, social studies). As a result, the Small-Group Differentiated Reading Model is modified to balance the reading needs of those students within the middle school structure. (See Figure 32.)

### Planning for the Language/Communication Arts Block

Similar to the self-contained classroom in the upper elementary grades, the 90-minute block in the middle school should contain both whole- and small-group instruction (see Figure 33 for an example of a seventh-grade departmentalized language arts classroom's daily reading block). In reality, the grouping configurations will be larger than that of the upper elementary classroom because of time constraints and larger class sizes. A sample rotation schedule is provided to demonstrate an efficient way to maximize small-group instruction in a limited amount of time (see Figure 34). Unlike that of the upper elementary school, the language arts block in the middle school includes reading, writing, and grammar instruction. The text used in the language arts block generally focuses on literature that supports grade-level standards.

Reading in content area text will need to be supported in the respective content area classroom. Although not addressed in this book, effective content area instruction must be supplemented with leveled texts to support the varying reading levels of

**FIGURE 33**
**Sample Daily Reading Block Schedule for a Seventh-Grade Classroom**

| Time | Grouping Configuration | Details |
|---|---|---|
| 8:15–8:45 (30 minutes) Monday–Wednesday<br><br>8:15–9:15 (60 minutes) Thursday and Friday | Whole class | **Reading**<br>• Read-aloud and shared reading (with basal if district mandated)<br>• Focus on specific comprehension strategy instruction and vocabulary development<br>**Writing and Grammar**<br>• Process writing instruction<br>• Grammar instruction<br>• Writing conferences |
| 8:45–9:15 (30 minutes) Monday–Wednesday | Small group A (two years below grade level) | • Complete small-group lesson plan |
| 9:15–9:45 (30 minutes) Monday–Wednesday | Small group B (at or slightly below) | • Complete small-group lesson plan |
| | Small group C (above grade level) | • Independent work day |

*Note.* Modified from *Small-Group Reading Instruction: A Differentiated Teaching Model for Intermediate Readers, Grades 3–8* (p. 118), by B. Tyner and S.E. Green, 2005, Newark, DE: International Reading Association. Copyright 2005 by the International Reading Association.

**FIGURE 34**
**Sample Weekly Schedule for Small-Group Reading Instruction in a Seventh-Grade Classroom**

| Monday | Tuesday | Wednesday | Thursday | Friday |
|---|---|---|---|---|
| 60 minutes for small-group reading: 8:45–9:15 (30 minutes) 9:15–9:45 (30 minutes) | | | 30 minutes for small-group reading: 9:15–9:45 | |
| A | C | A | B | A |
| B | B | C | | |

*Note.* Modified from *Small-Group Reading Instruction: A Differentiated Teaching Model for Intermediate Readers, Grades 3–8* (p. 118), by B. Tyner and S.E. Green, 2005, Newark, DE: International Reading Association. Copyright 2005 by the International Reading Association.

students. They will not become more proficient in reading in the content areas without texts that they can read. The lesson plans that are provided in this book can be adapted to support content area teachers who have a wide variety of readers in their class, particularly those reading below or above grade level.

### Description of the Groups

The needs of these intermediate students are successfully met when they are grouped according to ability. There really is no other way to effectively and efficiently meet the needs of all students. We are not advocating tracking groups of students; rather, we suggest implementing this model in a heterogeneously grouped classroom. This is reflected in the following example.

## Group A

This group consists of nine students who are currently reading two years or more below grade level. They are late in the evolving stage of reading development. This group meets with the teacher three times per week for small-group instruction.

## Group B

This group consists of 10 students who are currently reading at or slightly below grade level. They are nearing the end of the Maturing Reader stage and are well within the meaning level of spelling development. This group meets with the teacher three times per week for small-group instruction.

## Group C

This group consists of six students who are in the Advanced Reader stage. These students are able to read above grade-level expectations. Advanced readers meet with the teacher two times per week for small-group instruction; therefore, the majority of their reading is done independently.

### *Additional Support Personnel*

Historically, there has not been much supplemental support for readers who are performing below grade level in middle school. This exemplifies the need for small-group differentiated instruction in the language/communication arts block. At-risk students need to have some form of additional reading intervention. The support teacher (e.g., reading specialist/coach or special education, English as a second language, or Title I teacher) can use the small-group model as part of the daily intervention program. We have found that many intervention programs for struggling readers consist of a computer program or "homework help," neither of which assists students in becoming better readers.

### *Whole-Group Instruction in the Middle School Language/ Communication Arts Block*

Clearly, there is a need for whole-group instruction in the middle school language/communication arts block. When you consider the Common Core Standards and realize what the students are required to learn and be able to do independently, it becomes clear that teachers must use their time wisely. Again, our goal is to help teachers do just that.

We are very mindful of the time constraints and curricular mandates in the middle school classroom. As such, we have provided a sample schedule that breaks down the 90-minute block (see Figure 34). You will see that during this time frame, the teacher needs to provide exposure to the information that directly supports the appropriate grade-level standards. This includes knowledge of both information related to reading (e.g., text structure, elements of narrative and informational text) and information related to writing (e.g., writing process, types and purposes of writing, grammatical structure).

# Conclusion

Effectively managing small-group and whole-group instruction, along with independent reading activities, is not a task that should be taken lightly. In fact, this is a pivotal point in which a teacher can make the difference between the successful transformation of readers and status quo reading ability. Striking a balance between small-group, whole-group, and independent extension activities is crucial to the management of the total reading program. Embracing changes in instructional practices takes time, patience, and an understanding of the change process itself. However, the reward of more proficient readers far outweighs the effort needed to make these changes a reality.

# Assessing Student Performance in the Small-Group Differentiated Reading Models

Assessing student performance is critical for many reasons, including tracking student progress, assigning students to flexible groups based on individual need, and assisting in planning appropriate instruction. Assessing student performance in the Small-Group Differentiated Reading Models consists of several informal measures. Although we recognize the importance of formal, standardized, state-level assessments, they do not provide the quality of information necessary to guide a teacher's daily instruction. In many instances, the standardized assessment results are not available until the following school year after the students have matriculated to the next grade. Therefore, teachers cannot use the information as an instructional tool.

Prior to beginning small-group differentiated reading instruction, it is essential to assess the literacy knowledge of each student as it relates to fluency, word study, and comprehension. Using the assessment data, flexible small groups are established based on student needs in these areas. Flexible grouping refers to the teacher's ability to move students into and out of groups as needed. Assessment should be ongoing to ensure that students' instructional needs continue to be met. In our experience, the most powerful assessment data for intermediate readers come from daily teacher observation and interaction with the students within the small-group setting.

There are two types of assessments that will be used in the Small-Group Differentiated Reading Models: (1) pre- and postassessments and (2) ongoing, or formative, assessments. Pre- and postassessment data give the teacher information about overall reading progress and provide instructional reading levels. Ongoing assessments guide teachers in their daily instructional decisions.

The pre- and postassessments for fluency are designed to be completed every nine weeks or at the end of each quarter. In word study, the pre- and postassessments should be completed at the beginning and end of the year. For postcomprehension assessment, we recommend the use of an informal reading inventory. (See Table 10 for a brief description of these assessments and timelines for administering them.)

Ongoing assessments give teachers data to make sound, instructional decisions related to the instructional components that are administered on a continual basis. Teachers should use this formative assessment information to create flexible groups. In other words, if a student is performing above or below others in his or her small

**TABLE 10**
**Pre- and Postassessments Versus Ongoing Assessments for Intermediate Readers**

| Assessment | Fluency | Word Study | Comprehension |
|---|---|---|---|
| Pre- and post- | • 4 × 4 Oral Reading Fluency Rating Scale (available in the Assessment Materials section on the CD)<br>• Every nine weeks | • Cumulative spelling assessment<br>• Beginning and end of the year | • Informal reading inventory with narrative and informational passages (Student reads orally and silently.)<br>• Assess ability to summarize (retell) and answer different question types (literal, inferential, and application)<br>• At least two times per year (beginning and end) |
| Ongoing | • Teacher observation<br>• Weekly | • Weekly<br>• Per cycle (every eight weeks) | • Teacher observation<br>• Narrative text assessments<br>• Informational comprehension assessments<br>• Oral Questioning Response Checklist (available in the Assessment Materials section on the CD)<br>• Rubrics for written comprehension |

*Note.* Modified from *Small-Group Reading Instruction: A Differentiated Teaching Model for Intermediate Readers, Grades 3–8* (p. 99), by B. Tyner and S.E. Green, 2005, Newark, DE: International Reading Association. Copyright 2005 by the International Reading Association.

group, the teacher can identify another small group in the class that will be a better instructional fit.

This chapter provides ongoing assessment information for fluency, word study, and comprehension. We examine appropriate informal assessments that measure a student's instructional reading level along with specific aspects of oral and written comprehension. These aspects include a student's ability to summarize information, answer and create different types of comprehension questions, and demonstrate critical insight through oral and written responses. Note that there are no clearly delineated scores that teachers can use to move students from group to group. Rather, a teacher needs to analyze all available assessment data, including day-to-day observations in small-group instruction. These day-to-day observation data are critical when evaluating the placement of students in flexible groups.

# Fluency Assessment

Fluency assessment is a critical component of the small-group reading models. This is especially important for intervention and evolving readers. Informal measures that are both quantitative (i.e., providing numeric results) and qualitative (i.e., providing information about student behaviors) are helpful in assessing fluency. We discuss fluency assessment in the areas of rate (WPM), accuracy, phrasing, punctuation, and expression. Fluency progress is documented through pre- and postassessments as well as ongoing assessments. Although fluency is not part of the maturing or advanced lesson plans, it should be assessed using the pre- and postassessments to monitor student progress because fluency continues to play an important role in reading comprehension. The ongoing assessments for fluency are only applicable for the intervention and evolving readers.

## Pre- and Postassessment

Although reading fluency relates to both oral and silent reading, only oral reading fluency is assessed as it relates to this small-group model. Silent reading fluency becomes more important as students matriculate through the grades and is best assessed as it relates to comprehension, as discussed later in this chapter.

### Rate and Accuracy

A student's reading rate is assessed by determining the number of CWPM. It is used as the pre- and postassessment to gauge fluency progress.

Reading rate is reported most often in WPM. The following steps are necessary to accurately determine a student's reading rate:

1. Count the actual number of words in the text selection (no less than 150 words).
2. Multiply the number of words by 60.
3. Ask the student to read the appropriate instructional-level passage.
4. Time the student's reading of the passage in seconds (e.g., 120 seconds).
5. Divide the words read per minute by the number of seconds to get the WPM.

> **WPM Example**
>
> Number of words in the passage: 250
> Multiply by 60: $250 \times 60 = 15{,}000$
> Number of seconds to read the passage: 100
> Divide 15,000 by 100
> WPM = 150

To determine the CWPM, simply subtract the number of errors from the number of words read.

> **CWPM Example**
>
> Number of words in passage: 250
> Student errors: 10
> Number of words read correctly: $250 - 10 = 240$
> Multiply by 60: $240 \times 60 = 14{,}400$
> Number of seconds to read passage: 100
> Divide 14,400 by 100
> CWPM = 144

The next step is to determine which oral reading rates are acceptable for various grade levels. Although there are a number of studies that have established norms, Table 11 is based on large-scale norms for students in grades 3–5. Hasbrouck and Tindal (1992) normed over 7,000 students reading CWPM at three points (fall, winter, and spring) during the school year. (Note that CWPM will vary slightly from WPM in that the CWPM will typically be lower than WPM.) Table 11 also gives percentile information that will be helpful in tracking student progress. These norms were established regardless of a student's instructional reading level; thus, they gauge a student's ability to read at a particular grade level. For example, if you have a fourth grader whose instructional reading level is grade 3, you need to look at the grade 3 oral reading rates.

Oral reading rates for students in grades 6–8 are presented in Table 12. These norms were established for more than 3,500 students in a study conducted by Howe

**TABLE 11**
**Median Oral Reading Rates for Students in Grades 3–5**

| Grade | Percentile | Fall CWPM | Winter CWPM | Spring CWPM |
|-------|-----------|-----------|-------------|-------------|
|       | 75        | 107       | 123         | 142         |
| 3     | 50        | 79        | 93          | 114         |
|       | 25        | 65        | 70          | 87          |
|       | 75        | 125       | 133         | 143         |
| 4     | 50        | 99        | 112         | 118         |
|       | 25        | 72        | 89          | 92          |
|       | 75        | 126       | 143         | 151         |
| 5     | 50        | 105       | 118         | 128         |
|       | 25        | 77        | 93          | 100         |

*Note.* CWPM = correct words per minute. The data is from "Curriculum-Based Oral Reading Fluency Norms for Students in Grades 2 Through 5," by J.E. Hasbrouck and G. Tindal, 1992, *Teaching Exceptional Children, 24*(3), 41–44. Modified from *Small-Group Reading Instruction: A Differentiated Teaching Model for Intermediate Readers, Grades 3–8* (p. 101), by B. Tyner and S.E. Green, 2005, Newark, DE: International Reading Association. Copyright 2005 by the International Reading Association.

**TABLE 12**
**Median Oral Reading Rates for Students in Grades 6–8**

| Grade | Percentile | Fall CWPM | Winter CWPM | Spring CWPM |
|-------|-----------|-----------|-------------|-------------|
|       | 90        | 171       | 185         | 201         |
|       | 75        | 143       | 160         | 172         |
| 6     | 50        | 115       | 132         | 145         |
|       | 25        | 91        | 106         | 117         |
|       | 10        | 73        | 81          | 90          |
|       | 90        | 200       | 207         | 213         |
|       | 75        | 175       | 183         | 193         |
| 7     | 50        | 147       | 158         | 167         |
|       | 25        | 126       | 134         | 146         |
|       | 10        | 106       | 116         | 124         |
|       | 90        | 208       | 217         | 221         |
|       | 75        | 183       | 196         | 198         |
| 8     | 50        | 156       | 167         | 171         |
|       | 25        | 126       | 144         | 145         |
|       | 10        | 100       | 113         | 115         |

*Note.* CWPM = correct words per minute. The data is from *Standard Reading Assessment Passages (RAPs) for Use in General Outcome Measurement: A Manual Describing Development and Technical Features,* by K.B. Howe and M.M. Shinn, 2002, Eden Prairie, MN: Edformation. Modified from *Small-Group Reading Instruction: A Differentiated Teaching Model for Intermediate Readers, Grades 3–8* (p. 101), by B. Tyner and S.E. Green, 2005, Newark, DE: International Reading Association. Copyright 2005 by the International Reading Association.

and Shinn (2002). Again, these norms were established using CWPM and provide percentiles for three points during the school year (fall, winter, and spring). These norms can be used to monitor student progress in fluency development or compared with standard measures established by the school district. For students in these grades, please remember that fluency is only one indicator of reading progress. For example, if you have a student who falls below the 50th percentile for fluency, but all other assessment data show that the student comprehends grade-level material, fluency should not be a focus for instruction. Clearly, the student understands the information, and that is the most important thing.

### *Phrasing, Punctuation, and Expression*

In addition to quantitative data, a 4 × 4 Oral Reading Fluency Rating Scale (see the Assessment Materials section on the CD  ) should be used to assess qualitative skills in oral reading fluency. These skills include appropriate phrasing, attention to punctuation, smoothness, and expression. This instrument is a pre- and postassessment as students read an instructional-level passage individually. The teacher marks the rating scale in each of the four areas as he or she listens to the student read. The 4 × 4 Oral Reading Fluency Rating Scale is structured so that quarterly data can be recorded on the same sheet.

## Ongoing Assessment

Ongoing fluency assessment for intervention and evolving readers can be assessed easily in daily small-group instruction. Ongoing assessment data are collected on a weekly basis by making informal anecdotal notes during small-group reading instruction.

While listening to students read orally, the teacher makes notes concerning the qualitative fluency skills, such as those listed on the 4 × 4 Oral Reading Fluency Rating Scale. This gives the teacher a snapshot of the student's progress in fluency to supplement the pre- and postassessment data.

## Tracking Progress

Teachers can use an Oral Reading Fluency Class Profile (see the Assessment Materials section on the CD for separate profiles for grades 3–8) to record and track student fluency at established points during the school year. First- and fourth-quarter results can serve as the pre- and postassessments. For students performing at the intervention or evolving levels, a teacher may also choose to administer midyear or quarterly assessments. Oral reading fluency class profiles that are specific to each grade level provide median scores at three points during the school year so that the teacher can easily identify students who might need extra fluency practice and support.

Figure 35 displays the Oral Reading Fluency Class Profile for Mrs. Harmon's fifth-grade class. Mrs. Harmon plans to assess fluency in her classroom three times during the school year. Thus far, she has completed the fluency assessments for fall and winter. Notice that the median fluency rate is shown on each of the three scales. In the fall, nine of the students in the classroom scored below the median fluency rate of 105, although four of these students were close to the median and scored in the 90–100 range. Using this information, Mrs. Harmon supported her students with repeated readings of independent-leveled texts and additional oral reading practice, for which she gave specific feedback. Notice that the scores for the winter assessment show three additional students reaching grade-level scores on oral reading fluency.

# Word Study Assessment

Word study is assessed easily by administering and analyzing an informal word study assessment. The word study assessments can be used as pre- and postassessments and ongoing assessments. Pre- and postassessments should be given at the beginning and end of the year. Ongoing assessments should be administered weekly and again at the end of each cycle. Cycles typically last eight weeks each. Each of the eight weeks contains different features for study and corresponding word lists. If students are unable to achieve at least 90% on their weekly spelling assessment and 80% on their cycle assessment, teachers should spend more time teaching the given feature(s). Mastery is critical because the scope and sequence for word study is organized in such a way that the identified features build on one another.

## Pre- and Postassessment

Teachers first should administer the appropriate word study pretest to determine the specific strengths and areas of need for each student in the class (see the Assessment Materials section on the CD  for the word study pre- and postassessments). For students in grades 3 and 4, administer the evolving reader pretest. For students in grades 5 and 6, administer the maturing reader pretest. As discussed earlier, advanced readers do not participate in postassessment because the focus of their instruction is on meaning rather than word features.

When administering an assessment, have students first number their papers from 1 to 32, similar to a weekly spelling test. Read each word on the pre- and posttest lists in the following manner: Read the word, use the word in a sentence, and then read the word again. For example, "*Skipping.* The boy was so excited that he was skipping to school. *Skipping.*"

To score the pre- and postassessments, determine the score for each cycle area. To determine the cycle score, add the number of incorrect words within a given cycle. Then, use this score to determine a starting point of cycle instruction. A student is allowed one

## FIGURE 35
### Oral Reading Fluency Class Profile for Mrs. Harmon's Grade 5 Class

| Fall | | Winter | | Spring | |
|---|---|---|---|---|---|
| -180- | Laura (178) | -180- | Laura & Paul (180+) | -180- | |
| | Paul (175) | | | | |
| -170- | | -170- | Pedro (172) | -170- | |
| | | | ShaDerrika (161) | | |
| -160- | Pedro (160) | -160- | Jenae (160) | -160- | |
| | Jenae (154) | | | | |
| -150- | ShaDerrika (150) | -150- | Mark (150) | -150- | |
| | | | Adrien (145) | | |
| -140- | Mark (140) | -140- | Leuel (140) | -140- | |
| | Adrien (138) | | | | |
| -130- | Leuel (128) | -130- | Rodney (129) | -130- ←——→ (128) | |
| | Andre (120) | | Anna (125) | | |
| | | | Andre (125) | | |
| -120- | Rodney (119) | -120- | Jennifer (120) | -120- | |
| | | (118) ←——→ | Mason (120) | | |
| | | | Bill (119) | | |
| | Bill (114) | | John (118) | | |
| -110- | Lee (107) | -110- | Lee (115) | -110- | |
| (105) ←——→ | Mason (105) | | | | |
| -100- | Jennifer (100) | -100- | Michael (100) | -100- | |
| | John (96) | | Meredith (95) | | |
| -90- | Anna (95) | -90- | | -90 | |
| | Michael (90) | | | | |
| -80- | Meredith (83) | -80- | Spencer (82) | -80- | |
| | Spencer (78) | | Clyde (75) | | |
| -70- | | -70 | Dedrick (70) | -70- | |
| | Clyde (67) | | | | |
| -60- | Dedrick (60) | -60- | Pat (61) | -60- | |
| -50- | Pat (50) | -50- | | -50- | |
| -40- | | -40- | | -40- | |
| -30- | | -30- | | -30- | |
| -20- | | -20- | | -20- | |

Date: _____     Date: _____     Date: _____

Passage: _____     Passage: _____     Passage: _____

_____     _____     _____

_____     _____     _____

Comments: _____     Comments: _____     Comments: _____

_____     _____     _____

_____     _____     _____

*Note.* The arrows indicate the expected median fluency rate for this grade. Modified from *Small-Group Reading Instruction: A Differentiated Teaching Model for Intermediate Readers, Grades 3–8* (p. 103), by B. Tyner and S.E. Green, 2005, Newark, DE: International Reading Association. Copyright 2005 by the International Reading Association.

error per cycle. When a student makes two or more errors in a given cycle, this becomes the starting place for instruction. For example, in Figure 36, during the evolving reader year 2 preassessment, the student made one error in cycle 1, two errors in cycle 2, four errors in cycle 3, and three errors in cycle 4. Based on the student's errors, instruction should begin in week 1 of cycle 2. If a student has less than two errors per cycle on any given pretest, the teacher should administer the assessment for the next stage. For example, if a student spells all of the words on the evolving reader year 2 preassessment correctly, give the student the maturing reader year 1 preassessment.

## Qualifying for Intervention

For those students who score 50% or below on the evolving reader year 1 pretest, teachers should administer the intervention level 1 word study assessment. Refer to Chapter 3 for step-by-step instructions for determining the appropriate intervention level. Keep in mind that you will need to look at your classroom needs and realize that all students may not fit neatly into a particular group. As such, you will need to make the best instructional grouping decisions based on the data for your students.

## Ongoing Assessment

There are different types of ongoing assessments for different stages of readers. The first is a weekly assessment developed by the teacher. Using this weekly spelling assessment, a teacher will be able to identify whether the students have mastered the features studied in a given week and are ready to move forward. Part of the weekly spelling assessment should include an assessment of word meanings. We need to be aware of the importance of understanding as well as spelling. For example, teachers can ask students to define the words or use specific words in sentences to demonstrate meaning. Note that for advanced readers, this weekly assessment should be a vocabulary/meaning-based assessment.

The second ongoing assessment is the eight-week cycle assessment (see the Assessment Materials section on the CD 🔘 ). This assessment is given at the end of each cycle and will provide data that will allow a teacher to determine if students have internalized previous features studied. Administration for both ongoing assessments is the same as the pre- and postassessment instructions: Read the word, read the sentence provided, and then read the word again. Cycle assessments for advanced readers are vocabulary assessments that include Greek and Latin root words studied.

To score the ongoing assessments, determine the score based on a percentage. To determine this percentage, add the total number of correct words and divide by the number of test items. In the example in Figure 37, the student scored 88%. This score shows that the student is ready to move on; however, a further analysis of his errors shows that he would benefit from some additional work with doubling the consonant when adding suffixes. Therefore, the teacher should be sure to include a discussion of these features as he or she continues the word study sequence.

# FIGURE 36
## Sample Spelling Preassessment for an Evolving Reader in Year 2

Name: Mary H.

Date: August 20, 2011

Stage: Evolving

Year (circle one): 1 ②

Assessment (circle one): (Pre) Post

|  | Word | Student Spelling | Errors |
|---|---|---|---|
| 1 | bridge | bridge | |
| 2 | sailor | sailer | X |
| 3 | diminish | diminish | |
| 4 | furnish | furnish | |
| 5 | due | due | |
| 6 | shrank | shrank | |
| 7 | midfield | midfield | |
| 8 | intersect | intersect | |
| | Cycle 1 | | Number of Errors: 1 |
| 9 | antifreeze | antefreeze | X |
| 10 | promote | promote | |
| 11 | fragile | fragile | |
| 12 | safety | safty | X |
| 13 | punish | punish | |
| 14 | orchard | orchard | |
| 15 | elbow | elbow | |
| 16 | telegraph | telegraph | |
| | Cycle 2 | | Number of Errors: 2 |
| 17 | dictionary | dictionary | |
| 18 | beautiful | buootiful | X |
| 19 | satisfy | satisfy | |
| 20 | rotten | rotton | X |
| 21 | semicircle | semecircle | X |
| 22 | reproduce | reproduce | |
| 23 | preview | preview | |
| 24 | decompose | dicompose | X |
| | Cycle 3 | | Number of Errors: 4 |
| 25 | overcast | overcast | |
| 26 | medal | medal | |
| 27 | there's | there's | |
| 28 | employee | imployee | X |
| 29 | harmful | harmfull | X |
| 30 | monorail | monoraill | X |
| 31 | triangle | triangle | |
| 32 | knowledge | knowledge | |
| | Cycle 4 | | Number of Errors: 3 |
| | | Total Number of Errors: 10 Score (% correct): 67 | |

*Note.* Modified from *Small-Group Reading Instruction: A Differentiated Teaching Model for Intermediate Readers, Grades 3–8* (p. 138), by B. Tyner and S.E. Green, 2005, Newark, DE: International Reading Association. © 2005 by the International Reading Association.

# FIGURE 37
## Sample Ongoing Spelling Cycle Assessment for an Evolving Reader

Name: Thomas T.

Date: November 2, 2011

Stage: Evolving

Year (circle one):   ① 2

Cycle (circle one):   ① 2 3 4

| | Word | Student Spelling | Errors |
|---|---|---|---|
| 1 | trains | trains | |
| 2 | dishes | dishes | |
| 3 | carries | carries | |
| 4 | boys' | boys' | |
| 5 | walked | walkt | X |
| 6 | baked | baked | |
| 7 | treated | treated | |
| 8 | shouldn't | shouldn't | |
| 9 | she'll | sh'ell | X |
| 10 | they've | they've | |
| 11 | mistake | mistake | |
| 12 | unpack | unpack | |
| 13 | disable | disable | |
| 14 | downsize | downsize | |
| 15 | upturn | upturn | |
| 16 | shouting | shouting | |
| 17 | sobbing | sobbing | |
| 18 | shaping | shaping | |
| 19 | unwrap | unwrap | |
| 20 | misspell | misspell | |
| 21 | tracked | tracked | |
| 22 | ponies | ponies | |
| 23 | puffing | puffing | |
| 24 | babies | babies | |
| 25 | kitten's | kittin's | X |
| Total Number of Errors: 3<br>Score (% correct): 88% | | | |

*Note.* Modified from *Small-Group Reading Instruction: A Differentiated Teaching Model for Intermediate Readers, Grades 3–8* (p. 106), by B. Tyner and S.E. Green, 2005, Newark, DE: International Reading Association. © 2005 by the International Reading Association.

# Comprehension

Comprehension is the most challenging aspect of reading to assess, yet it is also the most important. If students are experiencing difficulty with comprehending a given text, the teacher needs to figure out where their comprehension is breaking down so that he or she will be able to tailor instruction to best meet their needs. We have included information on pre- and posttesting and ongoing comprehension assessments, which are all necessary for making effective instructional decisions.

## Pre- and Postassessments

An informal reading inventory is by far the most effective tool available to gauge a student's instructional reading level. This individualized assessment is used not only to determine reading level but also to provide quality information about how a student comprehends a given text. Informal reading inventories comprise a series of leveled passages (both narrative and content area informational) that typically begin at a pre-primer level and progressively become more difficult. Each inventory that we review in this section contains assessment for word recognition in isolation, word recognition in context, retelling, and comprehension questions. These are essential components for determining a student's reading level. This reading level takes into account not only word recognition accuracy but also understanding of a given passage.

The information gleaned from an informal reading inventory can be used to monitor progress over time. Specifically, the information provides the teacher with critical baseline and end-of-year data to show gains in reading ability. In this current age of teacher accountability, teachers need accurate, usable information. They need to be able to show where the students began and ended the year in reading. In other words, teachers need to show what impact their instruction had on the students' gain.

In the Small-Group Differentiated Reading Models, we use an informal reading inventory to make initial placements in reading groups and monitor yearly progress. In our experience, any informal reading inventory is quite lengthy, some taking several hours to administer. Therefore, we recommend that the following specific components be used to gauge an instructional reading level and provide in-depth comprehension data:

- Word recognition in isolation
- Word recognition in context
- Retelling
- Comprehension questions (literal, inferential, and application)

There are many commercial informal reading inventories available. The results from any given inventory are fairly comparable. However, we believe in consistency. Teachers need to give the same assessment at the beginning, middle (if applicable), and end of the year. If an entire district is tracking students' progress through an informal reading inventory, then the entire district needs to administer the same assessment.

The following informal reading inventories are widely used and respected in the reading community.

## Analytical Reading Inventory: Comprehensive Standards-Based Assessment for All Students Including Gifted and Remedial *(Woods & Moe, 2011)*

Key features include the following:

- Texts to determine students' independent, instructional, and frustration levels for narrative and informational passages (preprimer to grade 12)
- Word recognition in isolation
- Word recognition in context ability (miscue analysis)
- Assessment of different question types (literal, inferential, and application)
- Fluency rating scale
- Student predictions, prior knowledge, and retelling abilities
- Emotional status report
- Interest inventory/reading survey
- Silent and listening comprehension assessment
- A booklet of reading passages and a CD

The key features needed for small-group assessment include the following:

- Narrative and informational passages with accuracy rates and comprehension questions
- Word recognition in isolation (best indicator of a student's reading level)
- Retelling ability in instructional passages (summarizing)
- Assessment of different question types (literal, inferential, and application)

## Qualitative Reading Inventory–5 *(Leslie & Caldwell, 2011)*

Key features include the following:

- Texts to determine students' independent, instructional, and frustration levels for narrative and informational passages (preprimer to high school)
- Word recognition in isolation
- Word recognition in context ability (miscue analysis)
- Assessment of different question types (explicit and implicit)
- Student predictions, prior knowledge, and retelling abilities
- Silent and listening comprehension assessment

The key features needed for small-group assessment include the following:

- Narrative and informational passages with accuracy rates and comprehension questions

- Word recognition in isolation
- Retelling ability in instructional passages (summarizing)
- Assessment of different question types (explicit and implicit)

### Informal Reading Inventory: Preprimer to Twelfth Grade *(Roe & Burns, 2007)*

Key features include the following:

- Texts to determine students' independent, instructional, and frustration levels for narrative and informational passages (preprimer to grade 12)
- Word recognition in isolation
- Word recognition in context ability (miscue analysis)
- Assessment of different question types (main idea, detail, inference, sequence, cause and effect, vocabulary)
- Silent and listening comprehension assessment

Key features needed for small-group assessment include the following:

- Narrative and informational passages with accuracy rates and comprehension questions
- Word recognition in isolation
- Assessment of different question types (main idea, detail, inference, sequence, cause and effect, vocabulary)

## Ongoing Assessment

Ongoing assessments are those given by the teacher in response to the text selections read in the small group. Teacher observation is invaluable when students are seen in small groups on a regular basis. This observation provides the teacher with current information regarding the authentic ability of a student to process and understand text. This information is helpful, particularly when determining students' report card grades. We provide samples of what these data collection tools might look like with regard to in-group and extension activities (see the rubrics in the Assessment Materials section on the CD 🔘 ). Whatever the teacher decides to use to monitor student achievement, it must be easy to implement and manage. Most important, the tool must provide useful data.

## In-Group Assessments

The assessments used within small-group sessions are primarily of oral responses. Thus, the following tools are examples of such. Anecdotal notes are vital to track students' progress as they are engaged in informal comprehension conversations. These notes are particularly helpful in assisting the teacher with further instructional needs.

**Oral Questioning Response Checklist:** This simple checklist (see the Assessment Materials section on the CD ) allows the teacher to track the types of questions that he or she is asking as well as whether students are able to answer the questions correctly. The types of questions that students will ask and respond to will vary depending on the type of text. Students should be encouraged to participate in all levels of questioning and text types.

**Comprehension Reflection:** This is a teacher-created tool to be used with both text types that allows teachers to record and track their anecdotal notes. Teachers can choose to use this during or after their small-group instruction as a reflection of student responses as they relate to comprehending the text. Teachers could use the lesson plan to record this information and can use the information gleaned to plan follow-up instruction.

## Assessment of Extension Activities

Intermediate readers need to have the opportunity to write in-depth responses to text to demonstrate understanding. The written comprehension responses allow a teacher to critically analyze a student's insight of a particular text. As demonstrated by the lessons in this book, written extension activities need to be adapted to the comprehension goals of the lesson. We are not simply talking about reader response journals; intermediate readers need higher-level writing experiences.

Students will be asked to do an assortment of written extension activities. A teacher can decide between those that should be formally assessed (using a rubric) and those that should be informally reviewed or shared with the group. We provided some examples of rubrics that can be used with particular written comprehension extensions. We encourage teachers to create their own assessments based on their comprehension goals. You will notice that our example rubrics all contain spelling and grammar criteria. Intermediate readers need to be held accountable for the quality of their thoughts as well as their finished products.

Table 13 is an example of the rubric developed for the Inquiry Chart extension activity (Maturing Reader Informational Lesson Plan). Other examples of rubrics are provided in the Assessment Materials section on the CD .

**Written Questioning Response Sheet:** This sheet, which teachers can create by reserving the top portion of a sheet of paper for their questions and the bottom portion for student responses, can be used in conjunction with any text as an assessment of a student's level of understanding. Following the reading of a text, the teacher creates a question at each level (literal, inferential, and application) and asks for a written response from each student. Students also are responsible for identifying the question type.

## Informational Comprehension Assessments

These assessments (see the Assessment Materials section on the CD ) monitor a student's ability to identify the major elements of informational text. After the students

**TABLE 13**
**Inquiry Chart Extension Activity Rubric**

| Criteria | Exceeds Expectations (3 points) | Meets Expectations (1 or 2 points) | Below Expectations (0 points) | Points |
|---|---|---|---|---|
| Ideas/content | • Questions and/or ideas are clearly defined.<br>• At least four questions and/or ideas are listed. | • Questions and/or ideas are adequately defined.<br>• At least three questions and/or ideas are listed. | • Questions and/or ideas are unclear and/or fewer than three are listed. | |
| Sources | • Student researched and located outstanding sources.<br>• Sources are cited correctly. | • Student researched and located appropriate sources.<br>• At least three sources are cited correctly. | • Student researched and located only two appropriate sources.<br>• Fewer than three sources are cited correctly. | |
| Demonstrates skill in writing mechanics | • There are no writing/mechanics errors (spelling, grammar, typos, etc.). | • There are one to three writing/mechanics errors (spelling, grammar, typos, etc.). | • There are four or more writing/mechanics errors (spelling, grammar, typos, etc.). | |
| | | | Total Points: | |

complete one of the element assessments (cause and effect, sequencing, compare and contrast, main idea and supporting details), the teacher uses the rubric on the bottom of the assessment to evaluate the student's ability. These lower level assessments are most appropriate for evolving and intervention readers.

Using the information gathered from assessment data, teachers can plan small-group instruction more effectively. As mentioned previously, this information helps teachers make decisions about students' placement in flexible groups.

# Conclusion

The importance of assessment cannot be overlooked in the Small-Group Differentiated Reading Models. Pre- and postassessments as well as ongoing assessments are necessary to track students' progress accurately. Not only is the information used to flexibly group students, but also it can be useful in determining students' grades. The reading skills that are assessed directly correlate with the knowledge that the students need to know as outlined in the Common Core Standards. The manner in which teachers analyze the assessment results should be the framework for their instructional plan. The success of any reading program rests on the validity, reliability, and systematic use of assessment data.

# CONCLUSION

Teaching students how to become more proficient readers in the intermediate grades is not an easy feat. The diversity in the levels of readers in any intermediate classroom is the cornerstone of teachers' challenges. Intermediate students require a teacher who recognizes their individual strengths and areas of need and can effectively plan instruction that will meet those needs. We cannot make the mistake of thinking that just because many intermediate students can decode, they can comprehend as well. As students continue to develop and refine their critical reading skills, their teachers need to be skilled in all aspects of literacy. Differentiated reading instruction must become the standard if we are going to provide the opportunity for all students to reach their potential.

Students who enter the intermediate grades with deficits in reading face unique challenges, not only in language arts but also in every other content area. Reading is the centerpiece for learning across the curriculum. Foundational reading knowledge that relates to fluency, word study, vocabulary, and comprehension must be learned and mastered during the intermediate grades. In most instances, this is the last chance for students to participate in focused reading instruction. As students matriculate to high school and college, their success depends on their critical literacy competence, which must be built during the intermediate grades.

Struggling readers must be provided with specific instruction that will increase their overall reading ability as they face higher standards. Additionally, proficient readers need this instruction as well. The goal is for all students to receive instruction that addresses their individual literacy needs in order to make the most of their reading potential. Whole-class instruction alone does not provide the scaffolding that is essential to the development of good readers. Striking a balance between whole-class and small-group instruction allows all students the opportunity to maximize their learning. Differentiated reading instruction geared to the needs of all readers is no longer a luxury in the age of the Common Core Standards, high-stakes assessments, and teacher accountability: It is now imperative.

Many teachers of the intermediate grades readily admit that they are overwhelmed by the curricular mandates established by the district, state, and now the Common Core Standards. Unfortunately, without solid instructional reading practices in place, students and teachers will continue to fall short of these goals. All intermediate teachers must become teachers of reading—that is, knowledgeable about the reading process and assessments that they can use to guide their instruction. Further, these teachers need to know how to effectively implement the research-based strategies and extension activities that will best help their students at any given time.

Today, we know a great deal about teaching reading. We know what works and how to make it happen in a classroom. Our hope is that this new edition will continue to be a tool that teachers use to build their knowledge base, apply this knowledge in a variety of classroom situations, and meet the required standards.

Reading practices for students in the 21st century need to meet the demands of an incredibly fast-moving society. Literacy skills are necessary for the survival of each individual. Although we know that the job of an intermediate teacher can be underappreciated and daunting at times, we have seen incredible teachers who do not let the negatives overshadow their dedication to their profession and their excitement about their students' literacy gains. These are the teachers who are committed to making a difference for all of their students. These teachers are our role models as we seek to continually increase our knowledge and improve our pedagogy.

# REFERENCES

Allington, R.L. (1983). Fluency: The neglected reading goal. *The Reading Teacher, 36*(6), 556–561.

Armbruster, B.B., Anderson, T.H., & Ostertag, J. (1989). Teaching text structure to improve reading and writing. *The Reading Teacher, 43*(2), 130–137.

Armbruster, B.B., Lehr, F., & Osborn, J. (2001). *Put reading first: The research building blocks for teaching children to read: Kindergarten through grade 3*. Rockville, MD: The Partnership for Reading.

Atwell, N. (1998). *In the middle: New understandings about writing, reading, and learning* (2nd ed.). Portsmouth, NH: Boynton/Cook.

Bashir, A.S., & Hook, P.E. (2009). Fluency: A key link between word identification and comprehension. *Language, Speech, and Hearing Services in Schools, 40*(2), 196–200.

Bear, D.R. (1989). Why beginning reading must be word-by-word: Disfluent oral reading and orthographic development. *Visible Language, 23*(4), 353–367.

Bear, D.R. (1991). "Learning to fasten the seat of my union suit without looking around": The synchrony of literacy development. *Theory Into Practice, 30*(3), 149–157. doi:10.1080/004058491095

Bear, D.R., Invernizzi, M., Templeton, S., & Johnston, F. (2007). *Words their way: Word study for phonics, vocabulary, and spelling instruction* (4th ed.). Boston: Allyn & Bacon.

Beaver, J., & Carter, M.A. (2005). *Developmental reading assessment: Kindergarten through grade 3* (2nd ed.). Upper Saddle River, NJ: Pearson.

Beck, I.L., McKeown, M.G., McCaslin, E.S., & Burkes, A.M. (1979). *Instructional dimensions that may affect reading comprehension: Examples from two commercial reading programs*. Pittsburgh, PA: Language Research and Development Center, University of Pittsburgh.

Blachowicz, C.L.Z., & Fisher, P. (2000). Vocabulary instruction. In M.L. Kamil, P.B. Mosenthal, P.D. Pearson, & R. Barr (Eds.), *Handbook of reading research* (Vol. 3, pp. 503–523). Mahwah, NJ: Erlbaum.

Bloodgood, J.W. (1991). A new approach to spelling instruction in language arts programs. *The Elementary School Journal, 92*(2), 203–211.

Bloom, B.S. (Ed.). (1956). *Taxonomy of educational objectives: The classification of educational goals*. New York: Longman.

Carver, R.P. (1990). *Reading rate: A review of research and theory*. San Diego, CA: Academic.

Chall, J.S. (1979). The great debate: Ten years later, with a modest proposal for reading stages. In L.B. Resnick & P.A. Weaver (Eds.), *Theory and practice of early reading* (pp. 29–55). Hillsdale, NJ: Erlbaum.

Chall, J.S. (1983). *Stages of reading development*. New York: McGraw-Hill.

Chall, J.S. (1987). Developing literacy...in children and adults. In D.A. Wagner (Ed.), *The future of literacy in a changing world* (pp. 65–80). New York: Pergamon.

Cohen, R. (1983). Self-generated questions as an aid to reading comprehension. *The Reading Teacher, 36*(8), 770–775.

Cramer, R.L. (2001). *Creative power: The nature and nurture of children's writing*. New York: Longman.

Cudd, E.T., & Roberts, L.L. (1987). Using story frames to develop reading comprehension in a 1st grade classroom. *The Reading Teacher, 41*(1), 74–79.

Daggett, W.R., & Gendron, S. (2010). *Common Core State Standards Initiative: Classroom implications for 2014*. Rexford, NY: International Center for Leadership in Education. Retrieved May 23, 2011, from nserve.wetpaint.com/page/The+Common+Core+State+Standards+Initiative

Daneman, M., & Reingold, E. (1993). What eye fixations tell us about phonological recoding during reading. *Canadian Journal of Experimental Psychology, 47*(2), 153–178. doi:10.1037/h0078818

Daniels, H. (1994). *Literature circles: Voice and choice in the student-centered classroom*. York, ME: Stenhouse.

Dowhower, S.L. (1991). Speaking of prosody: Fluency's unattended bedfellow. *Theory Into Practice, 30*(3), 165–175. doi:10.1080/00405849109543497

Dowhower, S.L. (1999). Supporting a strategic stance in the classroom: A comprehension framework for helping teachers help students to be strategic. *The Reading Teacher, 52*(7), 672–688.

Duke, N.K., & Pearson, P.D. (2002). Effective practices for developing reading comprehension. In A.E. Farstrup & S.J. Samuels (Eds.), *What research has to say about reading instruction* (3rd ed., pp. 205–242). Newark, DE: International Reading Association.

Fielding, L.G., & Pearson, P.D. (1994). Reading comprehension: What works. *Educational Leadership, 51*(5), 62–68.

Fountas, I.C., & Pinnell, G.S. (1996). *Guided reading: Good first teaching for all children.* Portsmouth, NH: Heinemann.

Fowler, G.L. (1982). Developing comprehension skills in primary students through the use of story frames. *The Reading Teacher, 36*(2), 176–179.

Ganske, K. (2000). *Word journeys: Assessment-guided phonics, spelling, and vocabulary instruction.* New York: Guilford.

Gill, J.T., Jr. (1992). Development of word knowledge as it relates to reading, spelling, and instruction. *Language Arts, 69*(6), 444–453.

Griffin, C.C., Malone, L.D., & Kame'enui, E.J. (1995). Effects of graphic organizer instruction on fifth-grade students. *Journal of Educational Research, 89*(2), 98–107.

Gunning, T.G. (2002). *Assessing and correcting reading and writing difficulties* (2nd ed.). Boston: Allyn & Bacon.

Guthrie, J.T. (2005, March). *Teaching for engagement: The pathway to reading comprehension.* Paper presented at the George Graham Lecture in Reading, University of Virginia, Charlottesville.

Hale, J.B. (2008). *Response to Intervention: Guidelines for parents and practitioners.* Retrieved May 23, 2011, from www.wrightslaw.com/idea/art/rti.hale.htm

Hasbrouck, J.E., & Tindal, G. (1992). Curriculum-based oral reading fluency norms for students in grades 2 through 5. *Teaching Exceptional Children, 24*(3), 41–44.

Hasbrouck, J.E., & Tindal, G.A. (2006). Oral reading fluency norms: A valuable assessment tool for reading teachers. *The Reading Teacher, 59*(7), 636–644.

Hechinger, J. (2010, December 7). U.S. teens lag as China soars on international test. *Bloomberg.* Retrieved May 23, 2011, from www.bloomberg.com/news/2010-12-07/teens-in-u-s-rank-25th-on-math-test-trail-in-science-reading.html

Henderson, E.H. (1990). *Teaching spelling* (2nd ed.). Boston: Houghton Mifflin.

Henderson, E.H., & Templeton, S. (1986). A developmental perspective of formal spelling instruction through alphabet, pattern, and meaning. *The Elementary School Journal, 86*(3), 304–316.

Hennings, D.G. (2000). Contextually relevant word study: Adolescent vocabulary development across the curriculum. *Journal of Adolescent & Adult Literacy, 44*(3), 268–279.

Hoffman, J.V. (1992). Critical reading/thinking across the curriculum: Using I-charts to support learning. *Language Arts, 69*(2), 121–127.

Hook, P.E., & Haynes, C.W. (2009). Reading and writing in child language disorders. In R.G. Schwartz (Ed.), *Handbook of child language disorders* (pp. 424–444). New York: Psychology.

Howe, K.B., & Shinn, M.M. (2002). *Standard reading assessment passages (RAPs) for use in general outcome measurement: A manual describing development and technical features.* Eden Prairie, MN: Edformation.

Invernizzi, M., Abouzeid, M., & Gill, J.T. (1994). Using students' invented spellings as a guide for spelling instruction that emphasizes word study. *The Elementary School Journal, 95*(2), 155–167.

Invernizzi, M., & Hayes, L. (2004). Developmental-spelling research: A systematic imperative. *Reading Research Quarterly, 39*(2), 216–228. doi:10.1598/RRQ.39.2.4

Johnston, F.R. (2000). Spelling exceptions: Problems or possibilities? *The Reading Teacher, 54*(4), 372–378.

Jones-Kavalier, B.R., & Flannigan, S.L. (2006). Connecting the digital dots: Literacy of the 21st century. *Educause Quarterly Magazine, 29*(2). Retrieved May 17, 2011, from www.educause.edu/EDUCAUSE+Quarterly/EDUCAUSEQuarterlyMagazineVolum/ConnectingtheDigitalDotsLitera/157395

Katzir, T., Kim, Y., Wolf, M., O'Brien, B., Kennedy, B., Lovett, M., et al. (2006). Reading fluency: The whole is more than the parts. *Annals of Dyslexia, 56*(1), 51–82.

Keene, E.O. (2002). From good to memorable: Characteristics of highly effective comprehension teaching. In C.C. Block, L.B. Gambrell, & M. Pressley (Eds.), *Improving comprehension instruction: Rethinking research, theory, and classroom practice* (pp. 80–105). San Francisco: Jossey-Bass; Newark, DE: International Reading Association.

LaBerge, D., & Samuels, S.J. (1974). Toward a theory of automatic information processing in reading. *Cognitive Psychology, 6*(2), 293–323. doi:10.1016/0010-0285(74)90015-2

Leslie, L., & Caldwell, J. (2011). *Qualitative reading inventory–5* (5th ed). Boston: Allyn & Bacon.

Menke, D.J., & Pressley, M. (1994). Elaborative interrogation: Using "why" questions to enhance the learning from text. *Journal of Reading, 37*(8), 642–645.

Merriam-Webster. (2000). *Webster's tenth new collegiate dictionary.* Springfield, MA: Author.

Meyer, M., & Felton, R. (1999). Repeated reading to enhance fluency: Old approaches and new directions. *Annals of Dyslexia, 49*(1), 283–306.

Moats, L.C. (2000). *Speech to print: Language essentials for teachers.* Baltimore: Paul H. Brookes.

Morris, D. (2005). *The Howard Street tutoring manual: Teaching at-risk readers in the primary grades* (2nd ed). New York: Guilford.

Morris, D., Tyner, B., & Perney, J. (2000). Early Steps: Replicating the effects of a first-grade reading intervention program. *Journal of Educational Psychology, 92*(4), 681–693. doi:10.1037/0022-0663.92.4.681

Morse, O. (2007). *SOAPSTone: A strategy for reading* and *writing.* Retrieved May 17, 2011, from apcentral.collegeboard.com/apc/public/preap/teachers_corner/45200.html

National Center for Education Statistics. (2010). *The nation's report card: Reading 2009: National Assessment of Educational Progress at grades 4 and 8.* Retrieved May 18, 2011, from nationsreportcard.gov/reading_2009/reading_2009_report/

National Governors Association Center for Best Practices & Council of Chief State School Officers. (2010a). *Common Core State Standards for English language arts and literacy in history/social studies, science, and technical subjects.* Retrieved May 18, 2011, from www.corestandards.org/assets/CCSSI_ELA%20Standards.pdf

National Governors Association Center for Best Practices & Council of Chief State School Officers. (2010b). *Common Core State Standards for English language arts and literacy in history/social studies, science, and technical subjects: Appendix A.* Retrieved May 18, 2011, from www.corestandards.org/assets/Appendix_A.pdf

National Governors Association Center for Best Practices & Council of Chief State School Officers. (2010c). *In the states.* Retrieved May 17, 2011, from www.corestandards.org/in-the-states

National Institute of Child Health and Human Development. (2000). *Report of the National Reading Panel. Teaching children to read: An evidence-based assessment of the scientific research literature on reading and its implications for reading instruction* (NIH Publication No. 00-4769). Washington, DC: U.S. Government Printing Office.

Nelson, L. (1989). Something borrowed, something new: Teaching implications of developmental spelling research. *Reading Psychology, 10*(3), 255–274.

Ogle, D.M. (1986). K-W-L: A teaching model that develops active reading of expository text. *The Reading Teacher, 39*(6), 564–570. doi:10.1598/RT.39.6.11

Palincsar, A.S. (2003). Collaborative approaches to comprehension instruction. In A.P. Sweet & C.E. Snow (Eds.), *Rethinking reading comprehension* (pp. 99–114). New York: Guilford.

Palincsar, A.S., & Brown, A.L. (1984). Reciprocal teaching of comprehension-fostering and comprehension-monitoring activities. *Cognition and Instruction, 1*(2), 117–175.

Pearson, P.D. (1993). Teaching and learning reading: A research perspective. *Language Arts, 70*(6), 502–511.

Pearson, P.D., & Dole, J.A. (1987). Explicit comprehension instruction: A review of research and a new conceptualization of instruction. *The Elementary School Journal, 88*(2), 151–165.

Pearson, P.D., & Fielding, L. (1991). Comprehension instruction. In R. Barr, M.L. Kamil, P. Mosenthal, & P.D. Pearson (Eds.), *Handbook of reading research* (Vol. 2, pp. 815–860). White Plains, NY: Longman.

Pearson, P.D., & Gallagher, M.C. (1983). The instruction of reading comprehension. *Contemporary Educational Psychology, 8*(3), 317–344.

Pikulski, J.J., & Chard, D.J. (2005). Fluency: Bridge between decoding and reading comprehension. *The Reading Teacher, 58*(6), 510–519.

Pinnell, G.S., Pikulski, J.J., Wixson, K.K., Campbell, J.R., Gough, P.B., & Beatty, A.S. (1995). *Listening to children read aloud: Data from NAEP's Integrated Reading Performance Record (IRPR) at grade 4.* Washington, DC: Office of Educational Research and Improvement, National Center for Educational Statistics, U.S. Department of Education.

Pressley, M. (1990). *Cognitive strategy instruction that really improves children's academic performance.* Cambridge, MA: Brookline.

Pressley, M., & Afflerbach, P. (1995). *Verbal protocols of reading: The nature of constructively responsive reading.* Hillsdale, NJ: Erlbaum.

Pressley, M., Symons, S., Snyder, B.L., & Cariglia-Bull, T. (1989). Strategy instruction research comes of age. *Learning Disability Quarterly, 12*(1), 16–30.

Rasinski, T.V. (2000). Speed does matter in reading. *The Reading Teacher, 54*(2), 146–151.

Rasinski, T.V., & Padak, N.D. (1998). How elementary students referred for compensatory reading instruction perform on school-based measures of word recognition, fluency, and comprehension. *Reading Psychology, 19*(2), 185–216. doi:10.1080/0270271980190202

Rinehart, S.D., Stahl, S.A., & Erickson, L.G. (1986). Some effects of summarization training on reading and studying. *Reading Research Quarterly, 21*(4), 422–438.

Roe, B.D., & Burns, P.C. (2007). *Informal reading inventory: Preprimer to twelfth grade* (7th ed.). Boston: Houghton Mifflin.

Samuels, S.J. (1976). Automatic decoding and reading comprehension. *Language Arts, 53*(3), 323–325.

Samuels, S.J. (1979). The method of repeated readings. *The Reading Teacher, 32*(4), 403–408.

Samuels, S.J. (2002). Reading fluency: Its development and assessment. In A.E. Farstrup & S.J. Samuels (Eds.), *What research has to say about reading instruction* (3rd ed., pp. 166–184). Newark, DE: International Reading Association.

Samuels, S.J., Schermer, N., & Reinking, D. (1992). Reading fluency: Techniques for making decoding automatic. In S.J. Samuels & A.E. Farstrup (Eds.), *What research has to say about reading instruction* (2nd ed., pp. 124–144). Newark, DE: International Reading Association.

Santa, C.M., & Høien, T. (1999). An assessment of Early Steps: A program for early intervention of reading problems. *Reading Research Quarterly, 34*(1), 54–79. doi:10.1598/RRQ.34.1.4

Snow, C.E., Burns, M.S., & Griffin, P. (Eds.). (1998). *Preventing reading difficulties in young children*. Washington, DC: National Academy Press.

Stevens, K.C. (1982). Can we improve reading by teaching background information? *Journal of Reading, 25*(4), 326–329.

Sweet, A.P., & Snow, C. (2002). Reconceptualizing reading comprehension. In C.C. Block, L.B. Gambrell, & M. Pressley (Eds.), *Improving comprehension instruction: Rethinking research, theory, and classroom practice* (pp. 17–53). San Francisco: Jossey-Bass; Newark, DE: International Reading Association.

Templeton, S. (2002). Getting ready for systematic and sustained spelling instruction. *Voices From the Middle, 10*(1), 58–59.

Templeton, S., & Morris, D. (1999). Questions teachers ask about spelling. *Reading Research Quarterly, 34*(1), 102–112. doi:10.1598/RRQ.34.1.6

Tierney, R.J., & Pearson, P.D. (1985). Learning to learn from texts: A framework for improving classroom practice. In H. Singer & R.B. Ruddell (Eds.), *Theoretical models and processes of reading* (3rd ed., pp. 860–878). Newark, DE: International Reading Association.

Topping, K. (1987). Paired reading: A powerful technique for parent use. *The Reading Teacher, 40*(7), 608–609.

Torgesen, J.K., Alexander, A.W., Wagner, R.K., Rashotte, C.A., Voeller, K.K.S., & Conway, T. (2001). Intensive remedial instruction for children with severe reading disabilities: Immediate and long-term outcomes from two instructional approaches. *Journal of Learning Disabilities, 34*(1), 33–58.

Tyner, B. (2004). *Small-group reading instruction: A differentiated teaching model for beginning and struggling readers*. Newark, DE: International Reading Association.

Tyner, B. (2009). *Small-group reading instruction: A differentiated teaching model for beginning and struggling readers* (2nd ed.). Newark, DE: International Reading Association.

Tyner, B., & Green, S.E. (2005). *Small-group reading instruction: A differentiated teaching model for intermediate readers, grades 3–8*. Newark, DE: International Reading Association.

Vacca, J.A.L., Vacca, R.T., Gove, M.K., Burkey, L.C., Lenhart, L.A., & McKeon, C.A. (2011). *Reading and learning to read* (8th ed.). Boston: Allyn & Bacon.

Vygotsky, L.S. (1978). *Mind in society: The development of higher psychological processes* (M. Cole, V. John-Steiner, S. Scribner, & E. Souberman, Eds. & Trans.). Cambridge, MA: Harvard University Press.

Wixson, K.K. (1983). Questions about a text: What you ask about is what children learn. *The Reading Teacher, 37*(3), 287–293.

Wong, B.Y.L. (1985). Self-questioning instructional research: A review. *Review of Educational Research, 55*(2), 227–268.

Woods, M.L., & Moe, A.J. (2011). *Analytical reading inventory: Comprehensive standards-based assessment for all students including gifted and remedial* (9th ed.). Boston: Allyn & Bacon.

# Literature Cited

Baum, L.F. (1993). *The wizard of Oz*. New York: Tom Doherty. (Original work published 1900)

Giles, J. (1998). *The hare and the tortoise*. Austin, TX: Harcourt Achieve.

Inserra, R. (1999). *The dolphins*. Barrington, IL: Rigby.

LessonSnips. (2009). *Isaac Newton*. Retrieved May 23, 2011, from www.lessonsnips.com/lesson/isaacnewton

Lincoln, A. (1863, November 19). *Gettysburg address* [Speech, Bliss version]. Retrieved May 26, 2011, from www.papersofabrahamlincoln.org/Gettysburg%20Address.htm

Moore, H.H. (1997). The water cycle. In *A poem a day: 180 thematic poems and activities that teach and delight all year long* (p. 107). New York: Scholastic.

Silverstein, S. (2004). One inch tall. In *Where the sidewalk ends* (30th anniversary ed., p. 16). New York: HarperCollins.

Skidmore, J. (1997). *Hercules: The labors of Heracles from Greek mythology*. Retrieved May 17, 2011, from www.mythweb.com/hercules/index.html

Smith, A. (2001). *The nest on the beach*. Crystal Lake, IL: Rigby.

Strebe, D. (2009). *Map projection essentials*. Renton, WA: Mapthematics. Retrieved May 18, 2011, from www.mapthematics.com/Essentials.php

Thayer, E.L. (1888, June 3). Casey at the bat. *The San Francisco Examiner*.

CD CONTENTS

# Assessment Materials

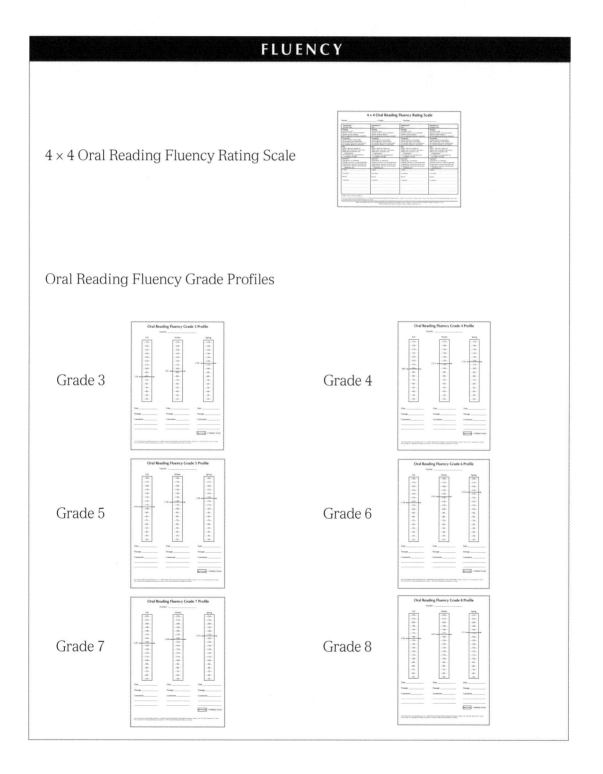

FLUENCY

4 × 4 Oral Reading Fluency Rating Scale

Oral Reading Fluency Grade Profiles

Grade 3

Grade 4

Grade 5

Grade 6

Grade 7

Grade 8

Word Study Pre- and
Postassessment Recording Form

Word Study Cycle Assessment
Recording Form

Intervention Reader Word Study
Assessments

Evolving Reader Word Study
Pre- and Postassessments

Evolving Reader Word Study Cycle
Assessments

Maturing Reader Word Study
Pre- and Postassessments

Maturing Reader Word Study Cycle
Assessments

Advanced Reader Word Study
(Meaning) Cycle Assessments

Oral Questioning Response Checklist

Informational Text Comprehension Assessment: Cause and Effect

Informational Text Comprehension Assessment: Sequencing

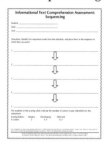

Informational Text Comprehension Assessment: Compare and Contrast

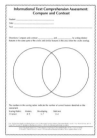

Informational Text Comprehension Assessment: Main Idea and Supporting Details

## SOAPSTone + Theme Rubric

## Types of Questions Rubric

## Inquiry Chart Rubric

## RAFT Rubric

# Word Study Materials

Note: Some sorts include a large amount of words. Teachers may choose to limit the number of word study cards that the group uses. We recommend that at least seven cards be included for each feature for sorting purposes.

Glossary of Word Study Terms

Intervention Reader Word Study Scope and Sequence

Intervention Reader Word Sort Directions

Intervention Reader Word Study Cards

Intervention Reader Dictated Sentences

## Evolving Reader Year 1 Word Study Scope and Sequence

## Evolving Reader Year 2 Word Study Scope and Sequence

## Evolving Reader Year 1 Word Sort Directions

## Evolving Reader Year 2 Word Sort Directions

## Evolving Reader Year 1 Word Study Cards

| bases | boxes | chances |
| --- | --- | --- |
| chops | classes | crashes |
| dishes | gases | glasses |
| hurts | lunches | nurses |
| rulers | sixes | streets |

## Evolving Reader Year 2 Word Study Cards

| stage | huge | page |
| --- | --- | --- |
| rage | age | wage |
| sage | edge | ledge |
| bridge | judge | budge |
| lodge | smudge | fudge |

## Maturing Reader Year 1 Word Study Scope and Sequence

## Maturing Reader Year 2 Word Study Scope and Sequence

## Maturing Reader Year 1 Word Sort Directions

## Maturing Reader Year 2 Word Sort Directions

## Maturing Reader Year 1 Word Study Cards

| | Maturing Reader Year 1 Word Study Cards | |
|---|---|---|
| certain | merchant | mermaid |
| nervous | person | service |
| circle | dirty | turtle |
| purple | gurgle | plural |
| current | alert | emerge |

## Maturing Reader Year 2 Word Study Cards

| | Maturing Reader Year 2 Word Study Cards | |
|---|---|---|
| analysis | analyses | basis |
| bases | crisis | crises |
| nemesis | nemeses | psychosis |
| psychoses | thesis | theses |
| addendum | addenda | bacterium |

## Advanced Reader Year 1 Word Study Scope and Sequence

## Advanced Reader Year 2 Word Study Scope and Sequence

## Advanced Reader Word Sort Directions

## Advanced Reader Year 1 Word Study Cards

## Advanced Reader Year 2 Word Study Cards

202

# Support Materials

Intervention Reader Lesson Plan

Evolving Reader Lesson Plan

Maturing Reader Lesson Plan

Advanced Reader Lesson Plan

FLUENCY

Read With Me

Record and Self-Reflect

# WORD STUDY

## Root Web

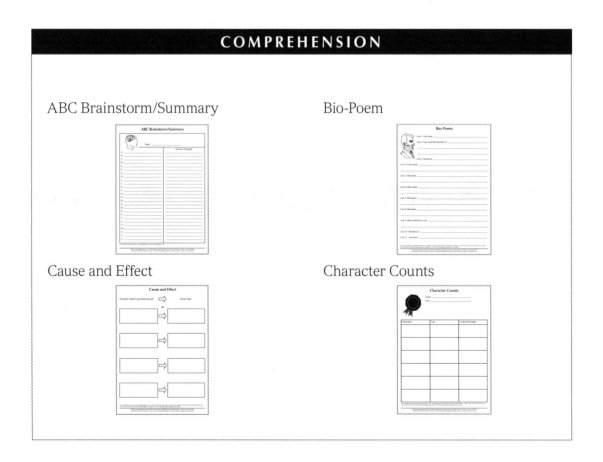

## Spelling Sort

## Sound Boxes

# COMPREHENSION

## ABC Brainstorm/Summary

## Bio-Poem

## Cause and Effect

## Character Counts

## Compare and Contrast With Meaning

## Directed Reading–Thinking Activity Sheet

## The Essentials

## Fact or Fib?

## Inquiry Chart

## K-W-L-R

## The Perfect Setting

## Problem–Solution

## Question Maker

## Questioning Guide for Informational Text

## Questioning Guide for Narrative Text

## RAFT Explained

## RAFT Paper

## Secret Sequence

## SOAPSTone + Theme Explained

## SOAPSTone + Theme

Story Map

Sum It Up

Timeline

Top 10 List

Very Important Predictions (VIP) Map

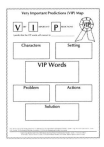

Vocabulary Word Map

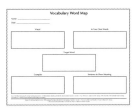

What's the Big Idea?

Word Study Matrix

You're the Reporter

INDEX

*Note.* Page numbers followed by *f* and *t* indicate figures and tables, respectively.